New edition coming March 2011!

MACROECONOMICS, SEVENTH EDITION

N. Gregory Mankiw

©2010 • 1-4292-1887-8

Part I. **Introduction**
1. The Science of Macroeconomics
2. The Data of Macroeconomics

Part II. **Classical Theory: The Economy in the Long Run**
3. National Income: Where It Comes From and Where It Goes
4. Money and Inflation
5. The Open Economy
6. Unemployment

Part III. **Growth Theory: The Economy in the Very Long Run**
7. Economic Growth I: Capital Accumulation and Population Growth
8. Economic Growth II: Technology, Empirics, and Policy

Part IV. **Business Cycle Theory: The Economy in the Short Run**
9. Introduction to Economic Fluctuations
10. Aggregate Demand I: Building the *IS-LM* Model
11. Aggregate Demand II: Applying the *IS-LM* Model
12. The Open Economy Revisited: The Mundell-Fleming Model and the Exchange-Rate Regime
13. Aggregate Supply and the Short-run Tradeoff Between Inflation and Unemployment.
14. A Dynamic Model of Aggregate Demand and Aggregate Supply

Part V. **Macroeconomic Policy Debates**
15. Stabilization Policy
16. Government Debt and Budget Deficits

Part VI. **More on the Microeconomics Behind Macroeconomics**
17. Consumption
18. Investment
19. Money Supply, Money Demand, and the Banking System

Epilogue: **What We Know, What We Don't**

MONEY, BANKING, AND FINANCIAL MARKETS, SECOND EDITION

Laurence M. Ball

©2012 • 1-4292-4409-7

Part I. **Foundations**
1. The Financial System
2. Money and Central Banks

Part II. **Financial Markets**
3. Asset Prices and Interest Rates
4. What Determines Interest Rates?
5. Securities Markets
6. Foreign Exchange Markets

Part III. **Banking**
7. Asymmetric Information in the Financial System
8. The Banking Industry
9. The Business of Banking
10. Bank Regulation

Part IV. **Money and the Economy**
11. The Money Supply and Interest Rates
12. Short-Run Economic Fluctuations
13. Economic Fluctuations, Monetary Policy, and the Financial System
14. Inflation and Deflation

Part V. **Monetary Policy**
15. Policies for Economic Stability
16. Monetary Institutions and Strategies
17. Monetary Policy and Exchange Rates
18. Financial Crises

Currently available
MONEY, BANKING, AND FINANCIAL MARKETS, FIRST EDITION
Laurence M. Ball
©2009 • 0-7167-5934-9

MACROECONOMICS
and the FINANCIAL SYSTEM

This volume containing part of Mankiw/Ball's *Macroeconomics and the Financial System* includes Chapters 15 through 19 only.

MACROECONOMICS
and the FINANCIAL SYSTEM

N. GREGORY MANKIW
Harvard University

LAURENCE M. BALL
Johns Hopkins University

Worth Publishers

Senior Publisher: Catherine Woods

Executive Editor: Charles Linsmeier

Senior Acquisitions Editor: Sarah Dorger

Executive Marketing Manager: Scott Guile

Consulting Editor: Paul Shensa

Senior Development Editor: Marie McHale

Development Editors: Jane Tufts and Barbara Brooks

Associate Media Editor: Tom Acox

Editorial Assistant: Mary Walsh

Associate Managing Editor: Tracey Kuehn

Project Editor: Dana Kasowitz

Photo Editor: Ted Szczepanski

Art Director: Babs Reingold

Cover and Text Designer: Kevin Kall

Production Manager: Barbara Anne Seixas

Composition: MPS Limited, a Macmillan Company

Printing and Binding: Quad/Graphics Versailles

Cover Artist: George Mamos

Library of Congress Cataloging-in-Publication Number: 2010932595

ISBN-13: 978-1-4292-5367-3

ISBN-10: 1-4292-5367-3

© 2011 by Worth Publishers

Printed in the United States of America

First Printing 2010

Worth Publishers

41 Madison Avenue

New York, NY 10010

www.worthpublishers.com

To Deborah and Patricia

about the authors

Christina Micek

N. Gregory Mankiw (pictured on the left) is Professor of Economics at Harvard University. He began his study of economics at Princeton University, where he received an A.B. in 1980. After earning a Ph.D. in economics from MIT, he began teaching at Harvard in 1985 and was promoted to full professor in 1987. Today, he regularly teaches both undergraduate and graduate courses in macroeconomics. He is also author of *Macroeconomics* (Worth Publishers) and *Principles of Economics* (Cengage Learning).

Professor Mankiw is a regular participant in academic and policy debates. His research ranges across macroeconomics and includes work on price adjustment, consumer behavior, financial markets, monetary and fiscal policy, and economic growth. In addition to his duties at Harvard, he has been a research associate of the National Bureau of Economic Research, a member of the Brookings Panel on Economic Activity, and an adviser to the Congressional Budget Office and the Federal Reserve Banks of Boston and New York. From 2003 to 2005 he was chairman of the President's Council of Economic Advisers.

Professor Mankiw lives in Wellesley, Massachusetts, with his wife, Deborah; children, Catherine, Nicholas, and Peter; and their border terrier, Tobin.

Laurence M. Ball (pictured on the right) is Professor of Economics at Johns Hopkins University. He received a B.A. in economics from Amherst College in 1980 and a Ph.D. in economics from MIT in 1986. He taught at New York University and Princeton University before his appointment at Johns Hopkins in 1994. He teaches both undergraduate and graduate courses in macroeconomics and is the author of *Money, Banking, and Financial Markets* (Worth Publishers).

Professor Ball's research areas include price adjustment and inflation, monetary and fiscal policy, and unemployment. He and Professor Mankiw have coauthored nine academic papers. Professor Ball is a research associate of the National Bureau of Economic Research and has been a visiting scholar at the Federal Reserve, the Bank of England, the Bank of Japan, the Central Bank of Norway, the Reserve Bank of Australia, the Reserve Bank of New Zealand, the Hong Kong Monetary Authority, and the International Monetary Fund.

Professor Ball lives in Baltimore with his wife, Patricia; son, Leverett; and their German shepherd, Bamboo.

brief contents

This volume containing part of Mankiw/Ball's *Macroeconomics* *the Financial System* includes Chapters 15 through 19. How the following brief table of contents is comprehensive: it pres all chapters in the full *Macroeconomics and the Financial System.*

contents

This volume containing part of Mankiw/Ball's *Macroeconomics and the Financial System* includes Chapters 15 through 19. However, the following detailed table of contents is comprehensive: it presents all chapters in the full *Macroeconomics and the Financial System*. The contents for the book in your hands starts on p. xviii.

part III Growth Theory: The Economy in the Very Long Run   191

Chapter 7 Economic Growth I: Capital Accumulation and Population Growth   193

This volume containing part of Mankiw/Ball's *Macroeconomics and the Financial System* includes Chapters 15 through 19. However, the following Preface is fully descriptive of the entire book.

preface

Economists have long understood that developments in the overall economy and developments in the financial system are inextricably intertwined. But if we needed reminding, the financial crisis and economic downturn that started in 2007 provided a wake-up call that is hard to ignore.

This book is designed for courses in intermediate-level macroeconomics that include ample coverage of the role of the economy's financial system. It is born of two parents. One of those parents is Greg Mankiw's text *Macroeconomics*. The other is Larry Ball's *Money, Banking, and Financial Markets*. Like any child, this book resembles both its parents but also has a personality of its own. As with a traditional book in macroeconomics, it covers such topics as monetary theory, growth theory, and the study of short-run economic fluctuations. But it also includes substantial material on asset prices, securities markets, banking, and financial crises. The integration of this material will foster interest in macroeconomics, especially among students looking toward careers in business and finance.

The great British economist John Maynard Keynes once remarked that an economist must be "mathematician, historian, statesman, philosopher, in some degree . . . as aloof and incorruptible as an artist, yet sometimes as near the earth as a politician." As this assessment suggests, students who aim to learn economics need to draw on many disparate talents. The job of helping students find and develop these talents falls to instructors and textbook authors.

When writing this book, our goal was to make macroeconomics understandable, relevant, and (believe it or not) fun. Those of us who have chosen to be professional macroeconomists have done so because we are fascinated by the field. More important, we believe that the study of macroeconomics and the financial system can illuminate much about the world and that the lessons learned, if properly applied, can make the world a better place. We hope this book conveys not only our profession's accumulated wisdom but also its enthusiasm and sense of purpose.

The Arrangement of Topics

Our strategy for teaching macroeconomics is first to examine the long run when prices are flexible and then to examine the short run when prices are sticky. This approach has several advantages. First, because the classical dichotomy permits the separation of real and monetary issues, the long-run material is easier for students to understand. Second, when students begin studying short-run fluctuations, they understand fully the long-run equilibrium around which the economy is fluctuating. Third, beginning with market-clearing models makes clearer the link between macroeconomics and microeconomics. Fourth, students learn first the material that is less controversial among macroeconomists. For all these reasons, the strategy of beginning with long-run classical models simplifies the teaching of macroeconomics.

Let's now move from strategy to tactics. What follows is a whirlwind tour of the book.

Part One, Introduction

The introductory material in Part One is brief so that students can get to the core topics quickly. Chapter 1 discusses the broad questions that macroeconomists address and the economist's approach of building models to explain the world. Chapter 2 introduces the key data of macroeconomics, emphasizing gross domestic product, the consumer price index, and the unemployment rate.

Part Two, Classical Theory: The Economy in the Long Run

Part Two examines the long run over which prices are flexible. Chapter 3 presents the basic classical model of national income. In this model, the factors of production and the production technology determine the level of income, and the marginal products of the factors determine its distribution to households. In addition, the model shows how fiscal policy influences the allocation of the economy's resources among consumption, investment, and government purchases, and it highlights how the real interest rate equilibrates the supply and demand for goods and services.

Money and the price level are introduced in Chapter 4. Because prices are assumed to be fully flexible, the chapter presents the prominent ideas of classical monetary theory: the quantity theory of money, the inflation tax, the Fisher effect, the social costs of inflation, and the causes and costs of hyperinflation.

Chapter 5 introduces the study of open-economy macroeconomics. Maintaining the assumption of full employment, this chapter presents models to explain the trade balance and the exchange rate. Various policy issues are addressed: the relationship between the budget deficit and the trade deficit, the macroeconomic impact of protectionist trade policies, and the effect of monetary policy on the value of a currency in the market for foreign exchange.

Chapter 6 relaxes the assumption of full employment by discussing the dynamics of the labor market and the natural rate of unemployment. It examines various causes of unemployment, including job search, minimum-wage laws, union power, and efficiency wages. It also presents some important facts about patterns of unemployment.

Part Three, Growth Theory: The Economy in the Very Long Run

Part Three makes the classical analysis of the economy dynamic by developing the tools of modern growth theory. Chapter 7 introduces the Solow growth model as a description of how the economy evolves over time. This chapter emphasizes the roles of capital accumulation and population growth. Chapter 8 then adds technological progress to the Solow model. It uses the model to discuss growth experiences around the world as well as public policies that influence the level and growth of the standard of living. Finally, Chapter 8 introduces students to the modern theories of endogenous growth.

Part Four, Business Cycle Theory: The Economy in the Short Run

Part Four examines the short run when prices are sticky. It begins in Chapter 9 by examining some of the key facts that describe short-run fluctuations in economic activity. The chapter then introduces the model of aggregate supply and aggregate demand as well as the role of stabilization policy. Subsequent chapters refine the ideas introduced in this chapter.

Chapters 10 and 11 look more closely at aggregate demand. Chapter 10 presents the Keynesian cross and the theory of liquidity preference and uses these models as building blocks for developing the *IS–LM* model. Chapter 11 uses the *IS–LM* model to explain economic fluctuations and the aggregate demand curve. It concludes with an extended case study of the Great Depression.

Chapter 12 looks more closely at aggregate supply. It examines various approaches to explaining the short-run aggregate supply curve and discusses the short-run tradeoff between inflation and unemployment.

Part Five, Macroeconomic Policy Debates

Once the student has command of standard long-run and short-run models of the economy, the book uses these models as the foundation for discussing some of the key debates over economic policy. Chapter 13 considers the debate over how policymakers should respond to short-run economic fluctuations. It emphasizes two broad questions: Should monetary and fiscal policy be active or passive? Should policy be conducted by rule or by discretion? The chapter presents arguments on both sides of these questions.

Chapter 14 focuses on the various debates over government debt and budget deficits. It gives some sense about the magnitude of government indebtedness, discusses why measuring budget deficits is not always straightforward, recaps the traditional view of the effects of government debt, presents Ricardian equivalence as an alternative view, and discusses various other perspectives on government debt. As in the previous chapter, students are not handed conclusions but are given the tools to evaluate the alternative viewpoints on their own.

Part Six, The Financial System and the Economy

Part Six enriches students' understanding of macroeconomics by exploring the financial system. Chapter 15 introduces financial markets and banks, emphasizing their roles in channeling funds from savers to investors and thereby spurring economic growth. It also discusses problems of asymmetric information in the financial system and how banks help overcome these problems.

Chapter 16 analyzes asset prices and interest rates. It discusses both classical theory, in which asset prices equal the present value of expected asset income, and the possibility of asset-price bubbles and crashes. The chapter also shows students how to calculate interest rates and returns on assets and explores the term structure of interest rates.

Chapter 17 surveys the markets for securities, including stocks, bonds, and derivatives. It addresses the mechanics of how securities markets operate and the decisions facing market participants, such as firms' decisions about which securities to issue and savers' decisions about which to buy. The chapter also presents a balanced discussion of a perennial debate: can anyone beat the market?

Chapter 18 discusses the banking industry: the different types of banks, how banks seek to earn profits and contain risk, the problem of bank runs, and government regulation of banking. The chapter also examines two key developments in recent history: subprime lending and the securitization of bank loans.

Finally, Chapter 19 examines financial crises. It starts with a general discussion of what happens in a financial crisis and how it affects the economy, then moves to a detailed analysis of the U.S. crisis of 2007–2009. The discussion emphasizes debates over government and central bank policies: How can policymakers contain crises when they occur? What regulatory reforms can prevent future crises? The chapter builds on what students have learned from earlier chapters about economic fluctuations, monetary and fiscal policy, and the financial system.

Alternative Routes Through the Text

We have organized the material in the way that we prefer to teach intermediate-level macroeconomics, but we understand that other instructors have different preferences. We tried to keep this in mind as we wrote the book so that it would offer a degree of flexibility. Here are a few ways that instructors might consider rearranging the material:

➤ Some instructors are eager to cover short-run economic fluctuations. For such a course, we recommend covering Chapters 1 through 4 so students are grounded in the basics of classical theory and then jumping to Chapters 9 through 12 to cover the model of aggregate demand and aggregate supply.

➤ Some instructors are eager to cover long-run economic growth. These instructors can cover Chapters 7 and 8 immediately after Chapter 3.

➤ An instructor who wants to defer (or even skip) open-economy macroeconomics can put off Chapter 5 without loss of continuity.

➤ An instructor who wants to emphasize the financial system can move to Chapters 15 through 19 immediately after covering Chapters 1 through 4 and 9 through 11.

We hope and believe that this text complements well a variety of approaches to the field.

Learning Tools

We have included a variety of features to ensure that the text is student-friendly. Here is a brief overview.

Case Studies

Economics comes to life when it is applied to understanding actual events. Therefore, the numerous case studies are an important learning tool, integrated closely with the theoretical material presented in each chapter. The frequency with which these case studies occur ensures that students do not have to grapple with an overdose of theory before seeing the theory applied.

FYI Boxes

These boxes present ancillary material "for your information." We use these boxes to clarify difficult concepts, to provide additional information about the tools of economics, and to show how economics relates to our daily lives.

Graphs

Understanding graphical analysis is a key part of learning macroeconomics, and we have worked hard to make the figures easy to follow. We often use comment boxes within figures that describe briefly and draw attention to the important points that the figures illustrate. They should help students both learn and review the material.

Mathematical Notes

We use occasional mathematical footnotes to keep more difficult material out of the body of the text. These notes make an argument more rigorous or present a proof of a mathematical result. They can easily be skipped by those students who have not been introduced to the necessary mathematical tools.

Chapter Summaries

Every chapter ends with a brief, nontechnical summary of its major lessons. Students can use the summaries to place the material in perspective and to review for exams.

Key Concepts

Learning the language of a field is a major part of any course. Within the chapter, each key concept is in **boldface** when it is introduced. At the end of the chapter, the key concepts are listed for review.

Questions for Review

After studying a chapter, students can immediately test their understanding of its basic lessons by answering the Questions for Review.

Problems and Applications

Every chapter includes Problems and Applications designed for homework assignments. Some of these are numerical applications of the theory in the chapter. Others encourage the student to go beyond the material in the chapter by addressing new issues that are closely related to the chapter topics.

Glossary

To help students become familiar with the language of macroeconomics, a glossary of more than 300 terms is provided at the back of the book.

Acknowledgments

We are grateful to the many reviewers and colleagues in the economics profession whose input helped to shape the two parents of this book, *Macroeconomics* (Mankiw) and *Money, Banking, and Financial Markets* (Ball). The former has been through seven editions, making the reviewers too numerous to list in their entirety. However, we are grateful for their willingness to have given up their scarce time to help improve the economics and pedagogy of this text.

We would like to mention those instructors whose recent input shaped the seventh edition of *Macroeconomics*, the first edition of *Money, Banking, and Financial Markets*, and this new book:

Burton Abrams
University of Delaware

Douglas Agbetsiafa
Indiana University at South Bend

Francis Ahking
University of Connecticut at Storrs

Ehsan Ahmed
James Madison University

Jack Aschkenazi
American InterContinental University

Jinhui Bai
Georgetown University

Clare Battista
California Polytechnic State University

Joydeep Bhattacharya
Iowa State University

Peter Bondarenko
University of Chicago

Michael Brandl
University of Texas at Austin

James Butkiewicz
University of Delaware

Tina Carter
Florida State University

Jin Choi
DePaul University

Ronald Cronovich
Carthage College

Massimiliano De Santis
Dartmouth College

Ranjit Dighe
State University of New York at Oswego

Aimee Dimmerman
George Washington University

John Driscoll
Federal Reserve Board

Ding Du
South Dakota State University

John Duca
Southern Methodist University

Fisheha Eshete
Bowie State University

Robert Eyler
Sonoma State University

James Fackler
University of Kentucky

Imran Farooqi
University of Iowa

David Flynn
University of North Dakota

Chris Foote
Federal Reserve Bank of Boston

Yee-Tien Fu
Stanford University

Doris Geide-Stevenson
Weber State University

Ismail Genc
University of Idaho

Rebecca Gonzalez
University of North Carolina at Pembroke

David R. Hakes
University of Northern Iowa

David Hammes
University of Hawaii at Hilo

Jane Himarios
University of Texas at Arlington

David Hineline
Miami University

Christopher House
University of Michigan

Aaron Jackson
Bentley College

Nancy Jianakoplos
Colorado State University

Bryce Kanago
University of Northern Iowa

George Karras
University of Illinois at Chicago

Roger Kaufman
Smith College

Manfred W. Keil
Claremont McKenna College

Elizabeth Sawyer Kelly
University of Wisconsin

Kathy Kelly
University of Texas at Arlington

Faik Koray
Louisiana State University

John Krieg
Western Washington University

Kristin Kucsma
Seton Hall University

Gary F. Langer
Roosevelt University

John Leahy
New York University

Mary Lesser
Iona College

Christopher Magee
Bucknell University

Michael Marlow
California Polytechnic State University

Robert Martel
University of Connecticut

W. Douglas McMillin
Louisiana State University

Jianjun Miao
Boston University

Meghan Millea
Mississippi State University

Robert Murphy
Boston College

John Neri
University of Maryland

Robert Pennington
University of Central Florida

Christina Peters
University of Colorado at Boulder

Ronnie Phillips
Colorado State University

Dennis Placone
Clemson University

Robert Reed
University of Kentucky

Jeffrey Reynolds
Northern Illinois University

David Romer
University of California at Berkeley

Brian Rosario
American River College

Joseph Santos
South Dakota State University

Naveen Sarna
Northern Virginia Community College

Mark Siegler
California State University at Sacramento

Robert Sonora
Fort Lewis College

David Spencer
Brigham Young University

Richard Stahl
Louisiana State University

Frank Steindl
Oklahoma State University

James Swofford
University of South Alabama

Henry S. Terrell
University of Maryland

Sven Thommesen
Auburn University

Brian Trinque
University of Texas at Austin

Nora Underwood
University of Central Florida

Kristin Van Gaasbeck
California State University at Sacramento

Rubina Vohra
New Jersey City University

Qingbin Wang
University at Albany

Charles Weise
Gettysburg College

Jaejoon Woo
DePaul University

Paul Woodburne
Clarion University

Bill Yang
Georgia Southern University

Noam Yuchtman
Harvard University

In addition, we are grateful for excellent research assistance from Stacy Carlson and Daniel Norris, students at Harvard, and Hai Nguyen, a student at Johns Hopkins.

The people at Worth Publishers have continued to be congenial and dedicated. We would like to thank Catherine Woods, Senior Publisher; Charles Linsmeier, Executive Editor; Sarah Dorger, Senior Acquisitions Editor; Scott Guile, Executive Marketing Manager; Marie McHale, Senior Development Editor; Paul Shensa, Consulting Editor; Tom Acox, Associate Media and Supplements Editor; Mary Walsh, Editorial Assistant; Steven Rigolosi, Director of Market Research and Development; Dana Kasowitz, Project Editor; Tracey Kuehn, Associate Managing Editor; Barbara Seixas, Production Manager; Barbara Reingold, Art Director; Vicki Tomaselli, Design Manager; Kevin Kall, Layout Designer; Karen Osborne, Copyeditor; Laura McGinn, Supplements Editor; and Stacey Alexander, Supplements Manager.

Many other people made valuable contributions as well. Most important, Jane Tufts, freelance developmental editor, worked her magic on this book, confirming that she's the best in the business. We are also grateful to Barbara Brooks for her invaluable editorial input. Alexandra Nickerson did a great job preparing the index. Deborah Mankiw and Patricia Bovers, our wives, provided invaluable suggestions and encouragement and graciously tolerated our absence as we spent many hours in front of our computer screens writing, editing, and fine-tuning this text.

Finally, we would like to thank our children, Catherine, Nicholas, and Peter Mankiw and Leverett Ball. They helped immensely with this book—both by providing a pleasant distraction and by reminding us that textbooks are written for the next generation.

N. Gregory Mankiw

Laurence Ball

August 2010

Supplements and Media

Worth Publishers has worked closely with Greg Mankiw, Larry Ball, and a team of talented economics instructors to put together a variety of supplements to aid instructors and students. We have been delighted at the positive feedback we have received on these supplements. Here is a summary of the resources available.

For Instructors

Instructor's Resources

Robert G. Murphy (Boston College) has written a comprehensive resource manual for instructors to appear on the instructor's portion of the Web site. For each chapter of this book, the manual contains notes to the instructor, a detailed lecture outline, additional case studies, and coverage of advanced topics. Instructors can use the manual to prepare their lectures, and they can reproduce whatever pages they choose as handouts for students. Professor Murphy has also created a Dismal Scientist Activity (www.dismalscientist.com) for each chapter. Each activity challenges students to combine the chapter knowledge with a high-powered business database and analysis service that offers real-time monitoring of the global economy.

Solutions Manual

Nora Underwood (University of Central Florida) has written the *Solutions Manual* for all of the Questions for Review and Problems and Applications.

Test Bank

Nancy Jianakoplos (Colorado State University) has written the *Test Bank*, which includes nearly 2,100 multiple-choice questions, numerical problems, and short-answer graphical questions to accompany each chapter of the text. The *Test Bank* is available on a CD-ROM. The CD includes our flexible test-generating software, which instructors can use to easily write and edit questions as well as create and print tests.

PowerPoint Slides

Ronald Cronovich (Carthage College) has prepared PowerPoint presentations of the material in each chapter. They feature animated graphs with careful explanations and additional case studies, data, and helpful notes to the instructor. Designed to be customized or used "as is," they include easy instructions for those who have little experience with PowerPoint. They are available on the companion Web site.

Online Offerings

Companion Web Site for Students and Instructors
(www.worthpublishers.com/mankiwball)

The companion site is a virtual study guide for students and an excellent resource for instructors. Robert G. Murphy (Boston College) and Brian Rosario (American River College) have updated the innovative software package for students. For each chapter in the textbook, the tools on the companion Web site include the following:

> ► *Self-Tests.* Students can test their knowledge of the material in the book by taking multiple-choice tests on any chapter. After the student responds, the program explains the answer and directs the student to specific sections in the book for additional study. Students may also test their knowledge of key terms using the flashcards.

> ► *Data Plotter.* Originally created by David Weil, Brown University, this tool enables students to explore macroeconomic data with time-series graphs and scatterplots.

> ► *Macro Models.* These modules provide simulations of the models presented in the book. Students can change the exogenous variables and see the outcomes in terms of shifting curves and recalculated numerical values of the endogenous variables. Each module contains exercises that instructors can assign as homework.

> ► *A Game for Macroeconomists.* Also originally created by David Weil, Brown University, the game allows students to become president of the United States in the year 2012 and to make macroeconomic policy decisions based on news events, economic statistics, and approval ratings. It gives students a sense of the complex interconnections that influence the economy. It is also fun to play.

> ► *Flashcards.* Students can test their knowledge of the definitions in the glossary with these virtual flashcards.

Along with the Instructor's Resources (see p. xxxi), the following additional instructor support material is available:

> ► *PowerPoint Lecture Presentations.* As mentioned earlier, these customizable PowerPoint slides, prepared by Ronald Cronovich (Carthage College), are designed to assist instructors with lecture preparation and presentations.

> ► *Images from the Textbook.* Instructors have access to a complete set of figures and tables from the textbook in high-resolution and low-resolution JPEG formats. The textbook art has been processed for "high-resolution" (150 dpi). These figures and photographs have been especially formatted for maximum readability in large lecture halls and follow standards that were set and tested in a real university auditorium.

> ► *Solutions Manual.* Instructors have access to an electronic version of the printed manual, which consists of detailed solutions to the Questions for Review and Problems and Applications.

BlackBoard

The Mankiw/Ball BlackBoard course cartridge makes it possible to combine Black-Board's popular tools and easy-to-use interface with the text's Web content, including preprogrammed quizzes and tests. The result is an interactive, comprehensive online course that allows for effortless implementation, management, and use. The files are organized and prebuilt to work within the BlackBoard software.

Additional Offerings

i-clicker

Developed by a team of University of Illinois physicists, i-clicker is the most flexible and most reliable classroom response system available. It is the only solution created *for* educators, *by* educators—with continuous product improvements made through direct classroom testing and faculty feedback. No matter their level of technical expertise, instructors will appreciate the i-clicker because the focus remains on teaching, not the technology. To learn more about packaging i-clicker with this textbook, please contact your local sales representative or visit www.iclicker.com.

Financial Times Edition

For adopters of this text, Worth Publishers and the *Financial Times* are offering a 15-week subscription to students at a tremendous savings. Instructors also receive their own free *Financial Times* subscription for one year. Students and instructors may access research and archived information at www.ft.com.

Dismal Scientist

A high-powered business database and analysis service comes to the classroom! Dismal Scientist offers real-time monitoring of the global economy, produced locally by economists and other professionals at Moody's Economy.com around the world. Dismal Scientist is *free* when packaged with this text. Please contact your local sales representative or go to www.dismalscientist.com.

The
Economist

The Economist has partnered with Worth Publishers to create an exclusive offer we believe will enhance the classroom experience. Faculty receive a complimentary 15-week subscription when 10 or more students purchase a subscription. Students get 15 issues of *The Economist* for just $15. That's a savings of 85 percent off the cover price.

Inside and outside the classroom, *The Economist* provides a global perspective that helps students keep abreast of what's going on in the world and provides insight into how the world views the United States.

Each subscription includes:

> *Special Reports.* Approximately 20 times a year, *The Economist* publishes a Special Report providing in-depth analysis that highlights a specific country, industry, or hot-button issue.

➤ *Technology Quarterly Supplements.* This supplement analyzes new technology that could potentially transform lives, business models, industries, governments, and financial markets.

➤ *Economist.com.* Unlimited access to *The Economist*'s Web site is *free* with a print subscription.

Included on *The Economist* Web site:

➤ *Searchable Archive.* Subscribers have full access to 28,000+ articles.

➤ *Exclusive Online Research Tools.* Tools include Articles by Subject, Backgrounders, Surveys, Economics A–Z, Style Guide, Weekly Indicators, and Currency Converter.

➤ *The Full Audio Edition.* The entire magazine or specific sections are available for download.

➤ The Economist *Debate Series.* The essence of Oxford-style debate is available in an interactive online forum.

➤ *Daily Columns.* These feature columns are available exclusively online, covering views on business, the market, personal technology, the arts, and much more.

➤ *Correspondent's Diary.* Each week, an *Economist* writer from a different country details experiences and offers opinions.

➤ *Blogs.* Blogs cover economics as well as U.S. and European politics.

To get 15 issues of *The Economist* for just $15, go to www.economistacademic.com/worth.

PART VI

The Financial System and the Economy

Introduction to the Financial System

"Economists themselves have not always fully appreciated the importance of a healthy financial system for economic growth."

—Ben Bernanke, 2010

The financial system is part of your daily life. You buy things with debit or credit cards, and you visit ATMs to get cash. You may have borrowed money from a bank to buy a car or pay for college. You see headlines about the ups and downs of the stock market, and you or your family may own shares of stock. If you travel abroad, you depend on currency markets to change your dollars into local money at your destination.

The financial system is also an important part of the overall economy. When the system works well, it channels funds from people who have saved money to people, firms, and governments with investment projects that make the economy more productive. For example, companies obtain loans from banks to build factories, which provide new jobs for workers and produce new goods for consumers. By increasing an economy's productivity, the financial system helps the economy to grow and the living standards of its citizens to rise.

At times, however, the financial system malfunctions and damages the economy. The U.S. financial crisis of 2007–2009 is a dramatic example of such a malfunction. Losses on subprime mortgages (home loans to people with weak credit histories) led to the failure or near-failure of many large banks. Bank lending contracted severely, resulting in lower consumption and investment. The Dow Jones index of stock prices fell more than 50 percent from 2007 to early 2009, shaking confidence in the economy and further reducing consumption and investment. Financial turmoil pushed the economy into a deep recession, with the unemployment rate rising from under 5 percent at the end of 2007 to 10 percent two years later.

The next few chapters explore financial systems in the United States and around the world. We discuss the different parts of these systems, such as banks and stock markets, and their economic functions. We discover how a healthy financial system benefits the economy, why the system sometimes breaks down, and what government can do to strengthen a country's financial system. In this chapter, we begin our study of the financial system with an overview of its two main parts: financial markets and banks.

15-1 Financial Markets

In economics, a market consists of people and firms that buy and sell something. **Financial markets** are made up of people and firms that buy and sell two kinds of assets. One type of asset is currencies of various economies, such as dollars and euros. We discussed currency markets in Chapter 5 (and you can learn more about them in a course on international economics). In this chapter, we focus on the second type of asset sold in financial markets: securities.

A **security** is a claim on some future flow of income. Traditionally, this claim was recorded on a piece of paper, but today most securities exist only as records in computer systems. The most familiar kinds of securities are bonds and stocks.

Bonds

A **bond**, also called a *fixed-income security*, is a security issued by a corporation or government that promises to pay the buyer predetermined amounts of money at certain times in the future. Corporations issue bonds to finance investment projects, such as new factories. Governments issue bonds when they need funds to cover budget deficits. When a corporation or government issues bonds, it is borrowing money from those who buy the bonds. The issuer receives funds immediately and pays the buyers back in the future. Because bond issuers owe money to bond purchasers, bonds are also called *debt securities*.

For example, you might pay $100 for a bond that pays you $6 a year for 10 years and then pays back the $100 at the end of the tenth year. To introduce some terms, the *face value* of this bond is $100, and the *coupon payment* is $6; the bond's *maturity* is 10 years.

Almost always, the total payments promised by a bond—the face value plus all coupon payments—exceed the price that a buyer pays for the bond. This means that bonds pay interest: the issuer pays buyers for the use of their funds. In our example of a 10-year bond, the interest rate is the coupon payment divided by the face value: $6/$100 = 6 percent. In other cases—for example, when a bond's face value differs from the price paid by the buyer—it takes some work to determine what interest rate the buyer receives. Chapter 16 shows how to calculate interest rates on bonds.

Bonds differ in their maturities, which range from a few months to 30 years or more. Bonds with maturities of less than a year have special names: they are called *commercial paper* when issued by corporations and *Treasury bills* when issued by the U.S. government.

Bonds also differ in the stream of payments they promise. For example, a *zero-coupon bond* yields no payments until it matures. To attract buyers, it sells for less than its face value. For example, you might pay $80 for a zero–coupon bond that pays $100 at maturity. (Again, Chapter 16 shows how to calculate the interest rate on such a bond.)

In our world, promises—including promises to make payments on bonds—are not always kept. Sometimes a bond issuer **defaults:** it fails to make coupon payments or pay the face value at maturity. A corporation defaults on its bonds if it declares bankruptcy. A government defaults if it doesn't have enough revenue to make bond payments.

UNCORRECTED PAGES

The risk of default varies greatly for different bonds. This risk is small for bonds issued by the U.S. government or by well-established, highly successful corporations. Default risk is larger for new corporations with unknown prospects or corporations that are losing money, because these companies may go bankrupt and stop making bond payments. The greater the risk of default, the higher the interest rate that a bond must pay to attract buyers.

Stocks

A **stock**, or *equity*, is an ownership share in a corporation. As of 2010, Exxon Mobil Corporation had issued about 5 billion shares of stock. If you own 50 million of these shares, you own 1 percent of Exxon Mobil and its oil refineries and are entitled to 1 percent of the company's future profits.

Companies issue stock for the same reason they issue bonds: to raise funds for investment. Like a bond, a share of stock produces a flow of income—but a different kind of flow. A bondholder knows exactly how much the bond will pay (unless the issuer defaults). The earnings from a company's stock are a share of profits, and profits are unpredictable. Consequently, buying stocks is usually riskier than buying bonds. People buy stocks despite the risk because stocks often produce higher returns.

Because stock is an ownership share, stockholders have ultimate control over a corporation. Stockholders elect a corporation's board of directors, which oversees the business and hires a president to run its day-to-day operations. In contrast, bondholders have no control over a corporation; a bond is simply a corporation's promise of future payments to the bond's buyer.

Stock and bond markets generate many challenging questions: How do firms decide how many bonds and shares of stock to issue, how do people decide which bonds and stocks to buy, and what determines the prices of these securities? How do developments in stock and bond markets affect the overall economy? We discuss these questions throughout the next few chapters.

15-2 Economic Functions of Financial Markets

What is the purpose of stock, bond, and other financial markets? Why do people participate in them, and why are they important for the economy? There are two main answers. First, financial markets channel funds from savers to investors with productive uses for the funds. Second, these markets help people and firms share risks.

Matching Savers and Investors

An economy's saving provides funds to finance investment. To capture this idea, Chapter 3 presented a model in which savers meet investors in a single market for loanable funds. Reality is more complicated: a system of markets and institutions helps channel funds from savers to investors. Stock and bond markets are two of the most important parts of this financial system.

We can illustrate the channeling role of securities markets with an example. Consider a young man named Britt. Unlike most people, Britt can throw a baseball 95 miles an hour, and he has a good curve ball, too. For these reasons, a baseball team pays him $10 million a year to pitch. Britt happens to be a thrifty person, so he does not spend all his salary. Over time, he accumulates a lot of savings and wonders what he should do with it.

If he just accumulates cash and puts it in a safe, Britt knows his savings will not grow. In fact, if there is inflation, the value of his money will fall over time. Britt wonders how he can use his wealth to earn more wealth.

In another city, Harriet, the owner of a software company, is pondering her future. Harriet is a person of great vision and has an idea that could make her rich: an application that sends smells from one smart phone to another.

Harriet wants to develop this app, which will let people send perfumes to their sweethearts and rotten-egg smells to their enemies. She knows this product, iSmells, will be highly profitable. Unfortunately, it is expensive to buy the computers and hire the programmers needed to make her idea a reality. Because her current business does not generate enough profits to finance this investment, Harriet fears that she won't be able to develop her great idea.

Financial markets can help both Harriet and Britt solve their problems. Harriet can obtain the funds for her investment from Britt (and people like him). Her company can issue new stock, which people like Britt will buy in the hope of sharing in Harriet's future profits. Harriet can also raise funds by selling bonds and using part of her future profits to make the payments promised by the bonds.

This is a win–win outcome. If Harriet develops iSmells and the app takes off, her company will flourish and Britt will earn large returns on the stocks and bonds that he buys. Harriet's investment will benefit other people as well: her workers will earn the high wages that a profitable business can pay, and people around the world will have fun exchanging smells.

This simple example captures the primary role of all the trillion-dollar financial markets in the real world. At any time, some people consume less than they earn and save the rest. Other people know how to use these savings for investments that earn profits, increase production and employment, and otherwise benefit the economy. When they work well, financial markets transfer funds from an economy's savers to its investors.

Risk Sharing

Financial markets have a second important role in the economy: they help people share risks. Even if investors could finance their projects without financial markets, the markets would exist to perform this risk-sharing function alone.

To see this point, let's suppose that Harriet is wealthy. If she uses most of her wealth, she could finance the expansion of her business without getting funds from anyone else and would not have to sell stocks or bonds in financial markets. She would retain full ownership of her firm and keep all the profits from iSmells.

Because the software business, like any industry, is risky, this strategy is probably unwise. Harriet's new software might be profitable, but there is no guarantee. It's possible that another firm will produce a better version of the software or that consumers will tire of smart-phone gimmicks and move on to the next technological toy.

In these cases, Harriet might not sell much software, and she could lose the funds she invested. Because of this risk, putting her money in a safe instead of into her company starts to look like a better idea. This strategy means giving up a chance for high software profits, but it is less risky.

Fortunately, Harriet does not have to choose between hoarding her money and risking it all on her company. Thanks to financial markets, she can fund her new investment, at least in part, by issuing stocks and bonds. This approach reduces the amount of her own wealth that Harriet must put into the firm and makes it possible for her to share the risk from her business with the buyers of her securities.

"Your mother called to remind you to diversify."

Harriet can use the wealth she doesn't spend on iSmells to buy stocks and bonds issued by other companies. She is likely to earn money on these assets even if her own business fares poorly. Harriet can also buy bonds issued by the U.S. and other governments. Such behavior is an example of **diversification**, the distribution of wealth among many assets.

Why is diversification desirable? Most of the time, some companies do well and others do badly. The software industry might boom while the steel industry loses money, or vice versa, and one software company may succeed while another fails. If a person's wealth is tied to one company, he loses a lot if the company is unsuccessful. If he buys the securities of many companies, bad luck and good luck tend to average out. Diversification lets savers earn healthy returns from securities while minimizing the risk of disaster.

Upcoming chapters discuss some sophisticated ideas about diversification and risk sharing, such as the markets for futures and options. At its core, however, the idea of diversification is simply common sense. The late James Tobin won the Nobel Prize in economics in 1981 largely for developing theories of asset diversification. When a newspaper reporter asked Tobin to summarize his Nobel-winning ideas, he said simply, "Don't put all your eggs in one basket."

But just because a principle reflects common sense doesn't mean that people follow it. The following case study offers an example of people who failed to heed James Tobin's advice, with disastrous consequences.

CASE STUDY

The Perils of Employee Stock Ownership

Many Americans save for their retirement through *401(k) plans*, named for the congressional act that created them. A 401(k) plan is a savings fund administered by a company for its workers. Saving through a 401(k) plan is appealing because any income contributed to the plan is not taxed. In addition, some companies match employee contributions to 401(k) plans.

A person who puts money in a 401(k) plan is offered a variety of assets to purchase. Usually the choices include shares in **mutual funds**. A mutual fund is a financial firm that buys and holds a large number of different stocks and bonds. Buying mutual fund shares is a relatively easy way to diversify your eggs into more than one basket.

A company's 401(k) asset offerings often include stock in the company itself, and some employees choose to put most of their 401(k) savings in their company's stock. As a result, their assets are not diversified. There seem to be several reasons for this behavior. Some employers encourage it, believing that workers are more loyal if they own company stock. Many workers are confident about their companies' prospects, so they view company stock as less risky than other securities. People are influenced by success stories such as that of Microsoft, where employees grew rich from owning company stock.

But putting all your eggs in one basket is disastrous if someone drops the basket, as happened at Enron, a huge energy company that went bankrupt in 2001. At Enron, 58 percent of all 401(k) funds, and all the savings of some workers, were devoted to Enron stock. During 2001, as an accounting scandal unfolded, Enron's stock price dropped from $85 to 30 cents. This drastic decline wiped out the retirement savings of many employees. One 59-year-old man saw the balance in his 401(k) account fall from $600,000 to $11,000.

The disaster was even worse because Enron laid off most of its employees. Workers lost their life savings at the same time they lost their jobs. Many suffered severe hardships such as the loss of their homes.

Since the Enron disaster, financial advisers have urged greater diversification in 401(k) plans. Many people have taken this advice to heart. One study estimates that, averaging over all companies, the percentage of 401(k) funds in company stock fell from 19 percent in 1999 to 10 percent in 2008.

The government has encouraged this trend through the Pension Reform Act of 2006, which limits companies' efforts to promote employee stock ownership. Before the act, some companies contributed their stock to 401(k) plans on the condition that workers hold on to the stock. Now employees must be allowed to sell company stock after three years of service.

Despite these changes, economists worry that too much 401(k) wealth remains in company stock. Company stock accounts for more than half of 401(k) assets at some large firms, including Procter & Gamble, Pfizer, and General Electric. In 2008–2009, GE employees saw their 401(k) balances plummet when GE Capital, a subsidiary that lends to consumers and businesses, suffered large losses. GE's stock price fell from $37.49 in December 2008 to $5.73 in March 2009, a decrease of 85 percent. In this case, the price recovered somewhat—it was $18.94 in March 2010—but the GE episode illustrates the perils of holding company stock.

Some economists think the government should take stronger action to address this problem. They propose a cap on the percentage of 401(k) money that goes to company stock. At this writing, however, no new laws appear imminent.[1] ∎

---

[1] For more on Enron's workers, see "Workers Feel Pain of Layoffs and Added Sting of Betrayal," *New York Times*, January 20, 2002, page A1. For recent trends in 401(k) plans, see Jack VanDerhei, Sarah Holden, and Luis Alonso, "401(k) Plan Asset Allocation, Account Balances, and Loan Activity in 2008," Issue Brief #335, Employee Benefit Research Institute, October 2009.

15-3 Asymmetric Information

When financial markets work well, they channel funds from savers to investors, and they help people reduce risk. But financial markets don't always work well. Sometimes they break down, harming savers, investors, and the economy. The problems of financial markets are complex, but many have the same root cause: **asymmetric information**, a situation in which one participant in an economic transaction has more information than the other participant. In financial markets, the asymmetry generally occurs because the sellers of securities have more information than the buyers.

Two types of asymmetric information exist in financial markets, *adverse selection* and *moral hazard*. These two concepts are outlined in Figure 15-1 and discussed in detail in the next sections.

Adverse Selection

In general, **adverse selection** means that the people or firms that are most eager to make a transaction are the least desirable to parties on the other side of the transaction. In securities markets, a firm is most eager to issue stocks and bonds if the values of these securities are low. That is the case if the firm's prospects are poor, which means that earnings on its stock are likely to be low and default risk on its bonds is high. Adverse selection is a problem for buyers of securities because they have less information than issuers about the securities' value. Because of their relative ignorance, buyers run a risk of overpaying for securities that will probably produce low returns.

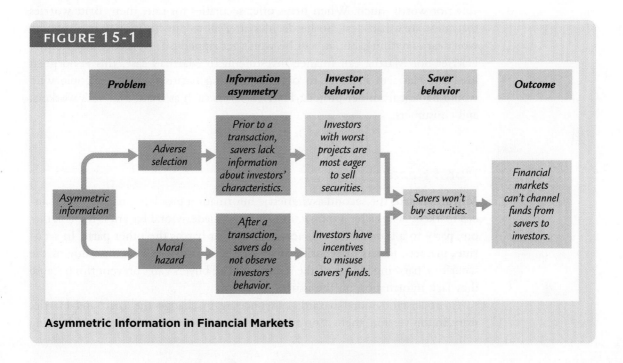

FIGURE 15-1

Asymmetric Information in Financial Markets

To illustrate adverse selection, let's return to the story of Harriet and Britt and add a third character, Martha. Like Harriet, Martha runs a software firm, and she would like to develop iSmells technology. But Martha is not as gifted as Harriet. Not only are there technical glitches in Martha's plans for the software, but she is a terrible manager. She is disorganized, and her abrasive personality results in high employee turnover. For all these reasons, Martha is less likely than Harriet to develop a successful product.

Both Martha and Harriet would like to finance their investments by selling securities to Britt. If Britt knew that Harriet is more talented than Martha, he would realize that Harriet's stock will probably produce higher earnings than Martha's and that Harriet is less likely to go bankrupt and default on her bonds. In short, he would prefer to buy Harriet's securities over Martha's. But remember: Britt's expertise is baseball, not software or business. The two women have equally glib sales pitches for their products, so both businesses seem like good bets to him. Because he doesn't know Martha or Harriet, can't evaluate their talents, and doesn't know the likelihood that each will succeed, Britt doesn't know the value of either woman's securities.

The story gets worse. Martha and Harriet understand their businesses, so they *do* know the value of their securities. They have more information than Britt. This information asymmetry produces adverse selection: Martha, the more inept businessperson, wants to issue more securities than Harriet. Why? Harriet knows that shares in her company are worth a lot. Therefore, while she wants to diversify by selling some stock to others, she wants to keep a relatively large amount for herself. Martha, on the other hand, knows her stock is not worth much because there's a good chance her company will fail. Therefore, she wants to unload all her stock onto other people and keep little or none for herself.

Britt doesn't understand software, but he does understand adverse selection. He realizes that when somebody is extremely eager to sell something, it is probably not worth much. When firms offer securities for sale, then, Britt worries that most are a bad deal. So he decides after all to put his money in a safe; he won't earn anything, but at least he won't get ripped off. Consequently, neither Harriet nor Martha can finance investment. In Martha's case, this is no great loss. But Harriet's inability to obtain financing harms the many people who would benefit from her project: Harriet, savers such as Britt, Harriet's workers, and consumers.

Moral Hazard

Moral hazard, the second asymmetric information problem prevalent in financial markets, arises after a transaction has been made. Moral hazard is the risk that one party to a transaction will act in a way that harms the other party. In securities markets, issuers of securities may take actions that reduce the value of the securities, harming buyers of the securities. The buyers can't prevent this because they lack information on the issuers' behavior.

To understand moral hazard, let's once again change the Britt-and-Harriet story. In this version, there is no adverse selection: Harriet is the only one looking for funding (there is no Martha) and everyone in securities markets, including Britt, knows that Harriet can produce great software. Britt would do well to buy Harriet's securities as long as Harriet performs as everyone expects her to and wisely uses the funds for software development.

But what if Harriet doesn't do what she's supposed to do? Software is a tough, competitive industry. Harriet has the skills to succeed, but she must work hard and keep costs low to earn profits. Unfortunately, as a human being, Harriet faces temptations. She wants to pay high salaries to herself and the friends who work for her. She wants some nice Postimpressionist paintings on her office wall. And she thinks it would be fun to leave work at 2:00 every Friday afternoon to party at trendy clubs.

If Harriet succumbs to these temptations, then costs rise, productivity falls, and her firm is less profitable. If the problems get out of hand, Harriet's firm could even go bankrupt. If Harriet had financed her business with her own wealth, she would have incentives to work hard and behave prudently because the cost of artwork and parties would come out of her own pocket. But these incentives disappear if Harriet's firm is financed by Britt. If Britt buys the firm's stock, then it is he, not Harriet, who loses if profits are low. If Britt buys bonds, it is he who loses if the firm goes bankrupt and defaults.

Asymmetric information underlies this example of moral hazard. Harriet knows how she runs her business and Britt doesn't, but he does know the fickleness of human nature. Before buying her securities, Britt might make Harriet promise to work hard and spend his money wisely. This promise would be meaningless, however, because Britt lives on the other side of the country and has no way of knowing whether Harriet is keeping her promise. If Britt could somehow see everything Harriet does, he could demand his savings back the first time she leaves work early. He could cancel her account at the art dealer and her reservations at the trendy clubs. But Britt is busy on the pitcher's mound and can't keep track of what happens at Harriet's office. So he refuses to buy Harriet's securities. Once again, Harriet cannot finance her investment, even though she has a great idea for a new product.

15-4 Banks

The story of Britt and Harriet has taken a bad turn. Because of asymmetric information, financial markets have failed to channel funds from savers to investors. But now a hero arrives on the scene: a bank. Britt deposits his money in the bank and earns interest. The bank lends money to Harriet for her investment. Ultimately, Britt's savings find their way to Harriet, and both people (and the economy as a whole) benefit.

Why can Harriet get money from a bank if she can't get it from financial markets? The answer is that banks reduce the problem of asymmetric information. We'll discuss how banks address asymmetric information later in this section. First, we need to understand some basics about banks.

What Is a Bank?

A bank is one kind of **financial institution**. A financial institution, also called a *financial intermediary*, is any firm that helps channel funds from savers to investors. A mutual fund is another example of a financial institution because it sells shares to savers and uses the proceeds to purchase securities from a number of firms.

A **bank** is a financial institution defined by two characteristics. First, it raises funds by accepting deposits. These include savings deposits and checking deposits that people and firms use to make payments. Both types of deposits earn interest, and savings deposits earn more than checking. Second, a bank uses its funds to make loans to companies and individuals. These are **private loans:** each is negotiated between one lender and one borrower. In this way, they differ from the borrowing that occurs when companies sell bonds to the public at large in financial markets.

In the past, banks were restricted to accepting deposits and making loans, but today, banks engage in many financial businesses. They trade securities, sell mutual funds and insurance, and much more. Still, what makes them banks are their deposits and loans.

There are several types of banks. For example, *savings and loan associations* are usually small, and much of their lending is to people buying homes. *Commercial banks* can be very large, and they lend for many purposes. We discuss the various types of banks in Chapter 18.

A note on terminology: in everyday language, the term "bank" is used more broadly than we have defined it. Some institutions are called banks even though they don't accept deposits or make loans. One example is an *investment bank*, a financial institution that helps companies issue new stocks and bonds. An investment bank is not really a bank in economists' sense of the term.

Banks Versus Financial Markets

Like financial markets, banks channel funds from savers to investors. Funds flow through a bank in a two-step process: savers deposit money in the bank, and then the bank lends the deposited money to investors. In financial markets, savers provide funds directly to investors by buying their stocks and bonds. For these reasons, channeling funds through banks is called **indirect finance** and channeling them through financial markets is called **direct finance.** Figure 15-2 illustrates these concepts.

Why Banks Exist

Indirect finance is costly. To cover their costs and earn some profit, banks charge higher interest on loans than they pay on deposits. In effect, banks take a cut of the funds they transfer to investors. Nonetheless, people like Britt and Harriet use banks because of the asymmetric information problems that hinder direct finance.

Banks help Harriet to expand her business, and they also help Britt because they pay him interest on his savings. The interest that Britt earns from his bank

FIGURE 15-2

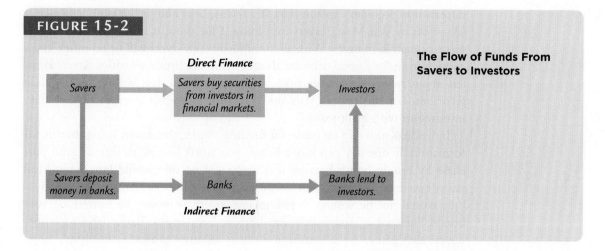

Direct Finance

The Flow of Funds From
Savers to Investors

Savers → Savers buy securities from investors in financial markets. → Investors

Savers deposit money in banks. → Banks → Banks lend to investors.

Indirect Finance

account may be less than the return on a security, but it's more than Britt would earn by putting his money in a safe.

Banks can help Britt and Harriet because they lessen the problems of asymmetric information that hobble securities markets. Banks overcome these problems by producing information about the investors that borrow from them. Greater information reduces both adverse selection and moral hazard in financial transactions.

Reducing Adverse Selection Banks reduce adverse selection by screening potential borrowers. If both Harriet and Martha want money, Britt can't tell who has a better investment project. But a good banker can figure it out.

When the two investors apply for loans, they must provide information about their business plans, past careers, and finances. Bank loan officers are trained to evaluate this information (and information from independent sources such as credit reporting agencies) and decide whose project is likely to succeed. A firm with a bad project may go bankrupt, and bankrupt firms default not only on any bonds they've issued but also on bank loans they've taken out.

Loan officers may detect flaws in Martha's plans or see that her past projects have lost money. They turn down Martha and lend money to Harriet, who has a record of success. Because the bank has gathered information, funds flow to the most productive investment.

Reducing Moral Hazard To combat moral hazard once a loan is made, banks include covenants in their loan contracts. A **covenant** is a statement about how the bank expects the borrower to behave, and it must be agreed upon by both the bank and the borrower. For example, Harriet's lender might include a covenant requiring that she spend her loan on computers—not parties at trendy clubs.

Banks monitor their borrowers to make sure they obey covenants and don't waste money. Harriet must send her bank periodic reports on her spending. If Harriet misuses her loan—thereby increasing the risk of bankruptcy and default—the bank can demand its money back. With such monitoring in place, it is safe for the bank to finance Harriet's investment.

Who Needs Banks? Some firms can raise funds by issuing securities; those that can't depend on bank loans to fund their investments. The asymmetric information problem explains why. If a firm is large and well established (such as Microsoft or Wal-Mart), savers may know a lot about it from the media or the security analysis industry. With all this information, savers will believe they know enough to make a good decision about buying the firm's securities. Savers know less about newer or smaller firms, however, and are less willing to buy their securities. For this reason, start-ups and small businesses need to finance their investments with bank loans.

Individuals also rely on banks for funding. Again, the reason is asymmetric information. If one day you buy a house, you won't be able to finance your purchase by issuing bonds because it is likely that no one would buy them. Most savers have heard of Microsoft but probably know little or nothing about you, so they would not be willing to risk giving you their money by purchasing your bonds. Fortunately, individuals can borrow from banks. Banks lend to homebuyers after gathering information on their incomes and credit histories.

15-5 The Financial System and Economic Growth

We have seen how the financial system helps individual savers, such as Britt, and investors, such as Harriet. Financial markets and banks also benefit the economy as a whole. When funds flow to good investment projects, the economy becomes more productive and living standards rise. In other words, a strong financial system spurs economic growth.

The Allocation of Saving

In Chapters 7 and 8, we used the Solow model to study economic growth. One of the model's central ideas is that an economy's output per worker depends on its saving rate. The more people save, the more funds are available for investment. With high saving, companies can build factories and implement new technologies. The economy produces more and its people become richer.

The Solow model has large elements of truth. We saw, for example, that differences in saving rates help explain differences in income across countries. Yet the model ignores the issues discussed in this chapter. It assumes that saving flows automatically to investors with productive projects. In fact, however, the right investors get funds only if the economy has a well-functioning financial system. An economy can save a lot and still remain poor if saving is not channeled to its best uses.

Financial systems vary across countries. Some countries, including the United States, have large stock and bond markets and banks that usually have ample funds. In these countries, it is relatively easy for individuals and firms with good investment projects to raise funds. In other countries, the financial system is underdeveloped; it is difficult for firms to issue securities, and bank loans are scarce. When a financial system cannot work properly, investors have trouble financing their projects and economic growth slows.

What explains these differences? One factor is government regulation. Some governments regulate securities markets to reduce the problem of asymmetric information. In the United States, for example, companies that issue securities must publish annual reports on their investments and earnings. This information lessens adverse selection, and savers are more willing to buy securities. Some countries lack such regulations.

Government policies also affect banks. In the United States, the government provides deposit insurance, which compensates people who lose deposits because a bank fails. Not all countries have such insurance. Chapter 18 discusses governments' involvement in banking in more detail.

Evidence on the Financial System and Growth

Many economists have studied the effects of financial systems on economic growth. Much of this research has occurred at the World Bank, a large international organization that promotes economic development. The research has found that differences in financial systems help explain why some countries are richer than others.

Figure 15-3 presents a portion of World Bank data drawn from 155 countries between 1996 and 2007. Panel (a) shows *stock market capitalization* in several groups of countries. This variable is the value of all stocks issued by corporations, expressed as a percentage of GDP. For example, a figure of 50 percent means the total value of stocks is half a year's output. Stock market capitalization measures investors' success in raising funds through the stock market.

Panel (b) shows total *bank loans*, again as a percentage of GDP. This variable measures banks' success in channeling funds from savers to investors.

The figure divides countries into four groups based on their real GDP per person. The high-income group contains a quarter of all countries, those with the highest real GDP per person. Upper-middle-income countries make up the next quarter, and so on. For each group, the figure shows the average levels of stock market capitalization and bank loans.

Figure 15-3 has a simple message: richer countries—those with higher real GDP per person—tend to have more developed financial systems than poorer countries. Rich countries have larger stock markets and more bank loans. These facts support the view that financial development aids economic growth.

By themselves, these graphs are not conclusive. They show a correlation between financial development and income levels, but correlation does not prove causation. Financial development could cause economic growth, but the opposite is also possible: perhaps countries grow rich for some other reason, such as good educational systems or robust foreign trade, and this growth causes them to develop stronger financial systems. Or perhaps some third factor causes both economic growth and financial development.

Much of the World Bank's research addresses the question of causality. One strategy is to compare countries with strong and weak financial systems in some past period, such as the 1960s. Researchers find that countries with stronger systems during the 1960s had faster economic growth in the decades *after* the 1960s.

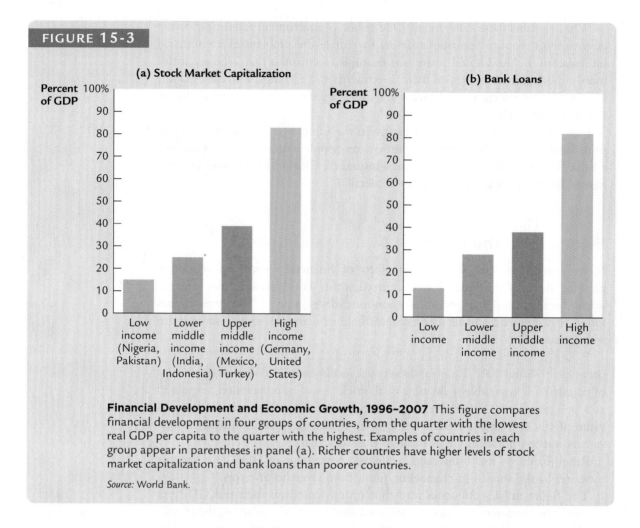

Financial Development and Economic Growth, 1996–2007 This figure compares financial development in four groups of countries, from the quarter with the lowest real GDP per capita to the quarter with the highest. Examples of countries in each group appear in parentheses in panel (a). Richer countries have higher levels of stock market capitalization and bank loans than poorer countries.

Source: World Bank.

This suggests that financial development comes first and causes growth, rather than vice versa.[2]

Let's examine two cases that illustrate how the financial system affects growth. The first, from U.S. history, discusses an unwise government policy that interfered with the financial system. The second discusses recent efforts to expand the financial systems of poor countries.

CASE STUDY

Unit Banking and Economic Growth

Today, large banks conduct business throughout the United States. You can find branches of Bank of America, for example, in most U.S. cities. This has not always been true. Before World War II, federal law allowed a bank to operate in

---

[2] Much of this research is summarized in Asli Demirguc-Kunt and Ross Levine, "Finance, Financial Sector Policies, and Economic Growth," World Bank Policy Research Working Paper 4469, January 2008.

only one state. Some states went further than federal law and restricted each bank to a single branch. A bank's customers could make deposits or seek loans at only one location. This restriction was called *unit banking*.

Proponents of unit banking believed that multiple branches would allow banks to become too large and powerful. Large banks might drive smaller banks out of business and exploit customers. Unit banking was most common in the Midwest, the home of the Populist political movement of the nineteenth century. Populists were angry at banks for seizing property from farmers who defaulted on loans.

In retrospect, most economists think unit banking was a mistake. It hurt both banks and their customers, for several reasons:

- Large banks benefit from *economies of scale*. They operate more efficiently than small banks. That is, they can offer services at a lower cost per customer. Unit banking increased costs at banks by keeping them small.

- With unit banking, a bank operated in only one town. If the town's economy did poorly, many borrowers defaulted on loans. The bank lost money and might be forced out of business. Having branches in different towns is a form of diversification: it reduces risk.

- Under unit banking, many small towns had only one bank, which operated as a monopoly. Customers had nowhere else to go if the bank charged high interest rates on their loans or provided poor service. In states that allowed multiple branches, banks from throughout the state could enter a town and increase competition.

For all these reasons, unit banking reduced the number of banks and their efficiency. The policy impeded the flow of funds from savers to investors. The result was lower economic growth.

Economists Rajeev Dehejia of Columbia University and Adriana Lleras-Muney of Princeton University analyzed the effects of unit banking. Their 2007 study compares states with unit banking to states that allowed multiple branches during the period from 1900 to 1940. As you might expect, the volume of bank loans was higher in states that permitted branching, confirming that branching helps move funds from savers to investors. The study's most important findings involve the effects of unit banking on the overall economy, including both the agricultural and manufacturing sectors. In states with branching, farms were larger in acres, and the value of farm machinery per acre was higher. Apparently the less constrained banking systems provided more funds for farmers to expand their farms and make them more productive. States with branching also had higher employment in manufacturing industries and higher manufacturing wages. Again this finding suggests that when banks were allowed to have branches, they were better able to channel funds to investors, in this case firms that wanted to build new and more productive factories. The study provides a concrete example of how policies that promote banking can contribute to a prosperous economy.[3] ■

---

[3] Rajeev Dehejia and Adriana Lleras-Muney, "Financial Development and Pathways of Growth: State Branching and Deposit Insurance Laws in the United States from 1900 to 1940," *Journal of Law and Economics* 50 (2007) 239–272.

Microfinance

Poor countries have severe shortages of jobs that pay decent wages. As a consequence, many people seek to support themselves by starting rudimentary businesses—making furniture or clothes, running small restaurants or shops, and so on. In many countries, women are especially likely to start their own businesses because discrimination limits their other opportunities.

A business requires an initial investment; for example, a furniture maker must buy tools and raw materials. Often the necessary funds are small by the standards of high-income countries but still exceed the wealth of would-be entrepreneurs. Most banks shy away from lending to the very poor, because they fear high default rates and because the interest payments on tiny loans do not cover the costs of screening and monitoring borrowers. Discrimination can make it especially difficult for women to get loans.

Without bank loans, many people are unable to start businesses that might lift them out of poverty. Others borrow from village moneylenders at exorbitant interest rates—sometimes 10–20 percent per *day*.

Microfinance seeks to fill this gap in developing countries' banking systems by providing small loans to poor people. The idea was pioneered by Muhammad Yunus, an economics professor in Bangladesh, who founded the Grameen Bank in the village of Jobra in 1974. Since then, microfinance institutions (MFIs) have sprung up in Africa, Asia, Latin America, eastern Europe, and even poor neighborhoods in New York and other U.S. cities.

MFIs are initially funded by governments, international organizations such as the World Bank, or private foundations. Their loans can be as small as $25, but they are large enough to fund simple businesses. Microfinance has grown spectacularly since its beginnings in a single village. As of 2010, MFIs had close to 100 million borrowers around the world.

MFIs try to overcome the problems that make conventional banks wary of lending to the poor. For example, some MFIs require that people borrow money in groups. The Grameen Bank lends to five would-be entrepreneurs at a time. This practice reduces the bank's costs per loan. In addition, it reduces the problem of moral hazard—the risk that borrowers will squander their loans and default. Credit is cut off to all five borrowers if any one borrower defaults, creating peer pressure to use loans prudently.

Many MFIs lend primarily to women. In part this reflects the institutions' desire to serve a group that faces discrimination elsewhere. But MFIs also cite their self-interest: they report that women default on loans less often than men. Overall, default rates on microloans are low—less than 2 percent at many institutions.

Many people think that microfinance has helped reduce poverty. In 2006, Muhammad Yunus and the Grameen Bank were awarded the Nobel Peace Prize, making Yunus the first economist to win a Nobel Prize in an area other than economics. In explaining its choice, the Nobel committee said that "loans to poor people without any financial security had appeared to be an impossible idea," but "Yunus and Grameen Bank have shown that even the poorest of the poor can work to bring about their own development."

The microfinance industry is changing as it grows. Most MFIs are nonprofit organizations supported by donations. In recent years, however, for-profit commercial banks have taken an interest in microfinance. These banks have observed the success of MFIs, especially the low default rates on their loans, and decided that microfinance can be profitable. Commercial banks have started making microloans in countries such as India, Colombia, and Senegal. Elsewhere, commercial banks support microfinance indirectly by lending money to MFIs.

Mexico's Compartamos ("let's share" in Spanish) is one of Latin America's largest microlenders, with a million borrowers. In 2006, it transformed itself from a nonprofit organization into a commercial bank. In 2007, it raised $500 million by issuing stock that is now traded on Mexico's stock exchange. Compartamos no longer relies on donations or government funding.

Many supporters of microfinance welcome the involvement of commercial banks because it increases the availability of microloans. Others, however, criticize the "commercialization" of microfinance. They allege that for-profit lenders charge excessive interest rates and deny loans to the poorest of the poor. Muhammad Yunus has criticized Compartamos, saying it is "raking in money off poor people desperate for cash."[4] ∎

Markets Versus Central Planning

Another way to grasp the importance of the financial system is to ask what happens if an economy lacks one entirely. Imagine a country with an economy run by the government. No private firms exist; everybody works for the government, which decides what goods and services to produce and who receives them. The government also decides what investment projects are worthwhile and orders that they be undertaken. No one raises funds for investment through financial markets or private banks.

This is not a fanciful idea, but rather a basic description of a **centrally planned economy**, also known as a *command economy*. This was the economic system under communist governments in the Soviet Union and Eastern Europe, which held power until the early 1990s. The economies of Cuba and North Korea are still based primarily on central planning.

If you have studied microeconomics, you learned that its central idea is the desirability of allocating resources through free markets. Market prices provide signals about what firms should produce and consumers should buy, thus guiding the economy to efficiency. Microeconomists take a dim view of central planning because a modern economy is too complicated for government officials to run without the help of markets.

The basic principles of free markets also apply to the financial system. Prices in financial markets, such as stock prices and interest rates, help channel funds to the most productive investments. This process does not work perfectly, but it

---

[4] For more on this controversy, see "Microfinance's Success Sets Off a Debate in Mexico," *New York Times*, April 5, 2008, page C1; and Robert Cull, Asli Demirguc-Kunt, and Jonathan Morduch, "Microfinance Meets the Market," *Journal of Economic Perspectives* (Winter 2009): 167–192.

beats the alternative of central planning. History shows that government officials do a poor job of choosing investment projects. To illustrate this point, the next case study examines history's most famous example of central planning.

CASE STUDY

Investment in the Soviet Union

In 1917, a communist revolution led by V. I. Lenin overthrew Czar Nicholas II of Russia. Lenin established the Soviet Union, which eventually grew to include Russia and 14 other "republics," from Ukraine in the west to Uzbekistan in central Asia. The economy of the Soviet Union was centrally planned.

Initially, the Soviet economy was mainly agricultural, and most of its people were poor. After Lenin's death in 1924, Josef Stalin took control of the government and began a push to "industrialize." Stalin and the leaders who succeeded him hoped to achieve rapid economic growth through investment in factories and modern technologies. Because Soviet planners controlled the economy's resources, they could dictate high levels of investment. From the 1930s to the 1980s, investment as a percentage of GDP was more than twice as high in the Soviet Union as in the United States and Western Europe.

At first, high investment produced rapid economic growth. In the 1950s and 1960s, Soviet planners predicted—and Western leaders feared—that the Soviet Union would become the world's most productive economy. But growth slowed in the 1970s and 1980s. Despite high investment, the Soviet Union fell further and further behind the West. Partly because of economic failure, the Soviet Union broke apart in the early 1990s. Russia and the other former republics shifted to economic systems based on free markets.

What went wrong with the Soviet Union? While many factors led to its downfall, it is clear, in retrospect, that an important factor was a misallocation of investment. Soviet planners chose projects poorly, so high investment did not lead to high output. Economic historians point to a number of mistakes:

- Planners put too many resources into prestige sectors of the economy that symbolized economic development, mainly heavy industry. The Soviets built too many factories to produce steel and too few to produce consumer goods. They invested in an unsuccessful effort to develop large airplanes. Starting in the 1950s, they spent heavily on their space program, which boosted national pride but strained the economy.

- Soviet planners overemphasized *short-run* increases in productivity. They were too hasty in trying to reach Western output levels. In 1931, Stalin said, "We are fifty or a hundred years behind the advanced countries. We must make good the distance in ten years. Either we do it or they will crush us." This attitude caused planners to neglect investments that were important for the long term. For example, they skimped on maintenance of roads and other infrastructure. This had little immediate effect, but over time the crumbling infrastructure became a drag on productivity.

- A related problem was that factory managers were evaluated based on annual production quotas. Managers focused on meeting current quotas rather than increasing long-run productivity. For example, they were reluctant to retool factories to use new technologies because this might disrupt production temporarily.

■ The power of government bureaucrats reduced efficiency. Plant managers were rewarded for following orders, not for thinking of innovative ways to raise output. In addition, managers competed for investment funds by lobbying the government. Those who were well connected or talented at lobbying received more resources than they needed, while other managers received too few.[5] ■

15-6 Conclusion

This chapter has surveyed the main parts of the financial system: securities markets and banks. We saw how securities markets transfer funds from savers to investors and how they help people share risks. We learned that asymmetric information problems, namely adverse selection and moral hazard, reduce the effectiveness with which securities markets channel funds. We explored how banks reduce asymmetric information problems and make it possible for investors who cannot issue securities to raise funds for their investments. Finally, we saw that the strength of a country's financial system is an important factor influencing its economic growth.

The next four chapters expand our analysis of the financial system. Chapter 16 discusses how prices in securities markets, such as stock and bond prices, are determined. Chapter 17 examines choices facing participants in securities markets, such as firms' decisions about issuing securities and savers' decisions about what securities to buy. Chapter 18 turns to the banking industry, discussing how banks make profits, the risks they face, and the role of government regulation. Finally, Chapter 19 discusses financial crises, examining both their causes and their devastating effects on economies.

Summary

1. The financial system has two central parts: financial markets (the markets for currencies and securities) and banks.

2. The securities sold in financial markets include bonds and stocks. When a corporation or government issues bonds, it is borrowing money from those who buy the bonds. In return, it promises the buyers predetermined

---

[5] For more on Soviet investment, see Gur Ofer, "Soviet Economic Growth, 1928–1985," *Journal of Economic Literature* 25 (December 1987): 1767–1833. This article was published shortly before the breakup of the Soviet Union.

payments at certain times. A stock is an ownership share in a corporation. A stockholder receives a share of the corporation's earnings.

3. The primary function of financial markets is to channel funds from savers to investors with productive uses for those saved funds. Financial markets also help people diversify their asset holdings, which reduces risk.

4. Financial markets can malfunction because of asymmetric information: sellers of securities (investors) know more than buyers. Adverse selection arises from asymmetric information about investors' characteristics. Investors with low chances for success are the most eager to sell securities. Moral hazard arises from asymmetric information about investors' actions. Investors have incentives to misuse the funds they receive from savers.

5. Financial institutions such as banks and mutual funds are firms that help channel funds from savers to investors. Banks raise funds by accepting deposits and use the funds to make private loans. Banks reduce adverse selection and moral hazard by gathering information to screen borrowers, putting covenants into loan agreements, and monitoring borrower behavior.

6. Saving can spur economic growth, but only if the financial system channels savings into productive investment. Poorly conceived government policies can hinder the operation of the financial system and reduce economic growth.

KEY CONCEPTS

Financial market	Mutual fund	Private loan
Security	Asymmetric information	Indirect finance
Bond	Adverse selection	Direct finance
Interest	Moral hazard	Covenant
Default	Financial institution	Microfinance
Stock	Bank	Centrally planned economy
Diversification		

QUESTIONS FOR REVIEW

1. What is a security?

2. What are the two main functions of the financial system?

3. What is the difference between a bond and a stock?

4. What is asymmetric information, and why is it a problem in financial markets?

5. What is adverse selection? How do banks reduce this problem?

6. What is moral hazard? How do banks reduce this problem?

7. Jennifer wants to get a loan from Citizens Bank to open a hair salon, but she is sometimes tempted to visit local casinos. What type of asymmetric information problem does this example illustrate? How might the bank solve this problem?

8. Ned wants a $10,000 loan from Capital One to open a sushi bar, but he filed for bankruptcy

eight years ago. What type of asymmetric information problem does this example illustrate? How might the bank solve this problem?

9. Why is a healthy financial system important for economic growth?

10. Why have centrally planned economies failed?

PROBLEMS AND APPLICATIONS

1. When financial markets channel funds from savers to investors, who benefits? Explain.

2. Suppose the owner of a corporation needs $1 million to finance a new investment. If his total wealth is $1.2 million, would it be better to use his own funds for the investment or to issue stock in the corporation? What if the owner's wealth is $1 billion?

3. If you were required to put all your retirement savings in the securities of one company, what company would you choose, and why? Would you choose the company you work for? Would you buy stock or bonds?

4. Suppose there are two investors. One has a project to build a factory; the other has a project to visit a casino and gamble on roulette. Which investor has a greater incentive to issue bonds? Which investor's bonds are a better deal for savers?

5. A company raises funds by issuing short-term bonds (commercial paper) and uses the funds to make private loans. Such a firm is called a *finance company*. Is a finance company a type of bank?

6. Firms such as Moody's and Standard & Poor's study corporations that issue bonds. They publish "ratings" for the bonds—evaluations of the likelihood of default. Suppose these rating companies went out of business. What effect would this have on the bond market? What effect would it have on banks?

7. National credit bureaus collect information on people's credit histories. They are likely to know whether you ever defaulted on a loan. Suppose that a new privacy law makes it illegal for credit bureaus to collect this information. What effect would this have on the banking industry?

8. When a bank makes a loan, it sometimes requires borrowers to maintain a checking account at the bank until the loan is paid off. What is the purpose of this requirement?

9. Microfinance institutions argue that (a) many traditional banks discriminate against women in lending and (b) women have lower default rates than men on loans from MFIs. Discuss how point (a) could explain point (b).

10. Go to www.planetrating.com, the site of Planet Rating, an organization that calls itself "the global microfinance rating agency." What is the main function of Planet Rating? How might its work help the microfinance industry to grow?

11. Do you know someone (such as a parent) who is working and saving for retirement? Does he or she have money in a 401(k) plan? What securities does the person hold through the plan? Does he or she follow the principle of diversification?

CHAPTER 16

Asset Prices and Interest Rates

We've long felt that the only value of stock forecasters is to make fortune tellers look good.

—*Warren Buffett*

At any time of the day, you can tap into financial news on your TV, computer, iPhone, or BlackBerry. You may learn, for example, that the price of Microsoft stock has risen from $35 at the start of the day to $37 at 2:00 P.M. but that it is still $8 below its high for the year. You may also see that the Dow Jones Index of stock prices has risen 89 points and that the price of a ten-year U.S. government bond has fallen from $998 to $995.

As the prices of stocks and bonds fluctuate, the owners of these assets see their wealth rise and fall. These price movements also affect the aggregate economy. In the 1990s, for example, U.S. stock prices rose rapidly and stockholders spent part of their gains on consumption goods. The boost to consumption helped fuel an economic boom in the second half of the decade. Subsequent declines in stock prices contributed to recessions in 2001 and 2007–2009.

As stock and bond prices scroll across your television or iPhone screen, their movements may appear mysterious. What economic forces determine asset prices? This chapter surveys the answers that economists give to this question. An asset entitles its owner to a future stream of income, so we first learn how to value an income stream and then examine how this valuation is used to determine an asset's price. We discuss the factors that cause asset prices to fluctuate over time, including the possibility of *bubbles* in which prices rise simply because of expectations that they will rise.

Throughout the chapter, we see that asset prices are closely related to interest rates. As a result, forces that cause interest rates to change, such as shifts in monetary policy, also help to explain asset-price movements. Finally, we examine the relationship between short-term and long-term interest rates and learn how this relationship helps us predict future interest rates.

16-1 Valuing Income Streams

Recall from Chapter 15 that a financial asset yields a stream of income in the future. The owner of a bond receives a payment when the bond matures and may receive coupon payments before then. The owner of a firm's stock receives part of the firm's future earnings. To find the value of an asset, we must determine the value of these income streams.

In making such valuations, the key principle is that payments have different values depending on when they are received. A dollar today is worth more than a dollar in the future because you can take today's dollar, put it in the bank, and earn interest on it. This process transforms one dollar today into more than one dollar in the future. Because of this principle, an economist's approach to asset pricing rests on a fundamental concept: the present value of an income stream.

Future Value

To compare payments at different times, economists begin with the concept of **future value**. The future value of a dollar is how many dollars it can produce in some future year. To understand this concept, suppose that banks pay a nominal interest rate of 4 percent. If you deposit a dollar today, it grows to $1.04 in a year. Thus, the future value of a dollar today is $1.04 in one year.

If you keep your money in the bank for a second year, it grows by another 4 percent. When $1.04 grows by 4 percent, it becomes $(1.04)(1.04)$, or $(1.04)^2 = \$1.082$. So a dollar today is worth $(1.04)^2$ in two years. If you keep the money in the bank for a third year, it grows by 4 percent again, becoming $(1.04)^3 = \$1.125$.

You should see the pattern. With a 4 percent interest rate, a dollar left in the bank for n years, where n is any number, grows to $\$(1.04)^n$. A dollar today is worth $\$(1.04)^n$ in n years.

The same principle applies to interest rates other than 4 percent. Let i be a nominal interest rate expressed in decimal form. (In decimal form, 4 percent is 0.04). A dollar today grows to $\$(1 + i)$ in one year, $\$(1 + i)^2$ in two years, and $\$(1 + i)^n$ in n years. So the future value of a dollar is given by

$$\text{Future Value of \$1 Today} = \$(1 + i)^n \text{ in } n \text{ Years.}$$

Present Value

We've seen how much a dollar today is worth in the future. Now let's turn this relation around to see how much a *future* dollar is worth *today*. This is the **present value** of a future dollar.

We can understand present value with a little algebra. We start by turning around the equation for future value:

$$\$(1 + i)^n \text{ in } n \text{ Years} = \$1 \text{ Today.}$$

Now divide both sides of the equation by $(1 + i)^n$:

$$\frac{\$(1 + i)^n}{(1 + i)^n} \text{ in } n \text{ Years} = \frac{\$1}{(1 + i)^n} \text{ Today.}$$

The left side of this equation simplifies and gives us the present value formula:

$$\text{Present Value of \$1 in } n \text{ Years} = \frac{\$1}{(1 + i)^n} \text{ Today.}$$

A dollar n years from today is worth $1/(1 + i)^n$ dollars today.

With a 4 percent interest rate, the present value of a dollar in n years is $\$1/(1.04)^n$. For example, the present value of a dollar in three years is $\$1/(1.04)^3 = \$0.889$. The present value of a dollar in twenty years is $\$1/(1.04)^{20} = \$0.456$.

Our analysis has a key implication: *a higher interest rate reduces the present value of future money.* Mathematically, a higher i reduces present value because it raises the denominator in the formula. The economic explanation is that a higher interest rate means a saver can trade a dollar today for more future dollars. Turning this around, at a higher interest rate, a future dollar is worth less today. For example, if the interest rate rises from 4 percent to 6 percent, the present value of a dollar in three years falls from $0.889 to $\$1/(1.06)^3 = \$0.840$. The present value of a dollar in twenty years falls from $0.456 to $0.312.

Series of Payments We can extend our reasoning to value a flow of money over multiple years. Suppose someone promises you $3 in two years and $5 in four years. Each dollar in two years is worth $\$1/(1 + i)^2$, so the $3 is worth $\$3/(1 + i)^2$. The $5 in four years is worth $\$5/(1 + i)^4$. Altogether, the present value of the future payments is $\$3/(1 + i)^2 + \$5/(1 + i)^4$.

To get a general formula for a series of payments, suppose you receive $\$X_1$ in one year, $\$X_2$ in two years, and so on up to $\$X_T$ in T years. The present value of this flow of money is

$$\text{Present Value} = \frac{\$X_1}{(1 + i)} + \frac{\$X_2}{(1 + i)^2} + \cdots + \frac{\$X_T}{(1 + i)^T}.$$

To practice using this formula, let's calculate the present value of a contract signed by baseball star C. C. Sabathia, a left-handed pitcher. After the 2008 season, the New York Yankees agreed to pay Sabathia $23 million per year for seven years, from 2009 through 2015. The total payments over the life of this contract are $7 \times \$23 = \$161$ million. To calculate the present value of the payments, let's assume an interest rate of 4 percent. In this case, the present value in 2008 was

$$\$23 \text{ million}/(1.04) + \$23 \text{ million}/(1.04)^2 + \cdots + \$23 \text{ million}/(1.04)^7.$$

If you plug these numbers into a financial calculator, you will find that the present value of Sabathia's salary in 2008 was about $138 million.

Payments Forever Some assets provide income indefinitely; there is no year T when the last payment is made. For example, a share of stock entitles the holder to a stream of earnings with no endpoint. A rare type of bond called a *perpetuity* pays interest forever.

In some cases, we can derive simple formulas for the present value of a perpetual income stream. One such case is a constant annual payment. If you receive a payment of $Z in all future years, the present value is[1]

$$\text{Present Value} = \frac{\$Z}{(1 + i)} + \frac{\$Z}{(1 + i)^2} + \frac{\$Z}{(1 + i)^3} + \cdots.$$

Using algebra, we can simplify this equation to

$$\text{Present Value} = \frac{\$Z}{i}.$$

Thus, a higher annual payment or lower interest rate means a higher present value. Conversely, a lower annual payment or higher interest rate means a lower present value. For example, if the interest rate is 4 percent, a payment of $100 per year forever has a present value of $100/(0.04) = $2500. If the interest rate falls to 2 percent, the present value of payments rises to $100/(0.02) = $5,000.

Another kind of perpetual income stream is a payment that grows over time at a constant rate. To analyze this case, let $Z be the payment in one year, and let g be the annual rate at which the payment grows. Each year, the payment is $(1 + g)$ times the previous payment: it is $Z(1 + g)$ in two years, $Z(1 + g)^2$ in three years, and so on. We assume the growth rate of payments is less than the interest rate ($g < i$). In this case, the present value of all payments is

$$\text{Present Value} = \frac{\$Z}{(1 + i)} + \frac{\$Z(1 + g)}{(1 + i)^2} + \frac{\$Z(1 + g)^2}{(1 + i)^3} + \cdots$$

This equation simplifies to:[2]

$$\text{Present Value} = \frac{\$Z}{(i - g)}.$$

Once again, the present value of payments depends on the initial payment Z and the interest rate i. In addition, present value depends on the growth rate g. When payments grow at a higher rate, their present value is higher. Mathematically, a higher g raises present value because it reduces $i - g$, the denominator in the formula.

Suppose again that $Z = \$100$ and $i = 4$ percent. If $g = 2$ percent, the present value of payments is $100/(0.04 - 0.02) = $100/(0.02) = $5,000. If g rises to 3 percent, the present value rises to $100/(0.04 - 0.03) = $100/(0.01) = $10,000.

Table 16-1 summarizes the key principles about present values that we have derived.

---

[1] *Mathematical note*: To derive this result, let $X = 1/(1 + i)$. We can write the previous equation as $PV = Z[X + X^2 + X^3 + \cdots] = ZX[1 + X + X^2 + \cdots]$. Footnote 2 on page 288 shows that $[1 + X + X^2 + \cdots] = 1/(1 - X)$. Therefore, $PV = ZX/(1 - X)$. Substituting in the definition of X and simplifying yields $PV = Z/i$.

[2] *Mathematical note*: To derive this result, let $X = (1 + g)/(1 + i)$ and write the previous equation as $PV = [Z/(1 + i)][1 + X + X^2 + \cdots]$. Footnote 2 on page 288 shows that $[1 + X + X^2 + \cdots] = 1/(1 - X)$. Therefore, $PV = Z/[(1 + i)(1 - X)]$. Substituting in the definition of X and simplifying yields $PV = Z/(i - g)$.

This derivation assumes $g < i$. If $i \geq g$, then the present value of payments is infinite.

TABLE 16-1

Present Values of Some Common Types of Payments

Payment (dollars)	Present Value (dollars)
$1 in n years	$\dfrac{1}{(1 + i)^n}$
A series of annual payments: $X_1, X_2, \ldots, X_T$	$\dfrac{X_1}{(1 + i)} + \dfrac{X_2}{(1 + i)^2} + \cdots + \dfrac{X_T}{(1 + i)^T}$
An annual payment of Z forever	$\dfrac{Z}{i}$
An annual payment that equals Z in the first year and grows at rate g	$\dfrac{Z}{(i - g)}$

16-2 The Classical Theory of Asset Prices

Now that we understand the concept of the present value of an income stream, we can use this concept to answer the question we raised earlier in this chapter: what factors determine the price of an asset, such as a stock or bond? Economists usually answer this question using the *classical theory of asset prices*, which is based on several ideas involving present values.

The Present Value of Income

An asset produces a flow of income. This flow might be a series of fixed payments (in the case of bonds) or a share of a company's profits (in the case of stock). According to the **classical theory of asset prices**, the price of an asset equals the present value of the income that people expect to receive from the asset:

Asset Price = Present Value of Expected Asset Income.

Notice the word "expected" in the theory. In many cases, nobody knows exactly how much income an asset will produce. For example, nobody is certain of a company's future profits, which determine the income from stock. Given this uncertainty, the classical theory says that asset prices depend on people's expectations, or best guesses, about asset income.

The rationale for the classical theory is simple. People purchase an asset because it yields a future stream of income. The present value tells us how much this income stream is expected to be worth and thus how much we should be willing to pay for the asset.

Suppose an asset's price is *below* the present value of its expected income stream. If the present value of the expected income is $100 and the asset price is $80, the asset is a great deal: buyers pay less than the asset is worth. Lots of savers will purchase the asset, and high demand will push up the price until it rises to $100.

Conversely, if an asset price exceeds the present value of expected income, then sellers receive more than the asset is worth. In this situation, the asset's owners will rush to sell it, and this increase in supply will push down the price.

The classical theory applies to many types of assets. For example, it says that the price of an apartment building equals the present value of net rental income from the building. Let's look more closely at the theory's implications for the pricing of two classes of assets, bonds and stocks.

Bond Prices The income from a bond includes the periodic coupon payments (if any) and the face value received at maturity. Let's say a bond has a maturity of T years, a face value of F, and an annual coupon payment of C. Assuming no chance of default, bondholders expect to receive all the promised payments. The payments are C in years 1 through $T - 1$ and $C + F$ in year T. The bond price is the present value of these expected payments. Using the second formula in Table 16-1, this present value is

$$\text{Bond Price} = \frac{C}{(1 + i)} + \frac{C}{(1 + i)^2} + \cdots + \frac{C}{(1 + i)^{T-1}} + \frac{(C + F)}{(1 + i)^T}.$$

For example, suppose a bond's maturity is 4 years ($T = 4$), annual coupon payments are \$5 ($C = \$5$), the face value F is \$100, and the interest rate is 4 percent. Using the previous equation,

$$\text{Bond Price} = \frac{\$5}{1.04} + \frac{\$5}{(1.04)^2} + \frac{\$5}{(1.04)^3} + \frac{\$105}{(1.04)^4} = \$103.63.$$

Stock Prices Someone who owns a firm's stock owns a share of the firm. However, firms' earnings do not flow directly to their stockholders. Instead, firms periodically pay stockholders a portion of earnings called **dividends**. If a company with 1 million shares announces a dividend of $2 per share, it will pay stockholders a total of $2 million in dividends.

Because dividends are the income from stock, a stock's price is the present value of expected dividends. If expected dividends per share are D_1 in the next year, D_2 in the year after that, and so on, then

$$\text{Stock Price} = \frac{D_1}{(1 + i)} + \frac{D_2}{(1 + i)^2} + \frac{D_3}{(1 + i)^3} + \cdots.$$

In any year, a firm's dividends can differ from its earnings. Indeed, some firms earn healthy profits yet pay no dividends at all. Instead, they might use their earnings to finance investment projects such as new factories or the development of new products.

Over the long run, however, dividends are tied closely to earnings. If a firm uses its current earnings for investment rather than dividends, the investment boosts future earnings. These future earnings allow the firm to pay higher future dividends. Therefore, any rise in earnings raises dividends at some point in time. The present value of dividends increases, raising the firm's stock price. Because of these connections, expectations about companies' earnings have strong effects on stock prices.

What Determines Expectations?

An asset price depends on the present value of *expected* asset income. What determines what people expect? The classical theory assumes that people form *rational expectations* (introduced in Chapter 12), which means that they optimally use all available information to forecast future variables such as income flows.

To understand the implications of rational expectations, let's revisit Harriet's software company, iSmells, which we discussed in Chapter 15. The price of the company's stock depends on people's expectations of its future earnings, which will determine the dividends it can pay.

Rational expectations of earnings are based on all available information about the company. For example, if Harriet announces a new product, expected earnings rise to reflect the product's likely impact. If the economy enters a recession, expected earnings adjust based on how Harriet's firm will be affected. Expected earnings also take into account the costs of producing software, the number of competitors the firm faces, and all other factors that affect how successful Harriet's firm is likely to be.

It is important to realize that rational expectations are not always accurate or correct. Unpredictable events—changes in production costs or consumer demand, successes and failures in developing new products, and so on—can cause a firm's actual earnings to differ from the earnings people expect. If people have incorporated all relevant, available information into their expectations, however, their expectations will be as accurate as possible and the differences between expected and actual earnings will be as small as possible.

What Is the Relevant Interest Rate?

In addition to depending on expectations about earnings, asset prices depend on interest rates, which determine the present value of asset income. What interest rates should we use in present value formulas? In the classical theory, different interest rates are relevant for different assets. The riskier an asset—that is, the more uncertainty about the income flow from the asset—the higher the interest rate.

To understand this effect of risk, recall our initial discussion of present value, where we saw that a dollar today is worth $1 + i$ dollars in a year. In this discussion, i is an interest rate that savers receive for sure—say, from a safe bank account. From now on, we will call this rate the **safe interest rate**, or *risk-free rate*, i^{safe}. With this notation, a dollar today is worth a certain $\$(1 + i^{safe})$ in a year. Conversely, a certain dollar in a year is worth $\$1/(1 + i^{safe})$ today.

When determining asset prices, however, we often have to value uncertain payments. For example, suppose the expected dividend in some year from a share of stock is $10. This is the best forecast, but the dividend could range between $8 and $12. People dislike such risk. With this uncertainty, the expected dividend from the stock is worth less than a certain $10.

How does risk affect present values? A dollar today is worth $1 + i^{safe}$ certain dollars next year. This means a dollar today is worth *more* than $1 + i^{safe}$ risky dollars next year, because risky dollars are less valuable than certain dollars. To put it differently, a dollar today is worth $1 + i^{safe} + \varphi$ risky dollars in a year, where

---

TABLE 16-2

Ideas Behind the Classical Theory of Asset Prices

- An asset price equals the present value of expected income from the asset.
- Expectations about income are rational. Expected income is the optimal forecast based on all available information.
- The interest rate in the present value formula is a risk-adjusted rate. It equals the safe interest rate plus a risk premium: $i = i^{\text{safe}} + \varphi$.

φ (the Greek letter phi) is a **risk premium**. A risk premium is a payment on an asset that compensates the owner for taking on risk.

The same reasoning applies to risky income at any point in the future. A dollar today is worth $(1 + i^{\text{safe}} + \varphi)^n$ risky dollars in n years. Turning this around, the present value of a risky dollar in n years is $1/(1 + i^{\text{safe}} + \varphi)^n$. In our equations for asset prices, the interest rate is the sum of the safe rate and the risk premium, $i = i^{\text{safe}} + \varphi$. We call this sum the **risk-adjusted interest rate**.

Assets carry varying degrees of risk. The greater the risk, the higher the risk premium. For example, stocks have higher risk premiums than bonds because, as we discuss in Section 16-6, the income from stocks is more volatile. A higher risk premium raises the risk-adjusted interest rate in the present value formula, reducing the present value of expected income. Therefore, a higher risk premium reduces an asset's price.

Table 16-2 summarizes the ideas behind the classical theory of asset prices.

The Gordon Growth Model of Stock Prices

Stock prices are among the most closely watched asset prices in an economy. The classical theory says a stock price is the present value of expected dividends per share. Using this idea to value stocks can be cumbersome, however, as it requires year-by-year forecasts of dividends into the distant future. Therefore, economists have sought easier ways to calculate stock prices.

One approach was proposed by Myron Gordon in 1959. Gordon pointed out that many firms raise dividends fairly steadily over time. To capture this behavior in a simple way, he assumed that expected dividends grow at a constant rate g. If expected dividends next year are D_1, expected dividends in the following years are $D_1(1 + g)$, $D_1(1 + g)^2$, and so on.

With the assumption of constant dividend growth, we can derive a firm's stock price from the last formula in Table 16-1. This formula says the present value of any steadily growing income stream is $Z/(i - g)$, where Z is the first payment and g is the payment growth rate. In Gordon's analysis, the first payment Z equals D_1, the first expected dividend, implying

$$\text{Stock Price} = \frac{D_1}{(i - g)},$$

where i is the risk-adjusted interest rate for the stock. This equation is called the **Gordon growth model** because it emphasizes the expected growth rate of dividends as a determinant of stock prices.

16-3 Fluctuations in Asset Prices

If you follow the financial news, you will notice that asset prices move around a lot. Because asset-price movements affect the value of firms and the wealth of consumers, they have significant effects on macroeconomic variables such as consumption, investment, and output. For these reasons, it is important to understand the basic forces behind asset-price movements.

Why Do Asset Prices Change?

The classical theory says an asset price is the present value of expected income from the asset. This present value changes if expected income changes or if interest rates change.

Stock prices change frequently because of changes in expected income from the stock. These changes occur when there is news (either good or bad) about a company's prospects. If a drug company patents a new wonder drug that helps people lose weight without changing their eating habits, rational expectations of the company's earnings rise. Higher expected earnings mean larger expected dividends for stockholders, so the stock price rises accordingly. If a car company's new model is recalled because of safety defects, its expected earnings and stock price fall. If there are signs that the whole economy is entering a recession, expected earnings and stock prices are likely to fall for many companies.

Such news has less effect on bond prices than on stock prices because the income from a bond is fixed as long as the issuer does not default. As a result, news about companies' prospects often has little effect on the expected income from bonds.

Changes in interest rates, however, affect the prices of both stocks and bonds. A higher interest rate reduces asset prices because it reduces the present value of any income flow. Recall that the relevant interest rate is the risk-adjusted rate, the economy's safe rate plus a risk premium ($i^{safe} + \varphi$). An asset price falls if the safe rate or the risk premium rises. The risk premium might rise because of greater uncertainty about income from the asset. For example, uncertainty about a firm's stock could rise if competitors enter its industry and people are unsure about how much business the firm will lose.

CASE STUDY

The Fed and the Stock Market

Throughout this book, we've seen that monetary policy influences many economic variables, including interest rates, output, and inflation. Monetary policy also influences asset prices. When central banks such as the Federal Reserve announce changes in policy, asset prices often react within minutes. Let's use the classical theory of asset prices to examine the reaction of stock prices.

In Chapter 11 we learned about the Fed's short-term policy instrument, *the federal funds rate*, which is the interest rate that banks charge one another for overnight loans. Suppose the Fed raises its target for this interest rate. This

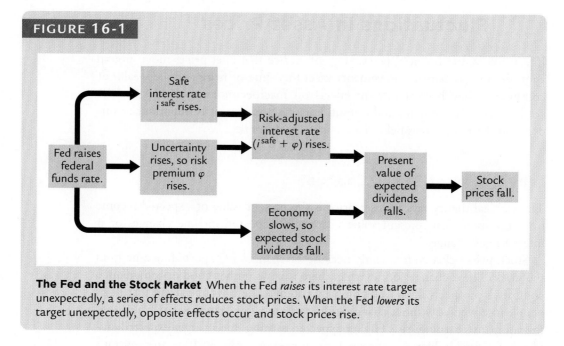

The Fed and the Stock Market When the Fed *raises* its interest rate target unexpectedly, a series of effects reduces stock prices. When the Fed *lowers* its target unexpectedly, opposite effects occur and stock prices rise.

action affects the stock market in several ways, which are summarized in Figure 16-1:

- The federal funds rate is a safe interest rate because banks are unlikely to default on overnight loans. Thus, the Fed's action raises the economy's safe interest rate. A higher safe rate reduces the present value of dividends received by stockholders, which decreases stock prices.

- The higher interest rate reduces spending by consumers and firms, which causes aggregate output to fall. Lower output reduces expected earnings for many companies. As a result, expected dividends for these companies fall, which again reduces stock prices.

- Some economists think an increase in the federal funds rate also increases risk premiums. The fall in output that results from the increase in the federal funds rate not only reduces expected earnings but also raises uncertainty, because it is hard to predict how badly companies will be hurt. Greater uncertainty means higher risk premiums, which raise the risk-adjusted interest rate and decrease present values and stock prices.

When the Fed raises its interest rate target, all three effects reduce the present value of dividends, pushing stock prices down. If the Fed reduces its target, the three effects work in reverse and stock prices rise.

A qualification: Fed actions have large effects *only when they are unexpected*. If people know the Fed is going to change interest rates, stock prices are likely to adjust in advance, and nothing happens when the Fed moves. In contrast, surprise rate changes cause sharp jumps in stock prices.

Fed Chairman Ben Bernanke studied the effects of Fed policies on the stock market during his career as an economics professor. He estimated the effects of interest rate changes on the stock market in a 2005 paper with Kenneth Kuttner of Williams College.

Bernanke and Kuttner examined the period from 1989 to 2002. They measured changes in stock prices on days when the Fed made surprise announcements about its federal-funds-rate target. On average, a rise in the target of 0.25 percent—say, from 4.0 percent to 4.25 percent—caused stock prices to drop suddenly by about 1 percent. A decrease in the target had the opposite effect: a cut of 0.25 percent *raised* stock prices by 1 percent.[3] ∎

Which Asset Prices Are Most Volatile?

All asset prices change over time, but some fluctuate more than others. Let's discuss why some asset prices are especially volatile.

Long-Term Bond Prices Changes in interest rates are the primary reason for changes in bond prices. (As noted earlier, expected income flows from a bond are constant unless default risk changes.) If interest rates in an economy rise, then all bond prices fall. But the size of the effect differs depending on bond maturities. A change in interest rates has a larger effect on prices of long-term bonds than on prices of short-term bonds.

The reason for this difference is that short-term bonds provide income only in the near future, while most payments on long-term bonds come later. The present value of payments is affected more strongly by the interest rate if the payments come later.

To illustrate this point, Table 16-3 compares bonds with maturities ranging from 1 year to 30 years. Each bond has a face value of $100 and coupon payments

TABLE 16-3

Bond Prices, Maturity, and Interest Rates

Years to Maturity	Price if $i = 4\%$	Price if $i = 6\%$	Percentage Fall in Price from Increase in i
1	$100.96	$99.06	1.89
2	101.89	98.17	3.65
3	102.78	97.33	5.30
4	103.63	96.53	6.85
5	104.45	95.79	8.29
10	108.11	92.64	14.31
15	111.12	90.29	18.75
20	113.59	88.53	22.06
25	115.62	87.22	24.57
30	117.29	86.24	26.48

Note: This table gives the prices of bonds with a face value of $100 and annual coupon payments of $5.

[3] See Ben Bernanke and Kenneth Kuttner, "What Explains the Stock Market's Reaction to Federal Reserve Policy?" *Journal of Finance* 60 (June 2005): 1221–1257.

UNCORRECTED PAGES

of $5 per year. The table shows the prices of the bonds when the interest rate is 4 percent and when it is 6 percent. The longer a bond's maturity, the greater the percentage fall in the price when the interest rate rises.

For example, the owner of a 1-year bond receives a single coupon payment of $5 plus the face value of $100, both paid after 1 year. When the interest rate rises from 4 percent to 6 percent, the present value of these payments, and thus the bond's price, falls from $100.96 to $99.06. This decrease is only 1.89 percent of the bond's initial price. In contrast, the owner of a 30-year bond receives a series of coupon payments over 30 years plus the face value at the end of 30 years. When the interest rate rises, the price of this bond falls from $117.29 to $86.24, a decrease in of 26.48 percent. Because the bond's payments are stretched over a long period, a rise in the interest rate wipes out a large part of its value.

Stock Prices Prices for stocks are more volatile than prices for bonds, even long-term bonds. Stock prices fluctuate greatly for two reasons. First, like long-term bonds, stocks yield income far into the future. A firm's dividends continue indefinitely, and changes in interest rates have large effects on the present value of this long-term income. Second, as we've discussed, news about firms and the economy cause changes in expected earnings and dividends and thus in stock prices. Fluctuations in stock prices caused by changes in expected earnings add to the fluctuations caused by changes in interest rates.

16-4 Asset-Price Bubbles

The classical theory of asset prices says an asset price equals the present value of expected income from the asset. Is this just a theory, or does it explain asset-price movements in the real world?

The answer to this question is controversial. Clearly there are elements of truth in the theory. We have seen, for example, that it helps explain how stock prices react to Federal Reserve policies. However, many economists believe that changes in asset prices can occur for reasons outside the classical theory, that is, for reasons other than changes in interest rates or expected income.

Sometimes, for example, asset-price increases are part of an **asset-price bubble**. In a bubble, asset prices rise rapidly even though there is no change in interest rates or expected income to justify the rise. Let's discuss how bubbles can occur and the debate over their relevance to the asset-price movements that we observe in the economy.

How Bubbles Work

When a bubble occurs, an asset price rises simply because people *expect* it to rise. To see how this might happen, suppose a famous stock analyst announces that the stock of Acme Corporation is hot: the stock price is likely to rise rapidly in the future. Let's assume the expert doesn't really have a good reason for this view; he is just trying to get attention with a bold prediction. Nonetheless, many people believe the expert and rush to buy Acme. This increased demand pushes up the price of the stock. The expert looks smart, and a bubble has begun.

Once a bubble begins, it feeds on itself. When Acme's price starts rising, more and more people decide the stock is hot. They buy Acme stock, pushing the price higher still. The stock looks even hotter, more buyers rush in, and so on.

As the bubble expands, Acme's price rises far above the level dictated by the classical theory: the present value of dividends per share. People pay more for the stock than it is really worth. They buy it because they expect the price to rise even higher in the future, and therefore they expect to be able to sell the stock for a profit.

The problem with bubbles is that they eventually pop. At some point Acme's price will rise so high that people begin to doubt whether price increases can continue. They stop buying the stock and start to sell what they have. This fall in demand for the stock and increase in supply cause the price to fall back toward the level dictated by the classical theory. Many people who bought Acme at the height of the bubble will lose a lot when the bubble bursts.

Bubbles can arise in many kinds of asset prices. From January 2002 to July 2006, for example, the price of the average house in the United States rose 71 percent. During that period, many people bought second homes or rental properties, believing that prices would continue to rise and that they would make lots of money when they sold their property. The bubble was also fueled by an increase in the availability of home mortgage loans. Lenders relaxed their standards for borrowers' incomes and credit histories, allowing more people to enter the housing market. This development increased housing demand and pushed up prices.

The peak of the housing bubble occurred in July 2006. Between then and April 2009, the average house price fell 33 percent. The losses to homeowners produced a surge of defaults on mortgage loans, which triggered the U.S. financial crisis of 2007–2009.

In addition to stocks and houses, history has seen bubbles in the prices of bonds, foreign currencies, precious metals, and commodities such as coffee and sugar. Perhaps the oddest bubble of all time occurred in Holland in the 1630s. The asset was tulip bulbs. A fad for tulips, recently introduced from Turkey, caused the prices of bulbs to rise rapidly, and people thought they could get rich by purchasing bulbs and reselling them after prices rose further. Many people borrowed large sums of money to buy bulbs. They suffered disastrous losses in February 1637, when the bubble ended abruptly and tulip bulb prices fell 90 percent.

Looking for Bubbles

Economists often debate whether bubbles are occurring in asset prices. Discussions of stock prices sometimes focus on the **price–earnings (P/E) ratio**, the price of stock divided by earnings per share. Using earnings over the recent past, economists compute P/E ratios for individual companies and the average P/E ratio for the stock market. Some think that high P/E ratios are evidence of bubbles.

To see why, recall the classical theory: a stock price equals the present value of expected dividends per share, which depends on expected earnings. It is difficult to test this theory, because we can't directly measure expectations of future earnings. But some economists argue that earnings in the recent past are a good guide to future earnings. If a stock price is unusually high compared to past earnings—if the P/E ratio is high—then the price is probably high relative to future earnings, meaning it is higher than it should be under the classical theory. A bubble may be underway.

According to the classical theory, high P/E ratios could be explained by low interest rates. Low rates raise the present value of future income and push up stock prices. In practice, however, stocks' P/E ratios sometimes rise without changes in interest rates, indicating a possible bubble.

It is important to note that a high P/E ratio indicates a bubble *only* if recent earnings are a good predictor of future earnings. If earnings are expected to grow rapidly, then recent earnings are not a good predictor of future earnings. For example, suppose a company is developing a promising new product. The company's current earnings are low, but earnings are expected to rise a lot when the product is introduced. According to the classical theory, high expected earnings imply a high stock price. With current earnings low, the classical theory predicts a high P/E ratio.

Economists have tried to determine the correct interpretation of P/E ratios. Do high ratios usually signal a bubble? Or are they more likely to reflect expectations of high earnings growth? Some researchers address this issue by examining what happens to stock prices *after* a period of high P/E ratios. Remember that bubbles eventually end. If a bubble has pushed up the P/E ratio, stock prices are likely to fall later. In contrast, if a high P/E ratio reflects high expected earnings, there is no reason to expect stock prices to fall. Examining later stock-price movements helps to isolate why the P/E ratio was high.

This approach was introduced in a 1998 paper by John Campbell of Harvard University and Robert Shiller of Yale University. Campbell and Shiller examined the P/E ratio for a large group of companies, the S&P 500. For a given year, they defined P as the average stock price for the group and E as average earnings per share over the previous 10 years. Campbell and Shiller then compared the P/E ratio to the change in stock prices over the following 10 years.

Figure 16-2 illustrates Campbell and Shiller's comparison for the period from 1918 through 2000. In this graph, the horizontal axis is the P/E ratio and the vertical axis is the average percentage change in stock prices over the next 10 years. We see a negative relationship: when the P/E ratio is high, stock prices are likely to fall. Campbell and Shiller concluded that high P/E ratios are usually caused by bubbles that dissipate in the future.

Campbell and Shiller's research was stimulated by a rapid rise in stock prices during the 1990s. The following case study discusses this period and stock-price fluctuations since then.

CASE STUDY

The U.S. Stock Market, 1990–2010

Figure 16-3 charts the Dow Jones Index of stock prices from 1990 through 2010. We see large swings in prices, which the ideas in this chapter can help us understand. Let's examine stock-price movements over three periods: 1990 to 2003, 2003 to 2007, and 2007 to 2010.

1990–2003: The Tech Boom and Bust The 1990s were a boom period for the stock market. The Dow Jones Index rose from about 2,500 at the start of the

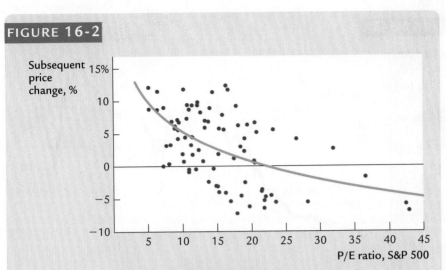

FIGURE 16-2

Evidence for Bubbles? Each point in this graph represents a year between 1918 and 2000. The horizontal axis is the price-earnings ratio for stocks in the S&P 500, based on average earnings over the previous 10 years. The vertical axis is the average percentage change in S&P prices over the following 10 years, adjusted for inflation. (The 10-year change after 2000 is estimated with data through 2009.) The orange "best fit" line through the data points indicates a negative relationship between these two variables: When the P/E ratio is high, stock prices are likely to grow slowly or fall over the following 10 years.

Source: Robert Shiller, Yale University (www.econ.yale.edu/~shiller/data.htm). Adapted from John Campbell and Robert Shiller, "Valuation Ratios and the Long-Run Stock Market Outlook," *Journal of Portfolio Management* 24 (Winter 1998) 11–26.

decade to over 6,000 in 1997, when Campbell and Shiller wrote their paper. The index continued to rise after that, peaking at 11,497 in the summer of 2000.

Companies' earnings rose during the 1990s, but not as fast as stock prices. This meant rising P/E ratios. From 1960 to 1995, the average P/E ratio for the Dow Jones Index was about 15. This ratio rose above 40 in 2000. P/E ratios were especially high for "tech" companies—those involved with computers, software, and the Internet. Many of these companies had P/E ratios over 100.

During the 1990s, many economists argued that a stock market bubble was under way. Federal Reserve Chairman Alan Greenspan supported this idea in a famous 1996 speech. Greenspan suggested that stock prices had been "unduly escalated" by "irrational exuberance," meaning prices had risen above the levels dictated by the classical theory.

Others argued that the high P/E ratios were in line with the classical theory. They pointed to the rapid spread of computer and Internet use in the 1990s. These technologies raised productivity and reduced costs in many industries, making it rational to expect rapid growth in companies' earnings. As we've discussed, expectations of high earnings growth imply a high P/E ratio in the classical theory.

Stock prices peaked in 2000, then fell for the next three years. The Dow Jones Index fell below 8,000 in 2003. Believers in a stock market bubble claimed

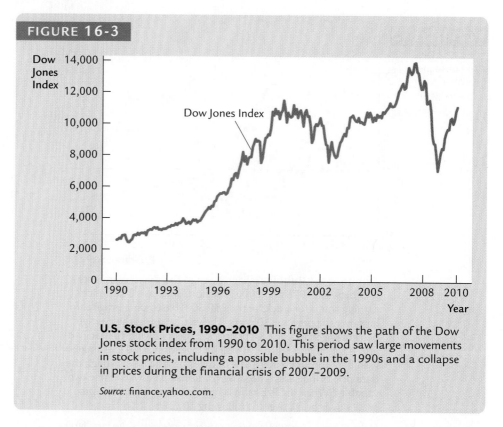

FIGURE 16-3

U.S. Stock Prices, 1990–2010 This figure shows the path of the Dow Jones stock index from 1990 to 2010. This period saw large movements in stock prices, including a possible bubble in the 1990s and a collapse in prices during the financial crisis of 2007–2009.

Source: finance.yahoo.com.

vindication. They interpreted the price declines as the bursting of the bubble and evidence that stocks were never really worth the prices of the late 1990s.

But again, not all analysts agree with this interpretation. Believers in the classical theory point to the effects of several bad-news stories between 2000 and 2003: the terrorist attacks of September 11, 2001; the discovery of false accounting at companies such as Enron; and the recession of 2001. These events reduced companies' expected earnings, possibly explaining the fall in stock prices. So the debate over stock bubbles continues.

2003–2007: Recovery As we see in Figure 16-3, stock prices started rising again in 2003. The Dow passed its 2000 peak in 2006 and reached 14,000 in mid-2007.

Initially, the rise in stock prices was driven by low interest rates. The Federal Reserve pushed rates down in 2003 because the economy remained weak after the 2001 recession. In 2004, the Fed started raising rates, but an economic recovery sustained the stock market boom. In contrast to the 1990s, the P/E ratio for the Dow was stable in the mid-2000s, suggesting that rising prices reflected increases in companies' earnings rather than a bubble.

2007–2010: The Financial Crisis and Its Aftermath Stock prices started falling in late 2007 as the housing bubble burst and disrupted financial markets. The decline accelerated after the failure of Lehman Brothers, a major investment bank, in September 2008. The Dow reached a trough of 6,547 in March 2009.

The financial crisis reduced stock prices through two channels. First, it reduced expectations of companies' future earnings and dividends. Initially, expected earnings fell for financial firms hit directly by the crisis. As the effects of the crisis spread through the economy, earnings forecasts also fell for nonfinancial firms.

Second, the financial crisis increased risk premiums. Unprecedented events created uncertainty about how bad the crisis would get. This uncertainty was reflected in large day-to-day swings in stock prices as traders reacted to the latest news. In the last four months of 2008, the Dow Jones Index rose or fell by 5 percent or more on nine different days. Uncertainty about companies' prospects raised risk premiums for their stocks.

In response to the financial crisis, the Federal Reserve pushed down the economy's safe interest rate (i^{safe}). As measured by the federal funds rate, the safe rate fell below 0.25 percent at the end of 2008. However, the decrease in the safe rate was smaller than the increase in risk premiums for stocks (φ). This difference implied an increase in risk-adjusted interest rates ($i^{\text{safe}} + \varphi$), which reduced the present value of future income. The combination of this effect and lower expected income caused stock prices to fall sharply.

In March 2009, the fall in stock prices ended. The Dow Jones Index rose over the next year and reached 11,000 in April 2010. Rising stock prices reflected a growing belief that the worst of the financial crisis was over, largely because of government and Federal Reserve efforts to save financial institutions from failure (discussed in Chapter 19). This optimism raised earnings forecasts for companies and reduced risk premiums, partially reversing the fall in stock prices during the crisis. As of April 2010, however, the Dow remained far below the 14,000 level it had reached in 2007. ■

16-5 Asset-Price Crashes

Believers in asset-price bubbles think that bubbles eventually end and prices fall. Sometimes this occurs gradually over a period of months or years. The bubble in U.S. stock prices was reversed over the period 2000-2003 and the housing bubble over 2006-2009. At other times, however, a bubble ends with an **asset-price crash**, as prices plummet over a very short period.

As discussed earlier, Holland's tulip bubble ended with a crash in 1637. In U.S. history, the most famous asset-price crashes have occurred in the stock market. In both 1929 and 1987, stock prices fell dramatically *within a single day*. Crashes can have disastrous effects on the economy if policymakers do not handle them well. Let's discuss how crashes occur.

How Crashes Work

Crashes are hard to explain with the classical theory of asset prices. Under that theory, prices fall sharply only if there is a large drop in the present value of expected asset income. This requires either a rise in interest rates or bad news about future income, and crashes often occur without such events. For example, when the stock market crashed on October 19, 1987, prices fell by 23 percent, yet interest rates were stable on that day, and there was no significant news about companies' earnings or dividends.

A crash is easier to explain if it is preceded by an asset-price bubble. At some point during a bubble, people start worrying that it will end. They would like to hold assets as long as prices rise but sell before the bubble bursts, so they watch for the end of the bubble.

At some point, a few asset holders get especially nervous and decide to start selling. Others notice this and fear that the bubble may be ending. They sell, too, hoping to dump their assets before prices fall too much. These actions push down prices, causing more people to sell. Pessimism about prices is self-fulfilling, just as optimism was self-fulfilling during the bubble.

Once a crash starts, it can accelerate rapidly. As prices fall, panic sets in, many asset holders try to sell at the same time, and prices plummet. Eventually, prices fall far enough to make the assets attractive again. At this point, prices may be *below* the present value of expected income, so it is more profitable to hold assets than to sell them. The rush to sell abates, and prices stabilize.

According to this reasoning, a crash is a risk whenever an asset-price bubble is under way. However, nobody knows how to explain why crashes occur on particular days. Sometimes there is a small piece of news, such as a report of low company earnings, that increases the nervousness of asset holders. But often the timing of a crash appears arbitrary. Even in retrospect, we do not know why the 1987 crash occurred on October 19 rather than some other day.

CASE STUDY

The Two Big Crashes

Stock prices rose rapidly during the Roaring Twenties: the Dow Jones Index climbed from 70 in 1921 to 365 in September 1929. This performance reflected excitement about new technologies, such as cars, radios, and electric appliances. The demand for stocks was also fueled by people's ability to "buy on margin," that is, to buy stock on credit, with only a small down payment.

In retrospect the experience of the 1920s looks like a classic bubble, but economists did not recognize this at the time. On October 17, 1929, the eminent economist Irving Fisher commented that "stock prices have reached what looks like a permanently high plateau."

It is not clear why the crash occurred just when it did. Increases in interest rates in early 1929 may have made stockholders nervous, because they reduced the present values of company earnings. In any case, the stock market fluctuated erratically for several months and then plummeted. The largest one-day decline occurred on "Black Monday," October 28, when the Dow dropped by 13 percent. This crash was followed by a series of smaller declines. In July 1932, the Dow reached a low of 41.

The 1987 crash was in some ways a repeat of 1929. It followed a rapid rise in prices: the Dow climbed from 786 in 1980 to 2,655 in August 1987. Some observers suggested that a bubble was under way, but again the crash was unexpected. The market started falling on October 14, and the bottom fell out on October 19, the second Black Monday. That day the Dow dropped 23 percent, easily beating the 1929 record for a one-day drop.

The 1987 crash was exacerbated by the use of computers to trade stocks. Computers sped up trading, so prices fell more quickly than in 1929. Moreover, in 1987 large stockholders such as mutual funds had systems of *program trading,* in which computers automatically sold stock if the market fell by a certain amount. These systems were designed to get rid of stocks quickly if a crash was under way. When the crash occurred, program trading worsened the vicious circle of falling prices and heavy selling.

Despite the similarities between the two crashes, their aftermaths differed. After October 1929, stock prices stayed depressed. The Dow did not climb back to its pre-crash level until 1954. In contrast, the market bounced back quickly after the 1987 crash. The Dow reached its pre-crash level in 1989 and kept rising through the 1990s.

The two crashes also had different effects on the overall economy. The 1929 crash contributed to the Great Depression of the 1930s, while economic growth was strong after the 1987 crash. Part of the explanation is the different behavior of the Federal Reserve. The Fed responded passively to the 1929 crash and the bank panics that followed. In 1987, the Fed lent money to financial institutions threatened by the crash, thus preventing a major disruption of the financial system. ■

Crash Prevention

Is there any way to prevent asset-price crashes? Both the federal government and stock exchanges have imposed rules for stock trading to make crashes less likely. Let's discuss two rules, one adopted after the 1929 crash and one after the 1987 crash.

Margin Requirements After the 1929 crash, Congress gave the Federal Reserve authority to establish **margin requirements**, limits on the amount that people can borrow to buy stock. Margin requirements have varied over time, but in recent years they have been around 50 percent. This means that stock purchasers must pay at least 50 percent of the cost with their own money.

This regulation tries to curtail the buildup of stock-price bubbles that precedes crashes. As we have discussed, the practice of buying on margin helped fuel the stock market boom of the 1920s. Margin requirements make such a price run-up less likely. When prices don't rise as high, there is less danger they will fall sharply.

Circuit Breakers After the 1987 crash, some securities exchanges established **circuit breakers**, requirements to shut down trading temporarily if prices fall sharply. These rules are motivated by the view that crashes are a vicious circle of panic and falling prices. A circuit breaker stops this process; it gives people time to calm down and assess the true value of their assets. If the circuit breaker works, the rush to sell subsides and prices stabilize when the exchange reopens. (In other words, panicky asset traders are like naughty four-year-olds: they behave more rationally after a "time out.")

At the New York Stock Exchange, current rules mandate a suspension of trading if the Dow Jones Index falls 10 percent within a day. The length of the suspension depends on the size of the fall and the time of day. For example, trading halts for an hour if prices fall 10 to 20 percent before 2:00 P.M. Larger decreases can halt trading for the rest of the day.

So far, trading on the New York Stock Exchange has been interrupted only once, on July 27, 1997. At that time the rules set smaller price declines as triggers for circuit breakers. The Dow Jones Index fell 7 percent, which was enough to shut down the exchange for the rest of the day.

16-6 Measuring Interest Rates and Asset Returns

In the previous sections, we have studied how asset prices are determined and why they change over time. With this background, we can define two concepts that are closely related to asset prices: a bond's yield to maturity and the rate of return on a stock or bond. In the rest of this book, we will see that these variables help determine what happens in asset markets. They influence savers' decisions about what stocks and bonds (if any) to purchase and firms' decisions about issuing stocks and bonds.

Yield to Maturity

Buying a bond means lending money to the company or government that issues the bond. In deciding whether to buy a bond, people compare the interest the bond pays to the interest they could receive on other bonds or on deposits in a bank account.

Comparing interest is not as straightforward as it might seem, however. Unlike the stated interest rate on a bank account, the interest rate on a bond is not always obvious. Consider a bond with a $100 face value, 4 years to maturity, coupon payments of $5 per year, and a price of $95. If you buy this bond, what interest rate will you earn?

Economists answer this question by calculating the bond's **yield to maturity**. This concept is based on the classical theory of asset prices. Earlier, we used this theory to derive an equation for the price of a bond:

$$\text{Bond Price} = \frac{C}{(1 + i)} + \frac{C}{(1 + i)^2} + \cdots + \frac{C}{(1 + i)^{T-1}} + \frac{(C + F)}{(1 + i)^T},$$

where C is the coupon payment, F is the face value, T is the maturity, and i is the interest rate. This equation tells us that a bond's price equals the present value of payments from the bond. We can use it to calculate the price if we assume a certain interest rate.

To measure yield to maturity, we turn this calculation around. We know the payments on a bond and the bond's price, and we use the previous equation to derive an interest rate. This interest rate is the bond's yield to maturity, the rate that makes the present value of the bond's payments equal to its price.

Recall the example of a bond with a 4-year maturity, a $100 face value, and $5 coupon payments. If the bond's price is $95, our bond-price equation implies

$$95 = \frac{5}{(1+i)} + \frac{5}{(1+i)^2} + \frac{5}{(1+i)^3} + \frac{105}{(1+i)^4}.$$

The yield to maturity is the interest rate i that solves this equation. Here, the solution is $i = 0.065$, or an interest rate of 6.5 percent.

A technical note: Usually, there is no easy way to solve equations like the last one. You have to use trial and error, plugging in different values for i until you find one that makes the right side equal to the 95 on the left. Fortunately, a computer or financial calculator can do this for you quickly.

Recall that the classical theory implies that asset prices move inversely with interest rates. In the case of bonds, this principle is true by definition: it follows from how we measure the yield to maturity. If the price on the left side of our equation goes up, the interest rate on the right must go down for the equation to hold.

In our example of a 4-year bond, if the price rises from $95 to $98, the yield to maturity falls from 6.5 percent to 5.6 percent. If this happens, you might hear on the news that "bond prices rose" or that "interest rates on bonds fell." These are two ways of saying the same thing.

The Rate of Return

Suppose you buy a stock or bond and hold onto it for a year. How much have you earned by holding the security? You have potentially increased your wealth in two ways:

1. The security may pay you directly. A bond may yield a coupon payment. If you own a company's stock, you do not directly receive the company's profits, but you may receive a dividend.

2. The price of the security may change. If the price rises, you own a more valuable asset, so your wealth rises. The increase in your wealth that comes from the price increase is called a **capital gain**. If the price of the security falls, you suffer a **capital loss** and your wealth decreases.

The total amount you gain from holding the security is the capital gain or loss plus any direct payment you receive. This total is called the **return** on the security:

$$\text{Return} = (P_1 - P_0) + X,$$

where P_0 is the initial price of the security, P_1 is the price after you hold it for a year, and X represents a direct payment. (X can be a coupon payment, C, or a dividend, D.)

The **rate of return** on a security is the return expressed as a percentage of the initial price. It is calculated by dividing the return by the price:

$$\text{Rate of Return} = \frac{\text{Return}}{P_0}$$

$$= \frac{(P_1 - P_0)}{P_0} + \frac{X}{P_0}.$$

The rate of return has two parts. The first is the percentage change in the security price; the second is the direct payment divided by the initial price.

Suppose in 2020 you buy a bond for $80. In 2021, the bond makes a coupon payment of $4 and the price rises to $82. Plugging these numbers into the formula, the rate of return is

$$\frac{(82 - 80)}{80} + \frac{4}{80} = 0.075, \text{ or } 7.5\%.$$

If the bond makes a coupon payment of $4 but the price falls from $80 to $75, the rate of return is

$$\frac{(75 - 80)}{80} + \frac{4}{80} = -0.013, \text{ or } -1.3\%.$$

As this example illustrates, the rate of return can be negative if a large enough capital loss occurs.

Returns on Stocks and Bonds

Figure 16-4 traces some data on rates of return. It shows the average rates of return on U.S. stocks and Treasury bonds from 1900 through 2009. You can see immediately that stock returns are more volatile than bond returns, reflecting the fact that stock prices fluctuate more than bond prices, as we discussed in Section 16-3. Changes in stock prices cause large swings in the rate of return. Notice the disastrous rate of return on stocks (−37.2%) during the financial crisis of 2008.

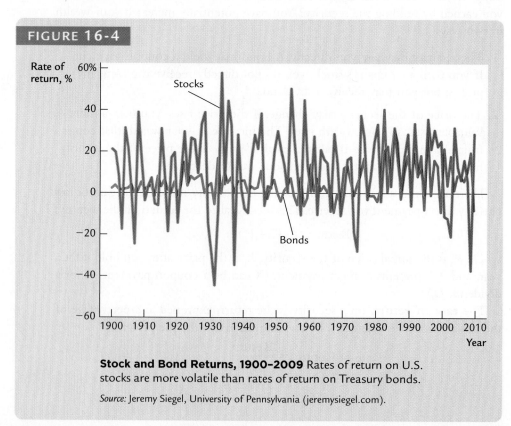

FIGURE 16-4

Stock and Bond Returns, 1900–2009 Rates of return on U.S. stocks are more volatile than rates of return on Treasury bonds.

Source: Jeremy Siegel, University of Pennsylvania (jeremysiegel.com).

While returns on stock are more volatile than those on bonds, the *average* rate of return is higher for stocks. For the period from 1900 through 2009, the average rate of return was about 11 percent for stocks and 5 percent for bonds. This difference should make sense. As we discussed earlier, savers choose assets with more uncertain (more volatile) income only if they are compensated with a risk premium—a higher average return.

Rate of Return Versus Yield to Maturity

People are often confused about the difference between the rate of return on a bond and its yield to maturity. Both variables tell us something about how much you earn by holding a bond, but they can behave quite differently. For example, a decrease in a bond's price can simultaneously cause an increase in the yield to maturity (because a bond's price and yield are inversely related) and a *negative* rate of return (because bondholders suffer capital losses). If you are thinking of buying a bond, which variable should you care about?

The answer depends on how long you are likely to hold the bond. If you hold the bond until it matures, the yield to maturity tells you what interest rate you receive. Fluctuations in the bond's price, which affect the rate of return, are irrelevant if you never sell the bond.

On the other hand, if you sell the bond after a year, you will receive the rate of return for the year. The yield to maturity does not matter if you don't hold the bond to maturity.

16-7 The Term Structure of Interest Rates

Using the concept of yield to maturity, we have seen how to measure the interest rate on a bond. In a modern economy, there are many different bonds that pay different interest rates. The FYI box "The Many Different Interest Rates" in Chapter 3 discusses why interest rates vary, including differences in credit risk and taxes. To conclude this chapter, we study one important factor that influences a bond's interest rate: its term.

"Term" is another word for time to maturity. Bond maturities range from a few months to 30 years or more. Different maturities usually imply different interest rates, even for bonds issued by the same borrower. Similarly, banks charge different interest rates on loans of different durations.

To illustrate this point, Figure 16-5 graphs the interest rates on two bonds for the period from 1960 to 2010. The securities are 10-year Treasury bonds and 90-day Treasury bills. We see that the two interest rates generally differ but that the difference is not stable. The Treasury bond rate is *usually* higher than the Treasury bill rate, but occasionally the Treasury bill rate is higher.

The relationships among interest rates on bonds with different maturities are called the **term structure of interest rates**. Let's discuss the factors that determine the term structure and why it changes over time.

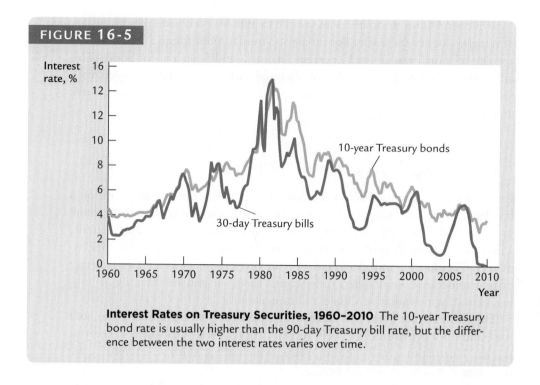

FIGURE 16-5

Interest Rates on Treasury Securities, 1960–2010 The 10-year Treasury bond rate is usually higher than the 90-day Treasury bill rate, but the difference between the two interest rates varies over time.

The Term Structure Under Certainty

To understand the term structure, we analyze savers' decisions about what bonds to buy. For now, let's make a major simplifying assumption: savers know the interest rates on all bonds, both today and in the future. For example, they know the rates on bonds that will be issued today, a year from now, and five years from now. We derive a theory of the term structure under this assumption of certainty, and then we look at what happens when savers are uncertain about future interest rates.

We start with an example involving one-year and two-year bonds. Suppose it is 2020, and Jane plans to save money for two years, until 2022. Jane is considering two ways to save: by purchasing one-year bonds and by purchasing two-year bonds. Let's compare the interest that Jane receives in the two cases.

Suppose first that Jane buys two-year bonds, and let $i_2(2020)$ denote the annual interest rate (the yield to maturity) on two-year bonds issued in 2020. Jane receives this interest rate for two years, for a total of $2i_2(2020)$. For example, if the interest rate is 4 percent, Jane receives a total of $2(4\%) = 8\%$ of her initial wealth.[4]

---

[4] This calculation uses an approximation. To see this, let's compute the earnings on a two-year bond exactly. If someone saves a dollar at an interest rate i_2, his wealth grows to $1 + i_2$ dollars after a year. His wealth after two years is $(1 + i_2)^2$ (see the discussion of future value in Section 16-1). The quantity $(1 + i_2)^2$ equals $1 + 2i_2 + (i_2)^2$. Subtracting off the saver's initial dollar yields his total earnings: $2i_2 + (i_2)^2$.

We've assumed that the earnings on a two-year bond are simply $2i_2$, which means we ignore the $(i_2)^2$ term. Economists often use this approximation because $(i_2)^2$ is small. For an interest rate of 4 percent (or 0.04 in decimal form), $(i_2)^2$ is 0.16% (0.0016). The total earnings on a two-year bond are $2i_2 + (i_2)^2 = 8\% + 0.16\% = 8.16\%$. Our approximation yields 8 percent, which is accurate enough for present purposes.

Now suppose Jane buys one-year bonds. She purchases these bonds in 2020 and they mature in 2021. At that point she can use the proceeds to buy new one-year bonds, which mature in 2022. The interest rates on one-year bonds purchased in 2020 and 2021 are $i_1(2020)$ and $i_1(2021)$, so Jane receives total interest of $i_1(2020) + i_1(2021)$. Recall that we're assuming certainty, so Jane knows both one-year rates in advance.[5]

From this information, we can derive a relationship between one- and two-year interest rates. The interest earnings from a two-year bond issued in 2020 must equal the total earnings from one-year bonds issued in 2020 and 2021. That is,

$$2i_2(2020) = i_1(2020) + i_1(2021).$$

This equation must hold if borrowers issue both one- and two-year bonds. If the two-year bonds offered more interest, savers like Jane would buy only two-year bonds, and the issuers of one-year bonds would have to raise interest rates to attract buyers. If two-year bonds paid less, issuers of these bonds would have to raise rates. When savers know current and future interest rates for certain, competition to sell bonds equalizes the interest payments for different maturities.

If we divide the last equation by 2, we get a formula for the two-year interest rate:

$$i_2(2020) = \frac{1}{2}[i_1(2020) + i_1(2021)].$$

The two-year rate is the average of the current one-year rate and the one-year rate in the following year. For example, if the one-year rate is 3 percent in 2020 and 5 percent in 2021, the two-year rate in 2020 is 4 percent.

This logic applies to any year. If $i_2(t)$ is the interest rate on a two-year bond issued in year t, $i_1(t)$ the rate on a one-year bond issued in year t, and $i_1(t + 1)$ the one-year rate in the following year, then

$$i_2(t) = \frac{1}{2}[i_1(t) + i_1(t + 1)].$$

The two-year rate in year t is the average of the one-year rates in years t and $t + 1$.

This formula also holds for periods other than a year. If t is a *month* and $t + 1$ is the following month, the formula says that the two-month interest rate is the average of two one-month rates.

Our logic extends beyond one- and two-period bonds to longer-term bonds. If $i_3(t)$ is the interest rate on a *three*-period bond, then

$$i_3(t) = \frac{1}{3}[i_1(t) + i_1(t + 1) + i_1(t + 2)].$$

The three-period interest rate is the average of the one-period rates in the current period, t, and the next two periods, $t + 1$ and $t + 2$.

---

[5] Once again we've used an approximation. The exact earnings from the one-year bonds are $i_1(2020) + i_1(2021) + [i_1(2020)] \times [i_1(2021)]$. We ignore the last term (the product of the two rates), which is small.

The rationale for this equation is similar to our reasoning about two-period bonds. Someone saving for three periods can buy either a three-period bond or a series of three one-period bonds. These strategies must produce the same earnings if savers buy both kinds of bonds.

Finally, we can write a general formula for any maturity. If $i_n(t)$ is the interest rate on an n-period bond in period t, then

$$i_n(t) = \frac{1}{n}\left[i_1(t) + i_1(t+1) + \cdots + i_1(t+n-1)\right].$$

The n-period interest rate is the average of one-period rates in the current period and the next $n-1$ periods. For example, the ten-year interest rate in 2020 is the average of the one-year rates in 2020 and the next nine years, 2021 through 2029.

The Expectations Theory of the Term Structure

So far, we have assumed that savers know the interest rates on all bonds, current and future. This simplifying assumption is not realistic. In 2020, savers know the current interest rates for all maturities, but they do not know with certainty what rates will be in 2021 or later.

To account for this fact, economists analyze the term structure with the **expectations theory of the term structure**. In this theory, savers do not know the future with certainty, but they have expectations about future interest rates. These expectations are rational: they are optimal forecasts given current information. Savers choose among bonds of different maturities based on their rational expectations about future interest rates.

In the expectations theory of the term structure, bonds of different maturities must produce the same *expected* earnings. If they don't, nobody will buy the bonds with lower expected earnings. This reasoning leads to

$$i_n(t) = \frac{1}{n}\left[i_1(t) + Ei_1(t+1) + \cdots + Ei_1(t+n-1)\right],$$

where E means "expected." This equation expresses the expectations theory of the term structure. It is the same as the previous equation, except it replaces actual future interest rates with expected rates. The n-period interest rate is the average of the current one-period rate and expected rates from $t+1$ to $t+n-1$.

Accounting for Risk

The expectations theory assumes that savers choose bonds based only on expected interest rates. This assumption ignores the role of uncertainty. Modifying the theory to account for risk makes it more realistic. As we discussed in Section 16-2, savers are risk averse. When asset returns are uncertain, savers demand higher expected returns as compensation.

To see the implications of risk for the term structure, recall another point from Section 16-2: long-term bond prices respond more strongly to changes in interest rates and are therefore more volatile than short-term bond prices. This means that holders of long-term bonds may experience large capital gains or losses, and this risk makes these bonds less attractive to savers.

Therefore, once we take risk into account, it is *not* true that long- and short-term bonds yield the same expected earnings, as the basic expectations theory assumes. If they did, savers would buy only short-term bonds, which are less risky. To attract buyers, long-term bonds must offer higher expected earnings.

Economists capture this idea by modifying the expectations theory of the term structure to include a **term premium** for long-term interest rates. This premium, denoted by τ (the Greek letter tau), is the extra return that compensates the holder of a long-term bond for the bond's riskiness. The following equation summarizes the expectations theory with a term premium:

$$i_n(t) = \frac{1}{n}\left[i_1(t) + Ei_1(t + 1) + \cdots + Ei_1(t + n - 1)\right] + \tau_n,$$

where τ_n is the term premium for an n-period bond. This equation says that the n-period interest rate is the average of expected one-period rates *plus* the term premium.

Bonds of different maturities have different term premiums. The quantity τ_2 is the premium for two-period bonds, τ_3 is the premium for three-period bonds, and so on. The longer a bond's maturity, the higher its term premium; for example, $\tau_3 > \tau_2$ and $\tau_4 > \tau_3$. A longer maturity means a more variable bond price and requires greater compensation for risk.

The Yield Curve

The term structure of interest rates can be summarized in a graph called the **yield curve**. The yield curve shows interest rates on bonds of various maturities at a given point in time.

Figure 16-6 shows a hypothetical yield curve for January 1, 2020. On that day, bonds with longer maturities have higher interest rates. For example, the three-month interest rate is 4 percent, the one-year rate is 5 percent, and the ten-year rate is 6 percent.

Yield Curve Shapes The yield curve looks different at different points in time. The shape of the curve depends on expectations about future interest rates. Figure 16-7 shows four possibilities. All assume the same one-period rate but reflect different expectations about future rates, which produce different interest rates at longer maturities.

As a first example, suppose that people expect the one-period interest rate to stay constant. The expected future rates—$Ei_1(t + 1)$, $Ei_1(t + 2)$, and so on—all equal the current rate $i_1(t)$. Substituting this assumption into our last formula for the n-period rate yields

$$i_n(t) = \frac{1}{n}\left[i_1(t) + i_1(t) + \cdots + i_1(t)\right] + \tau_n,$$

which simplifies to

$$i_n(t) = i_1(t) + \tau_n.$$

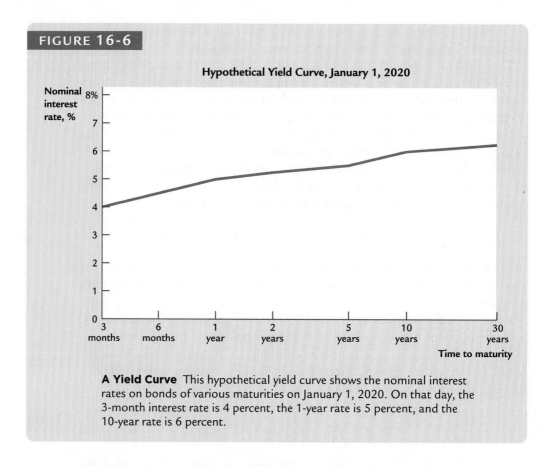

FIGURE 16-6

Hypothetical Yield Curve, January 1, 2020

A Yield Curve This hypothetical yield curve shows the nominal interest rates on bonds of various maturities on January 1, 2020. On that day, the 3-month interest rate is 4 percent, the 1-year rate is 5 percent, and the 10-year rate is 6 percent.

With the one-period rate expected to stay constant, the average of expected future rates equals the current one-period rate. The n-period rate is the one-period rate plus a term premium.

Recall that the term premium τ_n rises with a bond's maturity, n. Therefore, the last equation implies that the interest rate $i_n(t)$ rises with n. This case is captured by the green line in Figure 16-7. Rising term premiums cause the yield curve to slope upward.

The other lines in the figure illustrate cases in which the one-period interest rate is *not* expected to stay constant. The blue line is a yield curve that results when people expect the one-period rate to rise in the future. The average of expected future rates exceeds the current rate, pushing up long-term interest rates: they exceed the one-period rate by more than the term premium. In our graph, the yield curve is steep.

The red line is a yield curve that results when people expect the one-period interest rate to fall. The average of expected future rates is less than the current rate, reducing long-term rates and flattening the yield curve.

Finally, the orange line is an example of an **inverted yield curve**, a curve that slopes downward. This situation arises when people expect an unusually large fall in the one-period interest rate. This expectation reduces long-term rates by more than term premiums raise them, so long-term rates lie below the current one-period rate.

FIGURE 16-7

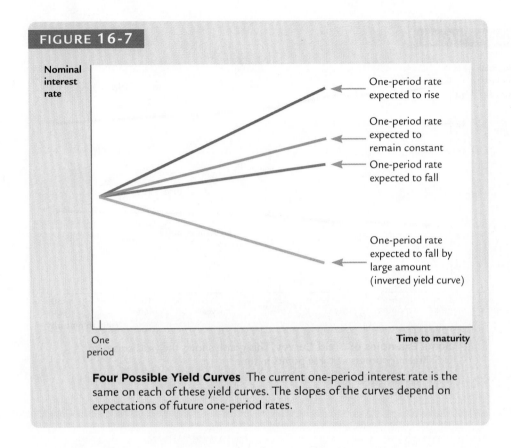

Four Possible Yield Curves The current one-period interest rate is the same on each of these yield curves. The slopes of the curves depend on expectations of future one-period rates.

Some Examples Figure 16-8 graphs actual yield curves for U.S. Treasury bonds in January 1981, June 1999, and December 2009. These cases illustrate some of the possible yield curves that we've discussed.

Notice first that interest rates were highest at all maturities in 1981. Inflation was high at that time, producing high nominal interest rates through the Fisher equation, $i = r + E\pi$ (discussed in Chapter 4). Interest rates were lowest in 2009, when the Federal Reserve was trying to end a deep recession.

The key features of the yield curves are their slopes. The yield curve for June 1999 has a common shape—a moderate upward slope. The interest rate is 4.6 percent at a maturity of three months, 5.6 percent at two years, and 6.0 percent at thirty years. The curve for December 2009 is steeper than usual, going from under 0.1 percent at three months to 4.5 percent at thirty years. Finally, the yield curve for January 1981 is inverted: rates fall with maturity over most of the curve.

Forecasting Interest Rates The expected path of interest rates determines the shape of the yield curve. Turning this relation around, the yield curve's shape tells us about the expected path of interest rates. An unusually steep curve, such as the one for December 2009, means that short-term interest rates are expected to rise. An inverted curve, such as the one for January 1981, means short-term rates are expected to fall sharply.

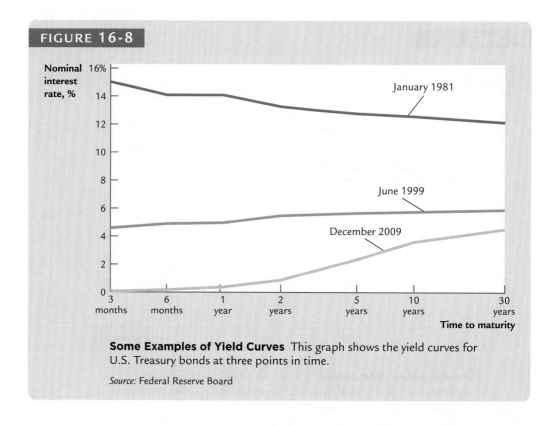

FIGURE 16-8

Some Examples of Yield Curves This graph shows the yield curves for U.S. Treasury bonds at three points in time.

Source: Federal Reserve Board

These facts imply a use for the yield curve: to forecast interest rates. If you are thinking of borrowing money in the future, you would like to know future interest rates. You can't know these rates for sure, but you can estimate them with the yield curve. The yield curve reveals the interest rate expectations of people who trade bonds. These are good forecasts because bond traders are well informed about interest rates.

CASE STUDY

Inverted Yield Curves

Because of term premiums, the yield curve usually has an upward slope. An inverted curve occurs only if short-term interest rates are expected to fall by a large amount. Why might this expectation arise?

Historically, most inverted yield curves have been caused by monetary policy—specifically, by efforts to reduce inflation. To fight inflation, the Federal Reserve slows the growth of the money supply, which pushes up the federal funds rate and other short-term interest rates. Higher interest rates reduce output temporarily, and lower output reduces inflation as indicated by the Phillips curve (discussed in Chapter 12).

In such an episode, the increase in short-term interest rates is temporary. People expect the Fed to reduce interest rates once inflation is under control. In fact, rates are likely to end up lower than they were before the Fed acted, because of lower inflation and the Fisher effect. The expected decrease in rates may be large enough to invert the yield curve.

In Figure 16-8, we saw that the yield curve for Treasury securities was inverted in 1981. At that time inflation was running near 10 percent, and the Federal Reserve was determined to reduce it. The Fed slowed money growth, and the three-month Treasury bill rate rose to 15 percent. The yield curve inverted because people expected large decreases in inflation and interest rates. Expectations turned out to be correct: the three-month Treasury bill rate fell to 8 percent in 1983 and 6 percent in 1986.

Another inverted yield curve occurred at the end of 2000. The Fed was worried that inflation might rise, because output had been growing at an unusually rapid pace. The Fed raised short-term interest rates to contain inflation, and the yield curve mildly inverted. In December 2000, the three-month rate was 6.0 percent, the one-year rate was 5.7 percent, and the thirty-year rate was 5.4 percent. ∎

16-8 Conclusion

Fluctuations in asset prices have important effects on the economy. Changes in the prices of stocks or of houses, for example, cause changes in consumers' wealth that affect aggregate demand and output. What causes asset prices to fluctuate? In answering this question, economists typically apply the classical theory of asset prices, in which the key factors are interest rates and expected asset income. Yet the classical theory may fail to explain some asset-price movements, including price increases during bubbles and price decreases during crashes.

In earlier chapters, we discussed how "the" interest rate is determined. In this chapter we have learned that there are various interest rates, and we also learned how to calculate them and studied the relationships among them. We found that long-term interest rates depend on expectations of future short-term rates and on term premiums.

With this background, we can take a closer look at the markets for assets and their roles in the economy. The next chapter discusses the people and firms that participate in asset markets and their decisions about what to buy and sell.

Summary

1. The present value of a future dollar is its worth in today's dollars. The present value of a dollar in n years is $\$1/(1 + i)^n$. We can use this formula to find the present value of a stream of income such as that generated by a bond or a share of stock.

2. The classical theory of asset prices says an asset price equals the present value of expected future income from the asset and assumes that expectations are rational.

3. The interest rate used to compute an asset price is a risk-adjusted rate; it equals the safe rate (i^{safe}) plus a risk premium (φ). The risk premium rises with uncertainty about future asset income.

4. A rise in expected asset income raises asset prices. A rise in interest rates reduces asset prices.

5. Some economists believe that asset prices are influenced by bubbles, which occur when prices rise above the present value of asset income. In a bubble, people pay high prices for assets because they expect prices to rise even higher.

6. An asset-price bubble may dissipate gradually or end with a crash when prices plummet in a short period of time. A crash occurs when asset holders lose confidence, sparking a vicious circle of selling and declining prices.

7. The interest rate on a bond is measured by the yield to maturity, the interest rate that makes the present value of the bond's payments equal to its price. The return on an asset is the change in its price plus any current payment (a coupon payment or stock dividend). The rate of return is the return as a percentage of the initial price. The rate of return on stocks is more volatile than the rate of return on bonds, but it is higher on average.

8. The term structure is the relationship among interest rates on bonds of different maturities (terms). The yield curve summarizes the term structure at a point in time. The shape of the yield curve depends on expectations about future interest rates. Economists use the yield curve to forecast future rates.

KEY CONCEPTS

Future value	Asset-price bubble	Return
Present value	Price-earnings (P/E) ratio	Rate of return
Classical theory of asset prices	Asset-price crash	Term structure of interest rates
Dividend	Margin requirements	Expectations theory of the term structure
Safe interest rate (i^{safe})	Circuit breaker	
Risk premium (φ)	Yield to maturity	Term premium (τ)
Risk-adjusted interest rate	Capital gain	Yield curve
Gordon growth model	Capital loss	Inverted yield curve

QUESTIONS FOR REVIEW

1. What is the future value of a dollar today? What is the present value of a dollar in the future?

2. What is the classical theory of asset prices?

3. What factors cause asset prices to change?

4. Which asset prices are most volatile? Why?

5. What happens in an asset-price bubble? What happens in an asset-price crash?

6. What is the difference between the yield to maturity on a bond and its rate of return?

7. Why can yield curves be used to forecast interest rates?

PROBLEMS AND APPLICATIONS

1. Suppose you win the lottery. You have a choice between receiving $100,000 a year for twenty years or an immediate payment of $1,200,000.

   a. Which choice should you make if the interest rate is 3 percent? If it is 6 percent?

   b. For what range of interest rates should you take the immediate payment?

2. Suppose a bond has a maturity of three years, annual coupon payments of $5, and a face value of $100.

   a. If the interest rate is 4 percent, is the price of the bond higher or lower than the face value? What if the interest rate is 6 percent?

   b. For what range of interest rates does the price exceed the face value? Can you explain the answer?

3. Suppose that people expect a company's earnings to grow in the future at the same rate they have grown in the past. Does this behavior satisfy the assumption of rational expectations? Explain.

4. Describe how each of the following events affects stock and bond prices:

   a. The economy enters a recession.

   b. A genius invents a new technology that makes factories more productive.

   c. The Federal Reserve raises its target for interest rates.

   d. People learn that major news about the economy will be announced in a few days, but they don't know whether it is good news or bad news.

5. Consider two stocks. For each, the expected dividend next year is $100 and the expected growth rate of dividends is 3 percent. The risk premium is 3 percent for one stock and 8 percent for the other. The economy's safe interest rate is 5 percent.

   a. What does the difference in risk premiums tell us about the dividends from each stock?

   b. Use the Gordon growth model to compute the price of each stock. Why is one price higher than the other?

   c. Suppose the expected growth rate of dividends rises to 5 percent for both stocks. Compute the new price of each. Which stock's price changes by a larger percentage? Explain your results.

6. Consider two bonds. Each has a face value of $100 and matures in ten years. One has no coupon payments, and the other pays $10 per year.

   a. Calculate the price of each bond if the interest rate is 3 percent and if the interest rate is 6 percent.

   b. When the interest rate rises from 3 percent to 6 percent, which bond price falls by a larger percentage? Explain why.

7. Suppose a bond has a face value of $100, annual coupon payments of $4, a maturity of five years, and a price of $90.

   a. Write an equation that defines the yield to maturity on this bond.

   b. If you have the right kind of calculator or software, find the solution for the yield to maturity.

8. Suppose the price of the bond in Problem 7 falls from $90 to $85 over a year. Calculate the bond's rate of return over the year.

9. Suppose it is 2020 and the one-year interest rate is 4 percent. The expected one-year rates in the following four years (2021 to 2024) are 4 percent, 5 percent, 6 percent, and 6 percent.

   a. Assume the expectations theory of the term structure, with no term premiums. Compute the interest rates in 2020 on bonds with maturities of one, two, three, four, and five years. Draw a yield curve.

   b. Redo part (a) with term premiums. Assume the term premium for an n-year bond, τ_n, is $(n/2)$ percent. For example, the premium for a four-year bond is $(4/2)\% = 2\%$.

10. Suppose it is 2020, the one-year interest rate is 8 percent, and the ten-year rate is 6 percent.

   a. Draw a graph showing a likely path of the one-year rate from 2020 through 2029.

   b. Why might people expect such a path for the one-year rate?

11. Using the expectations theory of the term structure, derive a formula giving the four-year interest rate in 2020 as a function of *two-year* rates in 2020 and the future.

12. Suppose that some event has no effect on expected interest rates but raises uncertainty about rates. What happens to the yield curve? Explain.

13. Go to bloomberg.com, which provides daily data on the Dow Jones stock index. Find a day within the last year when the index rose or fell by at least 2 percent. Consult news reports for that day and discuss why stock prices might have changed. Was the change consistent with the classical theory of asset prices?

CHAPTER 17

Securities Markets

Markets are constantly in a state of uncertainty and flux and money is made by discounting the obvious and betting on the unexpected.

—*George Soros*

If you are a college student, you may not be a saver right now, but someday you probably will be. Perhaps your brilliance and hard work·will make you rich. Even if your income is modest, you will probably set some of it aside for retirement. Either way, you will have to choose what to do with your savings.

Should you put your money in a bank? Should you buy securities such as stocks and bonds? Which securities are best? Should you buy individual securities or buy shares of a mutual fund, which owns many different securities?

People around the world face the problem of **asset allocation**, as do financial institutions that hold assets, such as banks and pension funds. Decisions about asset allocation produce the activity that we see in financial markets—the daily trading of securities worth billions of dollars.

This chapter discusses securities markets. We first meet the participants in these markets, including a variety of financial institutions. Then we discuss how the markets work—how governments and firms issue securities and how securities are traded.

Next we analyze the key choices facing securities market participants. These include firms' decisions about what securities to issue and savers' choices of asset allocation. Savers must decide how to split their wealth among broad classes of assets, such as stocks and bonds. They must also choose among individual securities, such as the stocks of different companies.

We turn last to another class of securities: *derivatives,* securities with payoffs tied to the prices of other assets. Markets for derivatives have grown rapidly in the last few decades. We discuss what derivative securities are, why they are traded, and the risks they can create.

17-1 Participants in Securities Markets

The players in securities markets include individual savers and many kinds of financial institutions. The key institutions are listed in Table 17-1. Some own large quantities of securities; some help people and firms to trade securities; some do both.

> ### TABLE 17-1
>
> **Major Institutions in Securities Markets**
>
> **Securities Firms**
>
> Mutual funds
> Hedge funds
> Brokers
> Dealers
> Investment banks
>
> **Other Financial Institutions**
>
> Pension funds
> Insurance companies
> Commercial banks

Individual Owners

Some securities are owned by individual people. In 2007 (the latest year with data available), U.S. citizens directly owned 28 percent of the stock of U.S. companies. They also owned most shares in mutual funds, which held another 25 percent of U.S. corporate stock.

Over time, stock ownership has spread to a larger fraction of the U.S. population. In 1983, only 19 percent of households owned any stock, either directly or indirectly through mutual funds. In 2008, 47 percent of households owned stock. One reason for this trend is the growth of 401(k) plans that channel workers' retirement savings into securities.

While many people own stock, a few hold disproportionately large amounts. In 2007, the wealthiest 1 percent of U.S. households owned 38 percent of stock held by individuals; the wealthiest 10 percent owned 80 percent.

Securities Firms

Among the financial institutions that participate in securities markets, one broad category is **securities firms**. These companies' primary purpose is to hold securities, trade them, or help others trade them. There are several types of securities firms: mutual funds, hedge funds, brokers and dealers, and investment banks.

Mutual Funds Recall from Chapter 15 that a mutual fund is a financial institution that holds a diversified set of securities and sells shares to savers. In effect, each shareholder owns a small part of all the securities in a fund. Buying mutual fund shares is an easy way for savers to diversify their assets, which reduces risk.

About 8,000 separate mutual funds exist in the United States. Most are run by large mutual fund companies such as Fidelity, Vanguard, and American Funds. Each company offers a menu of funds that feature different sets of securities.

Some funds hold a wide variety of stocks and bonds; others specialize. For example, some funds hold only Treasury bonds, and some hold only corporate bonds. Some specialize in stocks issued by large firms, and some specialize in small firms' stock. Some funds hold only U.S. securities, and some hold foreign securities.

Hedge Funds Like mutual funds, **hedge funds** raise pools of money to purchase securities. Unlike mutual funds, they cater only to wealthy people and institutions. Most hedge funds require clients to contribute $1 million or more.

A key difference between hedge funds and mutual funds involves government regulation. To protect small savers, the government limits the risks that mutual funds can take with shareholders' money. Hedge funds are largely unregulated because the government assumes that the funds' rich customers can look out for themselves. Light regulation means that hedge funds can make risky bets on asset prices. These bets sometimes produce large earnings, and sometimes large losses.

One common tool of hedge funds is **leverage**: funds borrow money from banks and use it to increase their security holdings. Larger security holdings magnify the funds' gains and losses when security prices change. Mutual funds are not allowed to use leverage to buy securities because of the risk of large losses. Another risky practice of hedge funds, forbidden to mutual funds, is trading derivative securities (discussed in more detail later in the chapter).

Money flowed into hedge funds in the early 2000s, and their total assets reached $3 trillion in 2007. During the ensuing financial crisis, asset values fell and savers withdrew money from hedge funds. In 2009, total hedge fund assets had fallen to $1.5 trillion.

Brokers and Dealers These firms help securities markets operate. A **broker** buys and sells securities on behalf of others. For example, if you want to acquire a share of Microsoft, a broker will buy it for you in a stock market. You pay a fee to the broker for this service.

You can choose between two types of brokers. A *full-service broker* has advisers who help clients choose which securities to buy. Leading full-service brokers include Merrill Lynch, Smith Barney, and Dean Witter. A *discount broker* provides less advice, or none at all; customers must choose securities on their own. Firms in this category include Charles Schwab, TD Ameritrade, and online brokers such as E* Trade.

A **dealer** buys securities for itself, not others, and earns profits by reselling them at higher prices. Typically, a dealer firm specializes in a narrow set of securities, such as Treasury bills or the stocks of certain companies. It holds an inventory of these securities and "makes a market" for them. The dealer stands ready to buy the securities when someone else wants to sell and to sell when someone else wants to buy.

Investment Banks This type of securities firm includes well-known names such as Goldman Sachs, Morgan Stanley, and Credit Suisse. An **investment bank** is not really a bank in economists' sense of the term, because it does not take deposits. Instead, investment banks have several functions in securities markets.

A traditional function is underwriting, a process we discuss in Section 17-2. As an **underwriter**, an investment bank helps companies issue new stocks and bonds. It advises the companies and markets the securities to potential buyers.

Investment banks also advise companies on *mergers and acquisitions,* or M&A. In these deals, two companies are combined or one company buys another. Investment banks research their client companies' potential profits from M&A and advise their clients about which deals to make and what prices to pay.

While underwriting and advising are their core functions, investment banks have also developed other ways to earn profits. Many investment banks buy and sell securities. Like hedge funds, they try to make money through risky bets on asset prices.

Investment banks also practice *financial engineering,* the development and marketing of new types of securities. One such security is the *junk bond,* a bond issued by a corporation with a low credit rating. Junk bonds were the brainchild of investment banker Michael Milken, whose firm, Drexel Burnham, started underwriting junk bonds in 1977. This innovation allowed more corporations to raise money in bond markets. More recently, investment banks have invented new derivative securities and securities backed by home mortgage loans, as discussed in upcoming case studies.

Other Financial Institutions

In addition to securities firms, several other financial institutions are important participants in securities markets because they buy large quantities of stocks and bonds.

Pension Funds Employers, both private firms and governments, establish pension funds to provide income to retired workers. Employers contribute money to the funds, and sometimes workers also make contributions. Pension funds use this money to purchase securities, and earnings from the securities provide retirement benefits.

Insurance Companies These companies sell life insurance and insurance for property, such as houses and cars. Purchasers of insurance pay premiums, which the companies use to buy securities. Earnings from the securities pay for insurance claims.

Commercial Banks In contrast to investment banks, commercial banks are institutions that accept deposits and make loans. Their primary assets are those loans—the money they are owed by borrowers. However, commercial banks also own securities, mainly government bonds. Banks hold bonds for liquidity: they can sell the bonds easily if they need cash.

Financial Industry Consolidation

In practice, the various types of institutions that participate in securities markets overlap because many firms engage in more than one business. For example, Merrill Lynch has long been a leader in both investment banking and brokerage. Over the last twenty years, mergers have produced large securities firms with multiple functions.

Two major events have contributed to consolidation in the financial industry. One was the 1999 repeal of the *Glass-Steagall Act,* which forbade commercial banks from merging with investment banks. With Glass-Steagal gone, mergers created conglomerates such as Citigroup and JP Morgan Chase, which own commercial banks and also perform most functions of securities firms. Chapter 19 discusses the reasons for these mergers.

The financial crisis of 2007–2009 was the second major event that has contributed to financial industry consolidation. During the crisis, financial institutions that were relatively healthy bought institutions in danger of failing. The following case study discusses two of these deals: the takeovers of the investment banks Bear Stearns and Merrill Lynch.

CASE STUDY

The Upheaval in Investment Banking, 2008

At the start of 2008, the five largest investment banks in the United States were Goldman Sachs, Morgan Stanley, Merrill Lynch, Lehman Brothers, and Bear Stearns. Over the course of the year, all these institutions faced crises that threatened their survival.

The story begins in the early 2000s. In that period, the five investment banks started issuing *mortgage-backed securities.* To create these securities, they purchased home mortgage loans from the original lenders and bundled them together. The buyers of the securities became entitled to shares of the interest and principal payments that borrowers made on the underlying mortgages.

Mortgage-backed securities had been issued before by other financial institutions (namely the mortgage agencies Fannie Mae and Freddie Mac, which we discuss in Chapter 18). The novel feature of the securities issued by the investment banks was that the mortgages backing them were *subprime*: they were loans to people with weak credit histories. Subprime borrowers must pay higher interest rates than traditional mortgage borrowers pay. As a result, securities backed by subprime mortgages promised high returns to their owners—as long as borrowers made their mortgage payments.

The investment banks sold some of their mortgage-backed securities to customers, but they kept others for themselves. Unfortunately, the decline in housing prices that started in 2006 caused a rash of defaults on subprime mortgages, because many borrowers couldn't afford their payments and couldn't sell their houses for enough to pay off their debts. As defaults rose, participants in financial markets realized that securities backed by subprime mortgages would produce less income than previously expected. Lower expected income reduced the prices of the securities, causing large losses to the investment banks and other owners of the securities.

Eventually, mounting losses created crises at the investment banks. In early 2008, rumors spread that Bear Stearns might go bankrupt. Other financial institutions stopped lending to Bear or buying its bonds because they feared that Bear would default on its obligations. Bear ran out of money to pay off its existing loans and commercial paper (short-term bonds) that was maturing.

In March 2008, lawyers for Bear Stearns started preparing a bankruptcy filing. At the last minute, the Federal Reserve intervened. The Fed brokered a deal in which JP Morgan Chase purchased Bear Stearns. As a result, Bear did not default on its debts. The firm ceased to exist, but many of its operations continued under the management of JP Morgan Chase.

Six months later, Lehman Brothers faced a similar crisis: doubts about its survival led other institutions to cut off lending to the firm. But in contrast to Bear's fate, nobody stepped in to save Lehman, and it declared bankruptcy on September 15, 2008. It went out of business and defaulted on its outstanding bonds and bank loans.

Lehman's failure shocked participants in financial markets and created fears that other investment banks would fail. On the same day as Lehman's bankruptcy, Bank of America purchased Merrill Lynch. Like Bear Stearns, Merrill was absorbed into a healthier institution.

Goldman Sachs and Morgan Stanley held fewer mortgage-backed securities than the other investment banks. They lost less and were able to remain independent but needed to reassure other financial institutions that they would survive. To do so, both firms became *bank holding companies (BHCs)* on September 21, 2008. This reorganization gave them the right to open commercial banks and to receive emergency loans from the Fed. In return, Goldman and Morgan accepted greater Fed regulation of their activities.

Despite these dramatic events, large investment banks still exist in the United States. As BHCs, Goldman Sachs and Morgan Stanley remain independent and continue to conduct investment-banking activities, including underwriting and securities trading. Merrill Lynch still operates as a broker and investment bank, albeit as a subsidiary of Bank of America. After losses in 2008, both Merrill and Goldman (but not Morgan Stanley) returned to profitability in 2009. ■

17-2 Stock and Bond Markets

Now that the players in securities markets have been introduced, let's discuss how they interact with one another. Savers and financial institutions participate in two kinds of markets. Firms and governments issue new securities in **primary markets**, and existing securities are traded in **secondary markets**.

Primary Markets

When a firm is founded, it can get funds from the owners' personal wealth and from bank loans. It may also attract funds from *venture capital firms*, which finance new companies in return for ownership shares. Up to this point, the firm is a *private company* with a small number of owners.

The Process of Issuing Securities As a firm grows, it may need more funds than it can raise as a private company. At that point, it turns to securities markets. It becomes a **public company**, a firm that issues stock and bonds that are traded in financial markets. A firm becomes public by making a first sale of stock, which is called an **initial public offering**, or **IPO**. Purchasers of the stock receive ownership shares in the firm. In return, the firm receives funds that it can use for investment.

Typically, a company's IPO is underwritten by investment banks. The company initiates this process by hiring a lead investment bank, which enlists other investment banks to form a *syndicate*. The syndicate members purchase the company's stock and resell it immediately to other financial institutions, such as mutual funds and pension funds. Shares are not offered directly to individual savers. Typically, investment banks sell the stock for 5 to 10 percent more than they pay for it.

A company announces an IPO in a formal document called a *prospectus*, which describes the stock being offered and the price. The prospectus also provides detailed information on the company, including financial statements and biographies of managers. The company's investment banks help prepare the prospectus. They also market the stock by sending their representatives around the country to make presentations to potential purchasers, such as mutual fund managers.

After a firm goes public, it returns to securities markets periodically to raise funds for investment. The firm can issue new stock, spreading ownership of the firm across additional buyers. It can also borrow money by issuing bonds. Investment banks underwrite these security issues, just as they underwrite IPOs.

The Need for Underwriters Investment banks earn large profits from underwriting. They receive a significant chunk of the money that firms raise by issuing securities. Why can't firms cut out investment banks and sell securities directly to the final purchasers?

The answer is that investment banks reduce the asymmetric information problem of adverse selection. Recall from Chapter 15 that firms may be most eager to issue securities when the value of the securities is low. To go public, a firm needs a track record to help people judge the value of its stock. Even then, potential stock purchasers are wary because they know less about the firm's business than the firm does. They fear that potentially unprofitable companies will try to sell securities at inflated prices.

Investment banks reduce this worry when they underwrite a firm's securities. They research the firm and try to ensure that it is sound and that its securities are priced reasonably. Investment banks convince other institutions of the securities' value by putting their own reputations on the line. If the Acme Corporation hires Goldman Sachs to underwrite its IPO, it has a better chance of selling its securities. Mutual fund managers may not have heard of Acme, but they've heard of Goldman Sachs, and they know that Goldman has a history of underwriting good securities.

Because reputation is so important, underwriting is a concentrated industry dominated by a small number of institutions. Since 2000, 10 investment banks have underwritten more than half of the securities issued around the world. It is hard for lesser-known firms to enter the underwriting business. If your friend Joe started Joe's Discount Investment Bank, he would probably have trouble selling securities. Mutual fund managers don't know Joe, so they would fear a rip-off.

We can better understand the role of underwriters by examining Google's IPO in 2004—one of the few that did *not* involve traditional underwriting.

UNCORRECTED PAGES

"Damn it, I don't want to know about my love life. Tell me about the bond market."

Instead, Google sold shares through an auction in which any institution or person could submit bids. Google hired Morgan Stanley and Credit Suisse to run the auction, but these firms did not research the company's finances or market Google's stock to possible buyers. As a result, they received only 3 percent of the IPO revenue, not the usual 5 to 10 percent charged by underwriters.

Google was able to modify the traditional IPO because it is an unusually well-known and successful company. Its reputation reduced the adverse selection problem. Many people were eager to buy Google stock, so the company didn't need the usual help from investment banks.

One issuer of securities has never hired an investment bank: the U.S. government. The government is even better known than Google, so it can sell bonds directly to savers and financial institutions. Most government bonds are issued through auctions run by the Treasury department and designed to produce the highest possible prices for the bonds.

Secondary Markets

After securities are issued in primary markets, their buyers often resell them in secondary markets. Then the securities are traded repeatedly among institutions and individual savers.

To understand this process, we first discuss how brokers help people enter securities markets. Then we discuss the main types of secondary markets: exchanges and over-the-counter (OTC) markets. OTC markets can be divided into dealer markets and electronic communication networks (ECNs).

The Role of Brokers A financial institution can buy securities directly from other institutions. Individual savers can buy bonds directly from the government in auctions. However, to buy stocks or corporate bonds, individuals need assistance from brokers.

If you want to buy securities, the first step is to establish an account with a broker. You can use a traditional broker, such as Merrill-Lynch, or an online broker, such as E*trade. You deposit money in your account so it is available to buy the securities you choose.

When you want to buy or sell, you contact your broker by phone or over the Internet. You place an order—let's say you want to buy 100 shares of Boeing, the aircraft manufacturer. You can place a *market order,* which tells the broker to buy Boeing for the best price he can find. Or you can place a *limit order,* telling him to buy only if the price reaches a certain level. The broker fills your order in different ways, depending on which type of secondary market he uses.

Exchanges Your broker may fill your order at an **exchange**, a physical location where brokers and dealers meet. Exchanges are used mostly to trade stocks, not bonds. The world's largest securities exchange is the New York Stock Exchange (NYSE), located on Wall Street in lower Manhattan. The stocks of roughly 3,000 companies are traded on the NYSE. Other cities with large stock exchanges include London, Frankfurt, Tokyo, and Sao Paolo.

Figure 17-1 illustrates how stocks are traded on the NYSE. You have asked your broker, Merrill-Lynch, to buy 100 shares of Boeing. Merrill has a *seat* on the exchange, allowing it to trade there. The person you contact at Merrill sends your order to one of the firm's *commission brokers,* who work on the floor of the exchange.

The commission broker walks to the *trading post* for Boeing stock. The trading post is a desk staffed by a broker-dealer called a **specialist**. The NYSE chooses one securities firm to provide a specialist for each stock (the specialist for Boeing works for Spear, Leeds, and Kellogg). The specialist manages the trading of that stock.

Brokers tell the specialist how many shares of Boeing they want to buy or sell and what prices they will accept. The specialist records this information and

FIGURE 17-1

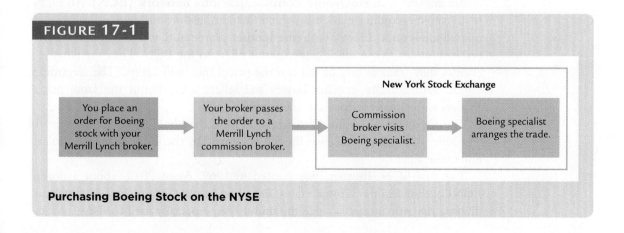

Purchasing Boeing Stock on the NYSE

arranges trades. Sometimes the specialist matches a broker who wants to buy stock with another who wants to sell. Other times, the specialist acts as a dealer, trading with brokers on behalf of her own firm. Either way, her job is to help brokers make the trades ordered by their customers.

Dealer Markets A secondary market that has no physical location—one that is not an exchange—is an **over-the-counter (OTC) market**. One type of OTC market is a **dealer market**, in which all trades are made with dealers. A computer network connects the dealers to brokers and other financial institutions that want to trade. Each dealer posts "bid" prices at which it will buy certain securities and "ask" prices at which it will sell.

The largest dealer market for stocks is the NASDAQ network. The initials stand for National Association of Securities Dealers Automated Quotation. Roughly 3,000 stocks are traded on the NASDAQ, the same number as on the NYSE. NASDAQ companies tend to be smaller, and many are in high-tech industries. Within the NASDAQ network, 20 or more firms may be dealers in a particular stock. If you tell your broker to buy or sell a stock for you, he looks for the dealer with the best price.

Most bonds, both corporate and government, are traded on dealer markets. Again, computer networks link dealers with other financial institutions that want to make trades. The biggest bond dealers are divisions of financial conglomerates such as Citigroup and JP Morgan Chase.

Dealers make profits from the **bid–ask spread**, the gap between the prices at which they buy and sell a security. The size of these spreads varies greatly. Spreads are smaller for more liquid securities, those that are easy to trade because there are many buyers and sellers. For the most liquid—Treasury securities—spreads are well under 0.1 percent of the price. Dealers can profit from small spreads by purchasing great numbers of securities and reselling them immediately.

Bid–ask spreads are higher for stocks, and higher still for corporate bonds. Spreads on these bonds can be several percentage points. The bond of a particular company may not be traded frequently. If a dealer buys the bond, it might take awhile to sell it, and the price could fall in the meantime. The bid–ask spread compensates the dealer for this risk.

Electronic Communication Networks An alternative to exchanges and dealer markets is an **electronic communications network (ECN)**. An ECN is an over-the-counter market in which financial institutions such as brokers and mutual funds trade directly with one another, a process that doesn't require dealers. Institutions that want to trade submit offers to the ECN. They say what securities they want to buy or sell and the prices they will accept. The electronic system automatically matches buyers and sellers who submit the same price. Traders pay a small fee for each transaction.

The advantage of trading through an ECN is that there is no bid–ask spread. The seller of a security receives the full price paid by the ultimate buyer. Dealers don't take a cut.

The first ECN, Instinet, was created in 1969. As of 2010, about a dozen ECNs operated in the United States, including Instinet, Island, and Archipelago. Trading has grown rapidly since the mid-1990s, especially for NASDAQ stocks.

UNCORRECTED PAGES

More than half of all trades in these stocks occur through ECNs rather than the NASDAQ dealer network.

Finding Information on Security Prices

Suppose you are adding up your wealth and want to know the current prices of the stocks and bonds you own. Daily newspapers such as the *Wall Street Journal* report prices from the previous day. A number of Web sites provide information that is updated more frequently. One popular site is bloomberg.com. The Bloomberg company was founded in 1981 by Michael Bloomberg (more recently mayor of New York City). Its Web site reports prices for many types of U.S. and foreign stocks and bonds. It also reports prices of shares in leading mutual funds.

Panel (a) of Figure 17-2 presents a page from the Bloomberg site, one that covers the 30 stocks in the Dow Jones index. During the trading day, this page is updated about every 20 minutes. It reports the price of each stock, the change in the price since the start of the day, and the number of shares traded. Clicking on a company symbol leads to more detailed information on the company, including past movements in its stock price, the price–earnings ratio, and dividend payments. Panel (b) shows this information for Boeing.

Each day the prices of some stocks rise and others fall. The overall behavior of stock prices is measured by **stock market indexes**, which average the prices for a group of stocks.

The Dow Jones is the oldest and most famous stock index. However, because the Dow covers only 30 stocks, it may not capture the movements of the whole market. The Standard & Poor's (S&P) 500 index is better for this purpose because it covers the 500 largest U.S. companies. The Wilshire 5000 index is even broader. The NASDAQ index covers all the companies that are traded in that market and is influenced strongly by the prices of tech stocks.

Web sites such as bloomberg.com provide data on a variety of stock market indexes. In Figure 17-2(a), information on the Dow appears above the prices of individual stocks. The Bloomberg site also provides indexes for sectors of the economy, such as transportation and utilities, and indexes for foreign stocks.

17-3 Capital Structure: What Securities Should Firms Issue?

So far we've discussed the mechanics of securities trading. Now we turn to the behavior of market participants—their decisions about which securities to sell and buy. We start with firms' decisions about issuing new securities.

The basic reason that firms issue securities is to raise funds for investment. A firm can raise funds by issuing either stocks or bonds. How does it choose between the two?

The mix of stocks and bonds that a firm issues is called its **capital structure**. Economists have long debated which capital structure is best. Let's discuss some of the key ideas in this debate.

FIGURE 17-2

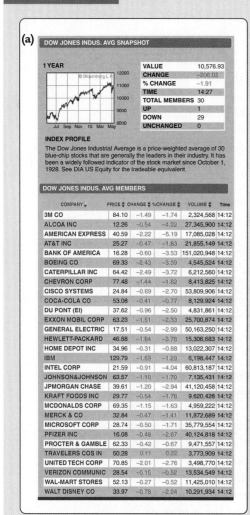

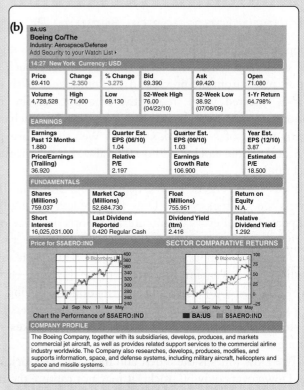

Stock Prices on Bloomberg.com (a) A page downloaded from bloomberg.com on 5/14/10 reports data on the 30 stocks in the Dow Jones index. For each stock, the page shows the current share price (in dollars), the change in the price since the start of the day (both the change in dollars and the percentage change), the number of shares traded (labeled "volume"), and the time at which these numbers were last updated. The top of the page provides information on the overall Dow index. (b) Clicking on "BOEING CO" leads to a page that gives detailed information on Boeing, including past movements in the stock price, the price–earnings ratio, and dividends.

Is Capital Structure Irrelevant?

The starting point for analyzing capital structure is the **Modigliani–Miller theorem (M and M theorem)**. This idea was proposed in 1958 by Franco Modigliani and Merton Miller, who both won the Nobel Prize in economics. Their view of capital structure is simple: capital structure doesn't matter. Stocks and bonds are equally good ways for firms to raise funds.

In making their argument, Modigliani and Miller assume that firms operate for the benefit of their stockholders. Stockholders give something up when a firm issues securities. If the firm issues new stock, current stockholders lose part of their ownership of the firm and receive smaller shares of the firm's future earnings. If the firm issues bonds, stockholders retain full ownership, but part of their earnings goes to interest payments. When firms issue securities, Modigliani and Miller argue, they should choose the type that minimizes the costs to current stockholders.

To determine these costs, Modigliani and Miller use the classical theory of asset prices. As we learned in Chapter 16, the classical theory says that the price of any security, whether a stock or a bond, equals the present value of expected income from the security.

The classical theory leads quickly to the conclusion that capital structure doesn't matter. Suppose a firm sells a share of new stock for $100. The present value of expected earnings that the buyer receives—and current stockholders give up—is $100. If the firm sells a bond for $100, the future payments again have a present value of $100. Either way, it costs $100 in present value to raise $100. Stocks and bonds are equally good deals for their issuers.

Why Capital Structure Does Matter

The M and M theorem implies that firms shouldn't care which securities they issue. However, few people take this idea literally. The theorem ignores several practical differences between stocks and bonds. Some of these factors encourage firms to issue stocks, and some favor bonds. As a result, most firms issue a mixture of the two.

Taxes Corporations pay taxes on their profits at rates up to 35 percent. In computing profits, corporations can deduct interest payments on bonds. Therefore, the more bonds a firm issues, the lower its taxes. In contrast, issuing stock does not affect corporate taxes.

These tax rules change the relative costs of securities. Ignoring taxes, the M and M theorem says it is equally costly to issue stocks and bonds. But the costs of issuing bonds are partly offset by their tax benefits, making them a cheaper way to raise funds.

Bankruptcy While issuing bonds has tax benefits, it also has a disadvantage: the risk of bankruptcy. When a firm sells bonds, it promises certain payments to bondholders. If the firm's earnings are low, it may not be able to make the payments. If it does not make the payments, it defaults, leading to bankruptcy. The more bonds a firm issues, the greater this risk.

Bankruptcy is costly. It triggers a legal process that requires expensive lawyers and accountants. Sometimes a bankrupt firm is forced to shut down, eliminating opportunities for future profits. Sometimes the firm continues to operate and eventually emerges from bankruptcy, but only after its business has been disrupted.

Firms can reduce bankruptcy risk by issuing stocks rather than bonds. If a firm's earnings are low, then stockholders receive low returns. The stockholders are disappointed, but the firm has not defaulted. Stocks don't require payments that the firm might have trouble making.

Adverse Selection As we discussed earlier, savers fear that firms will try to sell securities for more than their true value. This adverse selection problem affects capital structure because it is more severe for stocks than for bonds.

To see why, remember that adverse selection is caused by asymmetric information: buyers of securities know less than sellers. This asymmetry may be small when firms issue bonds. Buyers know exactly how much a bond pays as long as the issuer doesn't default, and they may know that default is unlikely. In contrast, stock purchasers are always uncertain about how much they will earn, and this uncertainty makes them worry about adverse selection.

The consequence is that some firms can issue bonds more easily than stock. To sell stock to nervous savers, these firms would have to accept low prices—less than the stock is really worth. In addition to the tax advantages, then, adverse selection is another reason to issue bonds.

Debt Maturity

So far, we've focused on the choice between stocks and bonds. When firms issue bonds, they must also choose the bonds' maturity. Firms can issue long-term bonds, which typically have maturities of 5 or 10 years, or commercial paper, with maturities under a year.

Generally, firms choose bond maturities based on their ability to pay off the bonds. A long-term investment project, such as a new factory, takes years to produce revenue. Firms finance these projects with long-term bonds, which they can pay off after revenue starts coming in.

Firms issue commercial paper when they need to borrow for short periods. This need often arises from the time lag between production and sales. For example, a swimwear company might produce bathing suits in the winter and sell them in the spring. It can issue three-month commercial paper to cover its winter production costs until it receives revenue in the spring.

17-4 Asset Allocation: What Assets Should Savers Hold?

We now turn from the issuers of securities to the buyers. Savers and institutions must choose their asset allocation, that is, how they split their wealth among different types of assets. We discuss the main factors in these decisions, focusing on the choice between stocks and bonds. We also touch on bank deposits, another asset held by savers.

The Risk-Return Tradeoff

Our discussion of stocks and bonds builds on Chapter 16's discussion of the rates of return on these securities. We saw that stocks have a higher average return over time. From 1900 through 2009, the nominal rate of return averaged about 11 percent for U.S. stocks and 5 percent for Treasury bonds. We can find average *real* returns by subtracting the inflation rate, which averaged 3 percent over the period 1900–2009, from the nominal rates. The real rate of return averaged 8 percent for stocks and 2 percent for bonds.

We also learned that stock returns are more volatile than bond returns: a saver can earn a lot on stocks, but she can also lose a lot. In 17 of the 110 years from 1900 through 2009, for example, nominal stock returns were less than -10 percent. In 2 years, 1932 and 2008, returns were near -40 percent. In contrast, returns on Treasury bonds have never been less than -10 percent.

When a saver chooses between stocks and bonds, she chooses between average return and safety. The choice is not all-or-nothing, however. The saver can split her wealth between the two assets, seeking a high return on part of it and keeping the rest safe. A key decision is the fraction of wealth to put into stocks. Raising this fraction raises the average return on total assets, but it also increases risk.

Calculating the Tradeoff Suppose that bonds have a real return of 2 percent (the actual average since 1900). Assume that this return is constant, so bonds are safe assets. (In reality, bond returns vary somewhat, but we assume this variation is small enough to ignore.) Stocks, by contrast, have variable returns. Assume that half the time the real return is 22 percent, and half the time it is -6 percent. The average return on stocks is

$$\frac{1}{2}[22\% + (-6\%)] = 8\%.$$

This average exceeds the return on bonds, but stocks are risky.

You have some wealth, say $100, to split between stocks and bonds. We'll use the letter s to denote the fraction of wealth you put in stocks. The fraction in bonds is $1 - s$. If $s = 0.6$, for example, you put $60 in stocks and $40 in bonds. The overall return on your wealth is a weighted average of stock and bond returns with weights of s and $1 - s$. That is,

$$\text{Return on Wealth} = s(\text{Return on Stocks})$$
$$+ (1 - s)(\text{Return on Bonds}).$$

As long as you hold some stock (s is positive), the return on your wealth is variable. If stock returns are high (22 percent), the return on your wealth is

$$\text{Return} = s(22\%) + (1 - s)(2\%)$$
$$= s(22\%) + 2\% - s(2\%)$$
$$= 2\% + s(20\%).$$

If stock returns are low (-6 percent), the return on your wealth is

$$\text{Return} = s(-6\%) + (1 - s)(2\%)$$
$$= s(-6\%) + 2\% - s(2\%)$$
$$= 2\% - s(8\%).$$

Using the last two formulas, we can see how the choice of s, the fraction of wealth in stock, affects your average return and risk. Given that high and low stock returns occur with equal probability, the average return on your wealth is

$$\text{Average Return} = \frac{1}{2}[2\% + s(20\%)] + \frac{1}{2}[2\% - s(8\%)]$$

$$= 1\% + s(10\%) + 1\% - s(4\%)$$

$$= 2\% + s(6\%).$$

The last line shows that a rise in s raises your average return.

Risk can be measured in several ways, but we will use one simple measure: the difference between the overall return on your wealth when stock returns are high and the overall return when stock returns are low. This difference shows how much your wealth can vary:

$$\text{Difference Between High and Low Returns on Wealth}$$

$$= [2\% + s(20\%)] - [2\% - s(8\%)]$$

$$= s(28\%).$$

A rise in the fraction s raises this measure of risk.[1]

Figure 17-3 shows the tradeoff you face in this example. It shows the risk and average return that result from different levels of stock ownership s. If $s = 0$ (you buy no stock), your average return is only 2 percent, but you face no risk. Both risk and return rise as s rises, reaching their highest levels at $s = 1$ (you buy only stock).

Saving in a Bank Account Buying stocks and bonds isn't the only way to save. Many people deposit some or all their wealth in bank accounts. What role do bank accounts play in asset allocation?

For present purposes, the answer is that bank accounts are similar to bonds. Bank accounts produce lower average earnings than stocks, but they are safe. In the example we just discussed, you can think of your holdings of "bonds" as your total safe assets, including bonds and bank accounts. Your key decision is how to split your wealth between these safe assets and risky stock.

Choosing the Mix

How should you respond to the risk–return tradeoff? Should you put a large fraction of your wealth in stock, accepting risk to seek high returns? Or should you play it safe and put most of your wealth in bonds and bank accounts?

These questions do not have absolute answers. The right asset allocation depends partly on personal preferences about risk. Some people are highly *risk averse*: they worry a lot about worst-case scenarios and find it painful to lose

---

[1] Economists often use another measure of risk, the standard deviation of returns. You know what this means if you have studied statistics. In our example, the standard deviation of the return on wealth is $s(14\%)$. An increase in s raises this standard deviation, as well as raising the difference in returns that we use to measure risk.

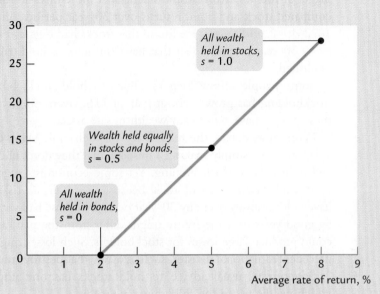

FIGURE 17-3

The Risk–Return Tradeoff In this example, bonds have a constant real return of 2 percent. The real return on stocks is 22 percent half the time and −6 percent half the time. Savers face a tradeoff between the average return on wealth and risk, which is measured here by the difference between the returns on wealth when stock returns are high and when they are low. An increase in s, the fraction of wealth in stocks, raises both the average return and risk.

money. These individuals should hold most of their wealth in safe assets and accept low returns to avoid risk. Individuals who can better tolerate risk should put most of their wealth in stocks.

Despite this role for personal preference, most economists think that a typical individual—someone with an average level of risk aversion—should hold more stocks than bonds. Financial planners who advise savers say the same thing. A common rule of thumb is that savers should hold two-thirds of their wealth in stocks and one-third in bonds. Some advisers say the share in stocks should be even higher than two-thirds.

Two basic factors underlie this advice. First, historically, average returns are not just higher for stocks than for bonds, but *much* higher. Over long periods, the differences in returns add up. If you put $100 in bonds and they produce their average real return of 2 percent, your wealth grows to $181 in 30 years. If you put $100 in stocks and they earn 8 percent, you end up with $1006.

Second, stocks are not really as risky as they first appear. We've seen that the returns on stock vary greatly from year to year. However, these fluctuations tend to average out over time, as good years offset bad years. People who hold stock for long periods, say 20 or 30 years, are likely to do well overall.

This point was popularized by a 1994 book, *Stocks for the Long Run,* by Jeremy Siegel of the Wharton Business School at the University of Pennsylvania. Siegel compared stock and bond returns over 30-year periods since 1871 (1871–1901, 1872–1902, and so on). He found that stocks had higher returns than bonds over every 30-year period, a fact that has continued to hold true since the book was published.

Some people follow Siegel's advice to hold stock, but many don't. While stockholding has grown, about half of U.S. savers still own no stock. Many of these people have significant wealth in safe assets.

Economists debate the reasons for this behavior. Many think that savers who avoid stock are simply making a mistake, that they don't understand the true risks and returns from stock holding. Yet some economists suggest that savers might have good reasons to avoid stocks because they really *are* risky. So far, stockholders haven't lost money over any 30-year period, because bad years have been followed by good years. But the future might differ from the past, and a run of bad luck could produce large losses for stockholders. Such losses might result from an unprecedented national disaster, such as a war that destroys much of the economy.[2]

Economists' usual advice to hold stocks has one important qualification, which we discuss in the following case study.

CASE STUDY

Age and Asset Allocation

Economists such as Jeremy Siegel argue that stocks are not very risky. However, the risks from stockholding grow with age, so older people should hold less stock than younger people.

Recall Siegel's point: stocks are safe because high and low returns average out over time. This argument applies to people who hold stocks for long periods. An older person has a shorter saving horizon: he is likely to start selling his assets soon to finance retirement. If this person holds stock, a few bad years can reduce his wealth significantly, and he won't have a chance to recoup these losses.

Another difference between young and old savers is that the young expect more future income from working. This prospect reduces the risk of holding stock. To see this point, suppose a 30-year-old puts all his savings in stock and the market crashes. Even if this person's wealth is wiped out, this event is not a disaster. The 30-year-old has several decades to earn money, rebuild his savings, and finance his retirement. In contrast, a current retiree who loses his wealth is in trouble, because he has no future earnings.

For these reasons, financial advisers tell savers to change their asset allocation as they age. You should start by holding mostly stock and then shift gradually toward bonds. One rule of thumb is that the percentage of your wealth in stocks should be at least 100 minus your age—at least 70 percent at age 30, 60 percent at age 40, and so on. ∎

---

[2] This idea is discussed by Robert Barro of Harvard University in "Rare Disasters and Asset Markets in the Twentieth Century," *Quarterly Journal of Economics* 121 (August 2006): 823-866.

17-5 Which Stocks?

So far, we have discussed the allocation of wealth among broad asset classes such as stocks and bonds. A saver must also choose specific assets within each class. We now consider this decision, focusing on the choice among stocks issued by different companies.

In Chapter 15 we saw that savers need to diversify the assets that they hold. Holding too much of one company's stock can be disastrous, as we saw in the case study "The Perils of Employee Stock Ownership." To reduce risk, savers should split the wealth they allocate to stock among a sizable number of stocks. One way to do this is to buy shares in a mutual fund.

By itself, the principle of diversification does not pin down which stocks to buy. A saver can achieve diversification with around 30 or 40 stocks; with that many, one company's misfortune can't hurt too much. Thousands of companies issue stock, so the possible combinations of 30 or 40 are vast. Someone—either the saver or a mutual fund manager—must choose which stocks to buy. Here we discuss some of economists' leading ideas about stock picking.

The Efficient Markets Hypothesis

Suppose you graduate from college and get a job at a mutual fund. Your boss asks you to recommend stocks for the fund to purchase. With little experience, you're not sure what to suggest. Fortunately, you remember a friendly finance professor. You decide to consult her, figuring that a finance professor must know how to pick stocks.

You may be surprised at the professor's advice. She is likely to tell you that it doesn't matter which stocks you pick. Rather than sweating over your decision, you can choose stocks randomly. Write the names of companies on pieces of paper, put them in a hat, close your eyes, and pull out your selections.

Is your professor joking? No, her advice is sincere, because she believes the **efficient markets hypothesis**. The efficient markets hypothesis says that no stock is a better buy than any other, a conclusion that justifies random choices. The efficient markets hypothesis is a central tenet of finance theory.

The efficient markets hypothesis follows from another finance principle, the classical theory of asset prices, which we learned about in Chapter 16. To see the connection, think about how you would choose stocks if you *didn't* draw names from a hat. You would look for good deals—stocks that are worth a lot relative to their prices. Recall from Chapter 16 that a stock's worth is the present value of expected dividends, so you should buy stocks with prices below this present value. In Wall Street lingo, you should buy stocks that are **undervalued assets**.

But the classical theory of asset prices says that a stock price always equals the present value of expected dividends and that expected dividends are the best possible forecasts (due to rational expectations). Thus, according to the classical theory, the price of a stock always equals the best estimate of the stock's value. This equality implies that there are no undervalued stocks.

Prices Follow Random Walks To understand the efficient markets hypothesis another way, let's think about movements in stock prices. When you pick stocks, you might try to forecast future price changes. If you can identify stocks with prices that are likely to rise, you can buy these stocks and earn capital gains when the price increases occur. If your forecasts are correct, your returns will exceed those on a random selection of stocks.

Once again, however, the efficient markets hypothesis says your strategy won't work. A stock price reflects expectations of a firm's dividends based on all available information. The price changes when expectations change in response to new information. For this information to change expectations and price, it must be a surprise—say, an announcement that the firm's recent earnings were higher than anticipated. If the information were known in advance, it would already be accounted for in expected dividends.

By definition, you can't predict surprises. Since only surprise information affects stock prices, changes in these prices are unpredictable. In statistical language, each price follows a **random walk**. You never know which prices are likely to rise, so once again stock picking is futile.

The Critique of Stock Picking The efficient markets hypothesis is controversial. It is popular among finance professors, but there are many doubters at securities firms. Analysts for mutual funds and brokers think they can do what the efficient markets hypothesis says is impossible: identify undervalued stocks.

The dividends a company can pay depend on its earnings. In looking for undervalued stocks, analysts produce forecasts of future earnings. These forecasts are based on many factors: companies' past performances, their current investment projects, competition in their industries, and so on. When forecasts for a company's earnings are high compared to its stock price, analysts recommend the stock. The securities firms they work for buy the stock and/or recommend it to clients.

Thousands of firms perform this analysis, and they put considerable resources into it. They pay high salaries to attract talented, hardworking analysts who gather lots of data and use sophisticated statistical techniques. They monitor companies continuously, so their forecasts always take into account the latest news.

Analysts argue that this effort pays off with good stock picks. But supporters of the efficient-markets hypothesis disagree, pointing out that the analysts' research and the resulting stock trades are actually forces that make the market efficient.

We can best see this point with an example. Assume that, initially, the price of Boeing stock equals the present value of expected dividends. The stock is neither under- nor overvalued. Then Boeing announces some good news: United Airlines has ordered 50 new planes. Analysts who follow Boeing read its news release and realize that the order will raise the company's earnings. Higher earnings will lead to higher dividends, so Boeing becomes undervalued at its current price. The analysts tell their firms to buy the stock.

This scenario plays out at many firms, creating a surge in demand for Boeing stock. High demand causes the stock price to rise and quickly reach a level that equals the new present value of dividends, which incorporates the news about the United order. At this point, Boeing is no longer undervalued. The analysts' efforts to identify an undervalued stock have caused the undervaluation to disappear.

Choosing Between Two Kinds of Mutual Funds

The efficient markets hypothesis is relevant to a decision facing many savers, the choice among stock mutual funds. There are two types of funds. An **actively managed fund** employs analysts who do the kind of research on companies that we have discussed. These funds buy and sell stocks frequently based on the analysts' recommendations.

In contrast, an **index fund** doesn't try to pick stocks. Instead, it buys *all* the stocks in a broad market index, such as the S&P 500. An index fund doesn't hire analysts to study companies—someone just looks up which stocks are in the index. The fund buys these stocks and then holds onto them, so it doesn't trade as often as an actively managed fund.

If you believe the efficient markets hypothesis, you should prefer index funds. The efficient markets hypothesis says that stocks picked by analysts will do no better, on average, than an index. And actively managed funds have the disadvantage of high fees. To pay analysts and traders, the funds usually charge shareholders 1 percent or more of their assets each year. Many index funds charge around a quarter of a percent. Once fees are deducted, returns are likely to be higher for index funds than for actively managed funds.

Many economists have examined returns on mutual funds. Generally, their data support the view that index funds produce higher returns, on average, than actively managed funds. This finding suggests that the efficient markets hypothesis has a large element of truth.

For example, about 1,300 actively managed stock funds operated over the decade 1995–2005. Averaging these funds together, the rate of return was 8.2 percent. Over the same period, the return on the S&P 500 was 10.0 percent. Of the actively managed mutual funds, 15 percent had a higher return than the S&P 500, and 85 percent had a lower return.

Notice that *some* funds beat the S&P index. What accounts for this success? There are two possible answers. One is that the managers of successful funds—the top 15 percent—are unusually talented. They can identify undervalued stocks even though the average manager can't. Given this interpretation, it might make sense to buy shares in actively managed funds if you can figure out which funds have the best managers.

Believers in the efficient markets hypothesis have a different view: successful fund managers are lucky. Different funds buy different sets of stocks. There is no good reason to prefer one portfolio to another. Nonetheless, over any period, news about companies will cause some stocks to perform better than others. Mutual funds that happen to own these stocks will have above-average returns.

According to this view, it's impossible to predict which mutual funds will beat a market index. You can see which funds have done so in the past. But since these funds were just lucky, there is no reason to think their success will continue. You should reject all managed funds and put your wealth in a low-cost index fund.

Once again, research supports the predictions of the efficient markets hypothesis. A number of studies have examined mutual funds with above-average returns over periods of one to five years. The studies ask whether these funds beat an index in subsequent years—and generally find that they don't.

Can *Anyone* Beat the Market?

Some economists interpret the efficient markets hypothesis as an absolute law: anyone who tries to beat a stock market index is wasting his time. Yet other economists have a less extreme view. They think that beating the market is difficult but not impossible, because exceptions to market efficiency exist. In any case, people keep trying to beat the market—to succeed where the average mutual fund fails. Many would-be market beaters fall into one of three categories, which we now discuss.

Fast Traders One strategy for beating the market relies on speed. To understand this approach, recall the logic behind the efficient markets hypothesis. If there is good news about a company, demand rises for the company's stock. Higher demand pushes the stock price to a level that reflects current expectations about earnings and dividends.

The efficient markets hypothesis assumes that stock prices respond instantly to news, but in reality, price adjustment takes a little time. For example, suppose there is good news about a NASDAQ stock. This news prompts buy orders to dealers who trade the stock. These dealers see decreases in their inventories, realize that demand has risen, and raise their ask prices for the stock.

This process may not take long. Dealers can respond to demand shifts within minutes or even seconds. But there is a brief period before a stock price adjusts to news when the stock is undervalued. Traders can profit from this undervaluation if they get their orders in quickly.

Many investment banks have departments that specialize in fast trading. Much of the work is done by powerful computers rather than by humans. The computers are programmed to react to news that will affect security prices, such as announcements of economic statistics. When triggered by such news, some computers can buy or sell securities within 3 milliseconds (0.003 second).

Behaviorists Fast trading exploits brief deviations from market efficiency. Another strategy is based on the view that inefficiencies persist, making some stocks undervalued for long periods. People who identify these stocks can beat the market even if they aren't especially fast. This view is held by believers in **behavioral finance**.

Recall that stock prices depend on expectations about companies' future earnings and dividends. The efficient markets hypothesis assumes rational expectations: people who forecast earnings, such as stock analysts, do as well as they can given their information. Behaviorists dispute this assumption. They argue that forecasters regularly make certain kinds of mistakes that lead to over- or undervaluation of stocks.

One mistake stressed by behaviorists is that forecasts made by stock analysts are overly "anchored": analysts form opinions about companies and then are reluctant to change them. If analysts have predicted that a company will do badly, they resist evidence to the contrary. If the company reports good news, analysts grudgingly raise their earnings forecasts, but not by as much as they should. With earnings forecasts too low, the company's stock is undervalued.

Some hedge funds use behavioral theories to try to identify undervalued stocks and beat the market. These funds are fairly new, so we can't yet judge their success. Some behavioral funds have performed well in recent years, but we need more data to tell whether this record reflects good strategies or good luck.

Geniuses? Many stock pickers are neither fast traders nor behaviorists. They just study companies, forecast earnings, and decide which stocks are undervalued. We have seen that most people who follow this approach can't beat the market. But maybe a few can.

In recent history, a handful of stock pickers have gained notoriety for beating the market repeatedly. One is Peter Lynch, who ran Fidelity's Magellan Fund from 1978 to 1990. Magellan's average return during this period was 29 percent. Also famous is William Miller of Legg Mason, whose fund beat the S&P 500 for 15 straight years, from 1991 through 2005.

Hard-core believers in the efficient markets hypothesis say that Lynch and Miller were lucky. If so, they were *very, very* lucky for a long time. The efficient markets hypothesis implies that a mutual fund has no better than a 1/2 probability of beating an index each year. The probability of winning 15 years in a row is at most $(1/2)^{15} = 0.00003$. Many observers doubt that anyone beats these odds through luck alone. They conclude that people such as Lynch and Miller really can pick stocks.

How do they do it? Efficient markets supporters stress that everyone has the same information about companies. Lynch and Miller read the same annual reports as other mutual fund managers and receive the same news releases. But perhaps some people have unusual skill in *interpreting* information. If a company creates a new product, for example, everyone hears about it. But a few geniuses have special insights about the product's likely success. They can forecast earnings better than the rest of the market.

When people name the best stock pickers, Peter Lynch and William Miller are often on the list. But one man is always at the top: Warren Buffett.

CASE STUDY

The Oracle of Omaha

Warren Buffett was born in Omaha, Nebraska in 1930, the son of a stockbroker. He earned a master's degree in economics and then worked in New York for Benjamin Graham, a famous stock picker of the 1940s and 1950s. In 1957, Buffett returned to Omaha and started a fund, Buffett Partnership Ltd. Its initial wealth was $105,000 from family and friends plus $100 of Buffett's own money. Buffett bought stocks through this company and a successor, Berkshire Hathaway.

The rest is history. From 1964 through 2009, the return on Berkshire Hathaway stock averaged 20.3 percent, compared to 9.3 percent for the S&P 500. If you had put $10,000 in an S&P index fund in 1964, you would have had about

$540,000 in 2009. If you had put $10,000 in Berkshire Hathaway in the same year, you would have had $43 million in 2009.

As of 2009, Buffett owned about 30 percent of Berkshire Hathaway's stock. His total wealth was $40 billion, making him the world's second-richest person (Bill Gates had $50 billion). Despite his success, Buffett still lives in a house that he bought for $32,000 in 1957, and, at age 79, he still runs Berkshire Hathaway full time.

How does Buffett pick stocks? He says he buys "great companies" with high earnings potential. In looking for such companies, Buffett "sticks with businesses we think we understand. That means they must be relatively simple and stable in character." This principle leads Buffett to avoid tech companies, such as Microsoft, whose businesses change rapidly.

Buffett assigns great weight to the quality of companies' managers. He looks for people who are smart and dedicated to making money for shareholders. He is leery of "empire builders"—managers who maximize their companies' size rather than profits. Buffett likes to meet managers personally to judge their abilities.

Over the years, Berkshire Hathaway has purchased large stakes in many companies, including the *Washington Post* (in 1973), GEICO (1976), Coca-Cola (1988), and Gillette (1989). Most of these acquisitions have proved profitable. For example, Coca-Cola's stock price in 1988 was $11. The company's recent earnings had been mediocre, and analysts predicted that its business would stagnate. Buffett realized that Coke had untapped potential for expanding overseas, using its world-famous brand name. After he bought the company's stock, Coke did expand overseas, and other analysts raised their earnings forecasts. By 1993, Coca-Cola's stock price was $75.

Buffett's reputation for brilliance grew during the recent financial crisis. Berkshire Hathaway's stock fell 10 percent in 2008, but that was much better than the 37 percent fall in the S&P 500. In September 2008, at the height of the crisis, Berkshire Hathaway bought $5 billion in Goldman Sachs stock. As the crisis diminished over 2009, Goldman's stock rose and Buffett earned large profits.

In November 2009, Berkshire Hathaway made the largest acquisition in its history: it purchased Burlington Northern railroad for $34 billion. This deal reflected Buffett's preference for traditional, stable industries. Buffett also knew Burlington Northern well, because Berkshire had owned 23 percent of the company since 2006.

In explaining the 2009 purchase, Buffett said he expected the demand for freight-train service to rise as the economy grew and high oil prices made trucking more expensive. It's too early to judge the success of the Burlington deal, but Buffett's record suggests that, once again, he was quicker than others to recognize a company's potential. ■

17-6 Derivatives

So far, this chapter has emphasized two kinds of securities, stocks and bonds. We now turn to another, more recently developed asset called a **derivative**. The payoffs from this security are tied to the prices of other assets; that is, the value of the security is "derived" from the other assets. Common types of derivatives include futures, options, and credit default swaps.

We first define these types of derivatives and describe how they are traded; then we discuss their uses. As you will see, some savers and financial institutions use derivatives to reduce risk, while others use them to make risky bets on asset prices.

Futures

A **futures contract** is an agreement to trade an asset for a certain price at a future point in time, the *delivery date*. One party agrees to sell the asset and another agrees to buy. The oldest futures contracts are those for agricultural products, such as grain and cotton. Farmers have traded these contracts for centuries. Futures also exist for nonagricultural commodities, such as oil and natural gas, and for securities, such as bonds and stocks.

Trading futures can produce either gains or losses. Generally, one side of a contract earns money at the expense of the other. Who wins depends on the price in the futures contract and the current price of the asset on the delivery date.

Let's consider an example. On January 1, 2020, Jack sells a futures contract for a Treasury bond to Jill. Jack promises to deliver the bond on July 1, and Jill promises to pay $100 on that date. When July 1 arrives, it turns out that Treasury bonds are trading for $110. Jill is in luck. She pays Jack the $100 they agreed on six months earlier, receives a bond, and can resell it for the current price of $110. These transactions yield Jill a profit of $10. Jack, on the other hand, receives only $100 for a bond worth $110. He loses $10.

Now let's change the story. Jack and Jill make the same deal on January 1, but the price of Treasury bonds on July 1 is $90. In this case, Jack wins: he receives $100 for a bond worth $90, gaining $10. Jill pays $100 for a $90 bond, losing $10.

Futures are traded on exchanges such as the Chicago Board of Trade and the Chicago Mercantile Exchange. People who want to trade hire brokers who work at the exchanges. A broker whose client wants to sell a certain contract looks for a broker whose client wants to buy. When the brokers meet, they arrange a trade.

When a trade occurs, both buyer and seller must post deposits with the futures exchange. These deposits are called *margins*. The purpose is to ensure that both parties fulfill their contract on the delivery day. A typical margin is 10 percent of the futures price. On January 1, when Jack and Jill trade a $100 bond future, each must deposit $10 with the exchange.

Options

A futures contract requires a transaction at the delivery date. An **option**, as the name suggests, may or may not produce a later transaction. If Jack sells Jill an option, she gains the right to trade a security with him—but not an obligation. Jill pays Jack a fee to receive the option.

A **call option** allows its owner to *buy* a security at a certain price, called the *strike price*. The option holder can make this purchase at any point before the option's expiration date, which is set in the contract. If he buys the security, he is said to *exercise* the option. A **put option** allows its owner to *sell* a security. Like a call option, it specifies a strike price and an expiration date.

Call and put options for stocks and bonds are traded on exchanges such as the Chicago Board of Options Exchange. As on futures exchanges, brokers for buyers and sellers meet to make deals. An option buyer immediately pays a fee to the seller. The seller makes a margin deposit to guarantee his performance if the buyer exercises the option.

Options also come from another source. Many companies create call options on their own stock and give them to executives as part of their pay. Options are valuable if stock prices rise, as the following example illustrates.

It is January 1, 2020. The current price of Google stock is $400. You buy a call option on one share of Google, with a strike price of $450 and an expiration date of July 1. You pay $20 for this option.

As long as Google's price is below $450, you don't exercise the option. You don't choose to buy the stock for more than it's worth. If July 1 arrives and the price is still below $450, the option expires. The $20 you paid for the option is a loss.

On the other hand, suppose that Google's stock rises to $500 on April 1. At that point, you might exercise the option. You can buy the stock for $450 and resell it for $500. You come out $30 ahead after accounting for the $20 you paid initially.

It is tricky to choose when to exercise an option. In our example, you earn a profit by exercising on April 1. But you might do even better by waiting. If the stock reaches $600 on May 1, you will earn more by exercising then. On the other hand, the stock might fall after April 1. If that happens, you will wish you had cashed in when the stock was high.

Credit Default Swaps

A **credit default swap (CDS)** is a derivative tied to debt securities, such as bonds and mortgage-backed securities, that promise certain future payments. A CDS buyer pays premiums, and payments on the CDS are triggered by defaults on the original securities. For example, Jack might sell Jill a CDS on bonds issued by the Acme Corporation. In this deal, Jill agrees to pay a series of premiums over some time period—say, the next five years. In return, Jack promises to make payments to Jill if Acme defaults on its bonds.

We can sometimes interpret a CDS as an insurance policy. Jill may buy a CDS on Acme bonds because she owns some of the bonds and therefore stands to lose if Acme defaults. With the CDS, she has "swapped" her default risk to Jack. Jack will compensate Jill for losses, just as her auto insurance company will compensate her for an accident.

A CDS differs from a conventional insurance policy in an important way. Jill can buy insurance on her car, but she *cannot* buy insurance on her neighbor Joan's car. Allstate won't agree to pay Jill for Joan's accidents, because they don't cost

Jill anything. In contrast, Jill *can* buy credit default swaps on Acme bonds even if she doesn't own the bonds. She will receive money if Acme defaults even though the default does not affect her directly.

The first CDSs were issued in 1997 by Chase Manhattan Bank (now part of JP Morgan Chase). They were tied to municipal bonds, but soon others were created for corporate bonds and mortgage-backed securities. The CDS market grew explosively from 2000 to 2007: the total payments promised in case of default grew from less than $1 trillion to $62 trillion.

In contrast to futures and options, credit default swaps are *not* traded on exchanges. Each CDS is negotiated privately between a buyer and a seller, with no margin deposit by either. CDSs are traded by many financial institutions, including commercial banks, investment banks, and insurance companies. A case study later in this chapter examines the role of CDSs in the 2007–2009 financial meltdown.

Hedging With Derivatives

Why do people trade derivatives? One purpose is to reduce risk through **hedging**. To hedge is to purchase an asset that is likely to produce a high return if another of one's assets produces a low or negative return. Hedging was the original purpose of credit default swaps: a security holder can reduce his default risk by purchasing a CDS on the security. Futures and options can also be used for hedging; let's look at some examples.

Hedging With Futures Hedging was the original purpose of agricultural futures. Imagine a farmer growing wheat and a miller who will buy the wheat when it is harvested in six months. Both parties face risk from fluctuations in the price of wheat. If the price is high in six months, the farmer will earn extra income, but the miller's costs will rise. The reverse happens if the price is low.

Wheat futures eliminate this risk. The farmer can sell a contract for wheat in six months, and the miller can buy this contract. The contract locks in a price for both parties.

Like commodities futures, financial futures can reduce risk. The owners of securities experience gains and losses when security prices change. To hedge, security holders make derivatives trades that produce profits if they suffer losses elsewhere.

For example, commercial banks hold large quantities of Treasury bonds. They stand to lose a lot if bond prices fall. A bank can reduce this risk by selling Treasury bond futures. If bond prices do fall, the bank earns profits from its sale of futures (like Jack in our earlier example). The profits on futures cancel the losses on bonds. If prices rise, the bank loses on futures but gains from its bond holdings. Either way, the bank's total profits are insulated from bond-price movements.

Hedging With Options Security holders can also reduce risk by trading options. One hedging strategy is a "protective put," which means a purchase of put options on securities you own. It protects against large losses on the securities.

For example, suppose you own shares in a mutual fund that holds the S&P 500. The current level of the S&P index is 1000. The index is likely to rise, but you worry about the possibility of a stock market crash. You might sleep better if you buy puts on the index—say, with a strike price of 900. In effect this option lets you sell stocks for 90 percent of their current value, even if prices fall lower. Your potential losses are limited.

You must pay for the put options, but you never use them if the S&P index stays above 900. Nonetheless, it may be prudent to purchase the puts: it is worth paying fees to reduce risk.

Speculating With Derivatives

Derivatives are also useful for **speculation**. This practice is the opposite of hedging, which reduces risk: speculators use financial markets to make risky bets on asset prices. Speculators earn a lot if they are right and lose a lot if they are wrong.

Suppose the current price of a Treasury bond is $100. Most people expect this price to stay constant, so the six-month futures price is also $100. You, however, are more insightful than most people. You realize that the Federal Reserve is likely to lower its interest rate target, pushing up bond prices. You can bet on this belief by purchasing the $100 Treasury bond futures. You will profit if Treasury bonds are selling for more than $100 in six months.

You can also use options to bet on Treasury bonds. If you think the price will rise, you might sell put options on the bonds—say, with a strike price of $100. As long as the actual price stays above $100, nobody exercises the options. The fees you receive for the options are pure profit.

The catch, of course, is that speculation requires you to predict asset prices better than other people, something the efficient markets hypothesis says is impossible. If it's really likely that the Fed will lower interest rates, everyone else knows this information, too, and the prices of futures and options have already adjusted to it, thus eliminating profit opportunities. According to the efficient markets hypothesis, speculation is pure gambling; you might as well play the slots.

Nonetheless, many financial institutions speculate with derivatives. Leading players include investment banks and hedge funds. The term "hedge fund" is a misnomer, because hedge funds don't hedge—they speculate.

Speculating with derivatives produced large gains and losses during the financial turmoil of 2007–2009. Credit default swaps played a large role in the story, as we see in the next case study.

CASE STUDY

Credit Default Swaps and the AIG Fiasco

Many credit default swaps issued in the 2000s were tied to subprime mortgage–backed securities, which we discussed in the earlier case study on investment banks. These CDSs differed somewhat from the type we've discussed before. A

UNCORRECTED PAGES

traditional CDS yields a payoff if the issuer of some security defaults on payments that it owes. In contrast, the sellers of CDSs on mortgage-backed securities promised to pay CDS buyers if the market prices of the underlying securities fell, even if the securities' issuers had not yet defaulted. This feature proved important over 2006–2008, when the prices of mortgage-backed securities fell and these outcomes triggered payments on CDSs.

Some firms had used credit default swaps to hedge the risk on mortgage-backed securities. In 2006, for example, analysts at Goldman Sachs started worrying that housing prices might fall. Goldman saw that it could lose money on the mortgage-backed securities it owned, so it started buying credit default swaps to hedge against this possible loss. It did so sooner than other investment banks, and this strategy helped limit its losses during the financial crisis.

Other firms used credit default swaps to speculate. Like Goldman Sachs, some hedge funds foresaw trouble in the housing market. They bet against mortgage-backed securities by purchasing credit default swaps on securities they didn't own. These bets paid off handsomely: researchers estimate that one hedge fund, run by John Paulson, earned $15 billion on CDSs.

If hedgers and speculators were buying credit default swaps, who was selling them? The answer in many cases was the American International Group, a conglomerate that primarily owns insurance companies. AIG's swaps promised payments of hundreds of billions of dollars if prices of mortgage-backed securities fell far enough.

AIG management thought the company was getting a good deal. It received a steady flow of fees from the sale of CDSs, and managers didn't expect to pay out much in return. They didn't anticipate the fall in housing prices and its effects on mortgage-backed securities. In 2006, an AIG report to government regulators said the likelihood of losses on CDSs was "remote, even in severe recessionary market scenarios."

This view was refuted spectacularly over the next two years. As the mortgage crisis unfolded, AIG had to make larger and larger payments to holders of its CDSs. In September 2008, when Lehman Brothers went bankrupt, it seemed likely that AIG would suffer the same fate.

At that point, the Federal Reserve stepped in. The Fed feared that a collapse of AIG would magnify the financial crisis, so it kept the company afloat with more than $100 billion in loans. The Treasury department also aided AIG by purchasing its stock. AIG survived, but the Fed and Treasury were widely criticized for their use of taxpayers' money. We return to this episode in Chapter 18. ■

17-7 Conclusion

This chapter has provided a survey of securities markets. We've examined the major types of markets, the people and firms that participate in them, and the tradeoffs they face in deciding which securities to buy and sell.

UNCORRECTED PAGES

Some lessons from this chapter will likely be relevant to your financial life. If you accumulate wealth, economists believe you should hold a large share in stocks—but shift toward safer assets as you age. In choosing which stocks to buy, you should be wary of brokers or mutual fund managers who claim they can outperform the market. The evidence suggests that beating the market is very difficult.

As you can probably tell, the behavior of securities markets is a vast topic. We have highlighted key issues, but you can learn much more by taking finance courses, either in an economics department or in a business school. Courses in corporate finance, for example, examine firms' capital structure in detail. Courses in asset pricing explore the factors determining the prices of stocks, bonds, and derivatives.

Summary

1. Securities firms are companies whose primary purpose is to hold securities, trade them, or help others trade them. These firms include mutual funds, hedge funds, brokers, dealers, and investment banks.

2. Corporations and governments issue securities in primary markets. Corporations sell their stocks and bonds through investment banks. By underwriting corporations' securities, investment banks reduce the problem of adverse selection. The U.S. government sells bonds through auctions.

3. After securities are issued, they are traded in secondary markets, including exchanges, dealer markets, and electronic communications networks.

4. Firms can finance investment by issuing stocks or bonds. The mix of the two that a firm chooses is called its capital structure.

5. Savers must choose how to split their wealth among different classes of assets, such as stocks and bonds. Stocks have higher average returns than bonds, but they are also riskier.

6. According to the efficient markets hypothesis, every stock's price equals the best estimate of its value, so no stock is a better buy than any other. It is futile to look for stocks that will produce higher-than-average returns.

7. Derivative securities are securities with payoffs tied to the prices of other assets. Futures contracts, options, and credit default swaps are examples of derivative securities.

8. Some people and institutions use derivatives to hedge against possible losses: they purchase derivatives that will produce high returns if other assets they own produce low or negative returns. Other people and institutions use derivatives to speculate: they make bets on asset prices that sometimes produce large profits and sometimes large losses.

KEY CONCEPTS

Asset allocation	Exchange	Random walk
Securities firm	Specialist	Actively managed fund
Hedge fund	Over-the-counter (OTC) market	Index fund
Leverage	Dealer market	Behavioral finance
Broker	Bid–ask spread	Derivatives
Dealer	Electronic communications network (ECN)	Futures contract
Investment bank		Option
Underwriter	Stock market index	Call option
Primary markets	Capital structure	Put option
Secondary markets	Modigliani–Miller theorem	Credit default swap (CDS)
Public company	Efficient markets hypothesis	Hedging
Initial public offering (IPO)	Undervalued asset	Speculation

QUESTIONS FOR REVIEW

1. What is a mutual fund? Is buying 200 shares of a mutual fund more or less risky than buying 200 shares of Walt Disney Company?

2. How do investment banks lessen the problem of adverse selection in securities markets?

3. What is the difference between primary and secondary markets for securities?

4. What factors influence a firm's decisions about its capital structure?

5. What are the benefits and costs to a person of holding a large fraction of her wealth in stock?

6. According to the efficient markets hypothesis, how should a saver choose among the stocks of different companies?

7. James, age 59, is close to retirement and wants to allocate 80 percent of his assets to stocks so that he can maximize his returns. Is this a good decision? Explain your answer.

8. Can a firm's stock be undervalued for a long period of time? Why or why not?

9. What is a futures contract? Describe a circumstance under which a person or firm would buy a futures contract.

PROBLEMS AND APPLICATIONS

1. When investment banks underwrite IPOs, they typically sell stock for 5 to 10 percent more than they paid for it. When they underwrite new stock for companies that are already public, the typical markup is 3 percent. What explains this difference?

2. As in Section 17-4, assume that bonds pay a real return of 2 percent. Stocks pay 22 percent half the time and −6 percent half the time. Suppose you initially have wealth of $100, and let X be your wealth after 1 year. What fraction of your wealth should you hold in stock under each of the following assumptions?

   a. You want to maximize the average value of X.

   b. You want to maximize the value of X when the return on stocks is −6 percent.

   c. You want to be certain that X is at least $100 (that is, you don't lose any of your initial wealth). Subject to that constraint, you maximize the average value of X.

3. Suppose two people are the same age and have the same level of wealth. One has a high-paying job and the other has a low-paying job. Who should hold a higher fraction of his or her wealth in stock? Explain.

4. Chapter 16 presented the classical theory of asset prices. In this chapter, we discussed two ideas that follow from the classical theory: the Modigliani–Miller theorem and the efficient markets hypothesis. How well do these two ideas fit real-world financial markets? Where does each fit on a spectrum from literally true to completely unrealistic?

5. Suppose everyone in the world becomes convinced that the efficient markets hypothesis is true. Will it stay true? Explain.

6. Research around 1980 showed that stocks of small firms had higher average returns than stocks of large firms. This finding gained much attention because it seemed to contradict the efficient markets hypothesis. It suggested a simple way to beat the market: purchase only small-firm stocks.

   a. Can you explain this deviation from market efficiency? (*Hint:* Think about the behavior in financial markets that leads to efficiency and why this behavior might not occur.)

   b. Would you guess that small-firm stocks have done better than large-firm stocks since 1980? Why or why not?

7. Recall that U.S. mutual fund companies offer about 8,000 separate funds. Suppose each fund has a 50 percent chance of beating the S&P 500 each year.

   a. Over a 5-year period, how many funds will beat the market in every year? What about a 15-year period?

   b. Based on the performance of William Miller's mutual fund from 1981 through 2005, would you say Miller is a genius? Explain.

8. In 1989, the economist Paul Samuelson rated Warren Buffett the greatest stock picker in the country. Yet Samuelson warned against buying Berkshire Hathaway stock. He wrote that "knowledge of Buffett's skills may be already fully discounted in the marketplace. Now that B-H has gone up more than a hundredfold, it is at a premium."

   a. Explain Samuelson's reasoning in your own words.

   b. People who followed Samuelson's advice have regretted it, because the returns on B-H stock since 1989 have been similar to earlier returns. What does this tell us about Buffett and/or the efficient markets hypothesis?

9. On its Web site, one mutual fund company describes its "disciplined and sophisticated investment strategies." (The term "investment" is used to mean the choice of securities.) Let's change the company's name to "Smith." With this alteration, the site says:

   > At the center of Smith's investment process is the Smith Investment Committee. It consists of a select group of senior investment professionals who are supported by an extensive staff. This staff provides multilevel analyses of the economic and investment environments, including actual and projected corporate earnings, interest rates, and the effect of economic forecasts on market sectors, individual securities, and client portfolios.

   Does this statement convince you to buy Smith mutual funds? Why or why not?

10. Suppose you hold most of your wealth in stock. What kinds of options should you buy or sell in each of the following circumstances?

    a. You think the stock market will probably do well, but you worry about a crash.

    b. You want to get a steady return on your assets. You don't care whether you get rich from a big rise in the market.

    c. You think there will soon be big news about firms' earnings, but you don't know whether the news will be good or bad.

11. Suppose you buy call options on Microsoft stock. Each option costs $2 and has a strike price of $40 and an expiration date of July 1. Discuss whether you would exercise the options in each of the following situations and why:

    a. It is March 1 and Microsoft's stock price is $30.

    b. It is March 1 and the stock price is $40.10.

    c. It is March 1 and the stock price is $50.

    d. It is June 30 and the stock price is $50.

    e. It is June 30 and the stock price is $40.10.

12. Suppose company A has a stable stock price. The price is not likely to change much in the next year. Company B has an uncertain stock price: it could either rise or fall by a lot. Would you pay more for a call option on A's stock or B's stock? Explain.

13. Use bloomberg.com to answer the following questions:

a. Which has done better over the last year, the U.S. stock market or the Brazilian stock market?

b. Which have done better over the last year, the stocks in the Dow Jones index or the NASDAQ index?

c. What was the rate of return on Boeing stock over the last year?

14. Go to buffettsecrets.com and study Warren Buffett's principles for choosing stocks. Do you think you could beat a stock index by following these principles? Explain.

CHAPTER 18

Banking

If you owe the bank $100, that's your problem. If you owe the bank $100 million, that's the bank's problem.

—J. Paul Getty

Chapter 15 described the central function of banks: reducing problems of asymmetric information. Adverse selection and moral hazard prevent some firms, especially those that are relatively unknown, from issuing securities in financial markets. These problems also prevent individuals from issuing securities. Firms and individuals that cannot raise funds by issuing securities turn to banks for loans.

In lending money, banks reduce adverse selection by screening borrowers and reduce moral hazard by establishing loan covenants and monitoring borrower behavior. Because of banks, small businesses can borrow money to expand, and people can borrow money to buy houses and cars.

This chapter takes a closer look at banking. We survey the many types of banks, from global giants such as Citigroup to banks that serve a single town. We also examine two changes in banking over the last quarter century that have had major consequences for the financial system and the macroeconomy: the growth of *subprime lenders*, a fringe of the banking industry whose customers have weak credit histories, and *securitization*, the creation of liquid securities backed by bank loans. These controversial practices both had roles in the financial crisis of 2007–2009.

We also examine banking from the point of view of bank managers. Like any business, a bank seeks to earn profits. It does so primarily by accepting deposits and lending them out at higher interest rates than it pays. We discuss banks' strategies for maximizing profits and look at the risks that banks face when they lend. We examine methods for containing risk and see what happens when risk management fails.

Finally, we discuss government regulation of banks. The main goal of regulation is to prevent bank failures. Toward that end, governments insure deposits and restrict risk taking by banks. Like the banks they supervise, regulators have experienced both successes and failures, and in the wake of the recent financial crisis there was pressure for the government to do more to regulate banks and other financial institutions.

18-1 The Banking Industry

We begin our study of banking by surveying the different types of banks, the distinct roles of large and small banks, and subprime lenders.

Types of Banks

Chapter 15 defined a *bank* as a financial institution that accepts deposits and makes loans. In the United States, this definition covers three types of institutions: commercial banks, savings institutions, and credit unions. A fourth category, finance companies, satisfies part of the definition: finance companies make loans but do not accept deposits. Figure 18-1 shows the total deposits and loans of these four types of institutions at the end of 2009.

Commercial Banks Commercial banks are the largest part of the banking industry. At the end of 2009, there were about 7,000 commercial banks in the United States. They had $8.3 trillion in deposits, including checking and savings deposits. They had $6.5 trillion in outstanding loans to a wide range of customers, including large corporations, small businesses, and individuals. Loans to individuals include home mortgages, car loans, student loans, and balances on credit cards.

Savings Institutions Savings institutions are also called *savings and loan associations (S&Ls)* or *savings banks.* At the end of 2009, savings institutions had about $900 billion in deposits and $800 billion in loans.

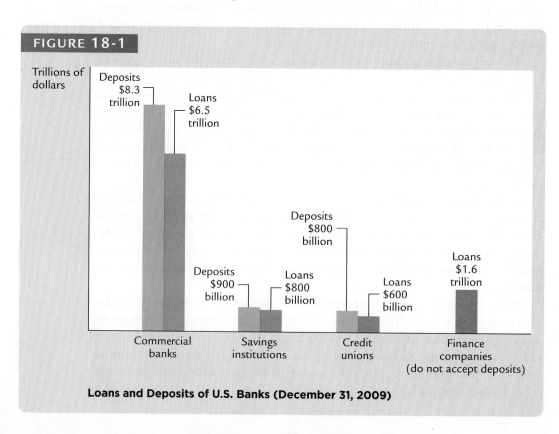

FIGURE 18-1

Loans and Deposits of U.S. Banks (December 31, 2009)

The original purpose of savings institutions was to serve households by accepting savings deposits and lending for home mortgages. Savings institutions were created in the nineteenth century, when commercial banks focused on business lending. Most savings institutions were established as *mutual banks*, meaning they were owned by their depositors and did not issue stock.

Over time, most savings institutions issued stock and ceased being mutual banks. They also expanded their businesses: today, savings institutions offer checking as well as savings accounts, and they make many types of loans. These changes have blurred the distinction between savings institutions and commercial banks, although the former still focus more on mortgages.

Credit Unions A **credit union** is a nonprofit bank. Like a mutual bank, it is owned by its depositors, who are called "members." Only members can borrow from the credit union. Membership is restricted to a group of people who have something in common. They might be employees of a company, members of a labor union, or veterans of a military service. Credit unions make several types of loans, including home mortgages, auto loans, and small personal loans. At the end of 2009, credit unions had $800 billion in deposits and $600 billion in loans.

Finance Companies Like banks, **finance companies** make loans; for example, they compete with banks in issuing mortgages and auto loans. At the end of 2009, finance companies had loans totaling $1.6 trillion. However, finance companies do *not* accept deposits. Instead, they raise funds by issuing bonds and borrowing from banks.

Many finance companies specialize in a certain kind of loan. For example, some lend to businesses for new equipment. Others are owned by manufacturing companies and lend to their customers. This group includes General Motors Acceptance Corporation (GMAC) and Ford Motor Credit Company, which make auto loans. Another market niche in which finance companies operate is subprime lending, which we discuss later in this chapter.

Large Versus Small Banks

In the United States, banks vary greatly in size. At one end of the scale are three giant commercial banks: Citibank, JP Morgan Chase, and Bank of America. Each of these banks has over a trillion dollars in total assets, which include outstanding loans and other assets, such as securities. The three banks have thousands of branches around the country and overseas. As of 2010, 15 U.S. banks had assets between $100 billion and $1 trillion, including Wells Fargo, PNC Bank, and Suntrust.

Many large banks are subsidiaries of *financial holding companies*—conglomerates that also provide the services of securities firms. For example, Citibank (a commercial bank) is part of Citigroup (a financial holding company). Citigroup has units that underwrite securities, sell mutual funds and insurance, and help people manage their wealth.

The smallest banks include **community banks**, commercial banks or savings institutions with less than $1 billion in assets. A community bank operates in a small geographic area by raising funds from local depositors and lending them to consumers and small businesses. An example is Harford Bank, based in Aberdeen, Maryland. In 2010, Harford had $250 million in assets and seven branches in Aberdeen and neighboring towns. Of the 7,000 commercial banks in the United States, more than 90 percent are community banks, but their total assets barely exceed $1 trillion. Most credit unions are also small, because they restrict membership to a narrow group of people. For example, The Johns Hopkins Federal Credit Union serves employees of the university and hospital that share its name. It has five branches and $300 million in assets.

Large and small banks coexist because each has advantages in some areas of banking. Only large banks have enough funds to lend to large corporations. In addition, large banks benefit from economies of scale: making a large number of loans reduces the cost per loan. If a bank issues credit cards, for example, it can manage the accounts of many cardholders with a single computer system.

Historically, small banks have existed because of legal restrictions on bank size. Before 1994, a bank could operate in only one state. And before World War II, some states had unit banking—a bank was restricted to a single branch (see the case study in Chapter 15).

Because these restrictions no longer exist, the number of small banks has declined as many merge with each other or are purchased by larger banks. The total number of commercial banks has fallen from a peak of 15,000 in 1984 to the current 7,000. Yet many small banks survive. Economists think the reason is that small banks are better than large banks at certain kinds of lending.

Community banks have a niche in small-business lending. Recall that lending requires information gathering. By focusing on a small area, community bankers come to know local businesses and the people who run them. As a result, they are better at screening borrowers than are banks from far away.

Credit unions reduce information problems by restricting loans to members. The fact that a borrower qualifies for membership provides information about his default risk. So does the history of his account at the credit union. This information helps loan officers screen out risky borrowers.

Subprime Lenders

Banks lend to millions of firms and individuals, yet not everyone can borrow from a bank. Loan officers deny credit to people whose default risk appears high, including people with low incomes or poor credit histories.

Government regulators encourage banks to be conservative in lending. They don't want banks to take risks that could lead to large losses. One reason is that the government insures bank deposits, so it stands to lose money if a bank fails.

People who can't borrow from banks often turn to **subprime lenders**, companies that specialize in high-risk loans. Subprime lenders include some finance companies, payday lenders, pawnshops, and illegal loan sharks. Each type of lender has methods for coping with default risk, which are summarized in Table 18-1.

Subprime Finance Companies The government regulates finance companies less heavily than banks. One reason is that finance companies do not accept

TABLE 18-1	
Subprime Lenders	
Type of Lender	**How Lender Copes with Default Risk**
Finance company	Credit scoring; high interest rates
Payday lender	Postdated checks; very high interest rates
Pawnshop	Very high collateral
Illegal loan shark	Very high interest rates; threats to defaulters

deposits, so the government doesn't owe insurance payments if a company fails. Light regulation allows finance companies to make loans that bank regulators might deem too risky. As a result, some finance companies specialize in subprime lending.

Finance companies make subprime mortgage loans, auto loans, and personal loans. Examples of subprime lenders are Household Finance Corporation (HFC), Countrywide Financial, and CitiFinancial. Many of these companies are subsidiaries of financial holding companies that also own commercial banks. CitiFinancial, for example, is part of Citigroup, and HFC is part of the HSBC Group.

Subprime lending, especially for mortgages, grew rapidly from the 1990s to 2007. This trend reflected the development of *credit scoring*, a process that reduces asymmetric information between borrowers and lenders. Credit bureaus such as Equifax, Experian, and TransUnion collect information on people's histories of borrowing and repaying and summarize them with credit scores. During the subprime boom, lenders grew increasingly confident that credit scores were accurate measures of default risk. By knowing a borrower's default risk, finance companies could offset expected losses from defaults by charging sufficiently high interest rates.

Subprime mortgage loans, for example, typically carried interest rates two to five percentage points above the best mortgage rates. Often, lenders added to their earnings by charging fees when a loan was made. When default rates on subprime mortgages started rising in 2007, new subprime mortgage lending dried up. Other kinds of subprime lending continue, however; one growth area is subprime credit cards.

Payday Lenders Payday lenders are companies that make small loans to people who need cash urgently. A typical loan is a few hundred dollars for a few weeks. Payday lenders include small companies with a single office and national chains such as Advance America and ACE Cash Express.

To borrow from a payday lender, a customer writes a check with some future date on it—often the next payday. The check covers the amount of the loan plus a fee. The lender gets repaid by cashing the check on the designated day unless the borrower repays the loan with cash or pays another fee to extend the loan.

Unlike banks, payday lenders gather little information about borrowers. They lend to anyone with a checking account and a pay stub to prove employment—or, in some cases, proof of unemployment benefits from the government. Instead of screening borrowers, payday lenders rely on the postdated checks to reduce defaults. A check is written for a day when funds are likely to be available. In addition, bounced-check fees at a borrower's bank encourage the borrower to make sure the check clears.

Payday lenders also compensate for default risk with *very* high interest rates. A common fee is 15 percent of the loan amount: for $200 in cash, you write a check for $230. For a four-week loan, this fee is equivalent to an annual interest rate of 515 percent! Surveys suggest that the average annual rate on payday loans is around 400 percent.

Most states have *usury laws* that set legal limits on interest rates, often around 40 percent per year. In the 1990s, however, payday lenders lobbied state legislatures to exempt them from usury laws, and they succeeded in many states. These legal changes led to rapid growth in the industry. As of 2010, payday lenders had more than 20,000 offices in the United States, most located in low-income areas. Studies estimate that 15 percent of U.S. households have borrowed from payday lenders.

Payday lenders are controversial. Critics allege that they practice *predatory lending*: they take unfair advantage of borrowers who are poor and uninformed about financial matters. According to this view, default rates are not high enough to justify three-digit interest rates on payday loans. And people who take out the loans often get into financial trouble.

Payday loans are dangerous because a borrower may still be short on cash when the loan is due. In this case, some people take out a larger loan to "roll over" both the initial loan and the fee. Sometimes a loan is rolled over again and again. With high interest rates, the borrower quickly runs up a large debt.

Criticism of payday lending led North Carolina and Georgia to ban the practice in the early 2000s. Under a 2006 law, the federal government ended payday lending to military personnel. Aside from the military, however, payday lending remains legal in 33 states.

Payday lenders defend their business. They say their loans help people facing emergencies to stave off disaster. For example, a payday loan can be used to pay rent when someone faces eviction. Some research supports the view that payday lending has benefits. After Georgia banned the practice, the state saw a 9 percent increase in personal bankruptcies, a 13 percent increase in bounced checks, and a 64 percent increase in complaints against debt collectors.[1]

Pawnshops Like a payday lender, a **pawnshop** is a source of small, short-term loans. It protects against default with very high collateral. A borrower deposits an item he owns and receives a loan for 30 to 50 percent of the resale value. The pawnshop has the right to sell the collateral if the loan is not repaid.

---

[1] See Donald P. Morgan and Michael R. Strain, "Payday Holiday: How Households Fare After Payday Credit Bans," *Federal Reserve of New York Staff Report* #309, November 2007. For a harsh critique of payday lending, visit the Web site of the Center for Responsible Lending. For a defense, see the Web site of the Community Financial Services Association, an organization of payday lenders.

There are roughly 13,000 pawnshops in the United States. A pawnshop's typical loan is $75 to $100 for 60 or 90 days. Common collateral includes jewelry, televisions, and—in some states—guns. About 80 percent of borrowers repay their loans and get back the collateral.

Pawnshops appeared in Europe in the fifteenth century and have existed in the United States since colonial times. The industry grew rapidly from the 1970s to the 1990s. Since then, business has leveled off because of competition with payday lenders.

Illegal Loan Sharks Another source of subprime loans is illegal **loan sharks**. These lenders charge interest rates that violate usury laws. Loan-sharking is a traditional business of organized crime.

Loan sharks' disregard for the law helps them cope with default risk. They can encourage repayment with threats of violence. They can seize defaulters' property without the trouble of getting a court judgment.

Yet loan-sharking is a declining industry. Many customers have switched to legal payday lenders or pawnshops. Today loan sharks operate mainly in immigrant communities. They sometimes require immigration papers as collateral for loans.

The last organized-crime figure convicted of loan-sharking was Nicodemo Scarfo Jr., of Philadelphia. In 2002, he was sentenced to 33 months in prison for charging an interest rate of 152 percent. Scarfo's defenders point out that he charged less than most payday lenders.

18-2 Securitization

Traditionally, when a bank makes loans, the loans become assets of the bank. The flow of interest on the loans is the bank's primary source of revenue. Over the last generation, however, this basic feature of banking has changed. Today, banks sell many of the loans they make rather than holding them as assets, and the loans are transformed into securities that are traded in financial markets. This **securitization** of loans has had benefits for banks and the economy, but it also played a role in the financial crisis of 2007–2009.

The Securitization Process

Figure 18-2 illustrates the securitization process. Banks and finance companies make loans to borrowers and then sell them to a large financial institution, the securitizer. This institution gathers a pool of loans with similar characteristics; for example, a pool might be $100 million worth of mortgage loans to people with certain credit scores. The securitizer issues securities that entitle an owner to a share of the payments on the loan pool. These securities are bought by financial institutions, including commercial and investment banks, pension funds, and mutual funds. The initial buyers often resell the securities in secondary markets.

UNCORRECTED PAGES

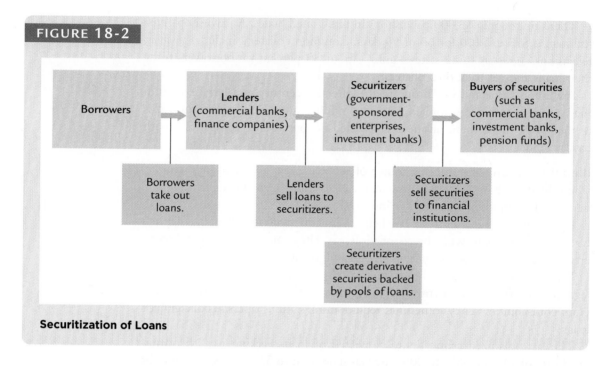

FIGURE 18-2

Securitization of Loans

Fannie and Freddie

Home mortgages are the type of loan most often securitized. The two largest issuers of **mortgage-backed securities** (MBSs) are the Federal National Mortgage Association, commonly known as Fannie Mae, and the Federal Home Loan Corporation, or Freddie Mac. The government created Fannie Mae in 1938 as part of President Franklin Roosevelt's New Deal; it created Freddie Mac in 1970. The purpose was to increase the supply of mortgage loans and thereby help more people achieve "the American Dream" of homeownership.

Fannie and Freddie are an unusual kind of institution called a *government-sponsored enterprise (GSE)*. They are private corporations with stocks that are traded on the New York Stock Exchange but are linked to the government: they were established by the government, the president appoints some of the directors, and they have a long-standing right to borrow money from the U.S. Treasury.

Fannie and Freddie raise funds by issuing bonds and then use the funds to purchase mortgages. Before the recent financial crisis, Fannie and Freddie were highly profitable institutions due in large part to their links to the government. In theory, Fannie or Freddie could go bankrupt, but people have long believed the government would save them if they got in trouble (as indeed happened in 2008). The belief that the government stood behind Fannie and Freddie meant their bonds were considered safe. As a result, the bonds paid low interest rates, and Fannie and Freddie could raise funds more cheaply than other financial institutions.

Initially, Fannie and Freddie held onto all the mortgages they bought with the funds they raised. In the 1970s, however, they started issuing mortgage-backed securities, which they sold to other financial institutions. This business grew rapidly, and today over half of U.S. mortgage debt is securitized by Fannie or Freddie.

From the 1970s to the early 2000s, Fannie and Freddie purchased only prime mortgages, those that appear to have low default risk based on borrowers' incomes and credit scores. In the early 2000s, they began to purchase subprime mortgages in an effort to increase the supply of mortgages to low-income people. However, the securities they sell to other institutions are still backed entirely by prime mortgages. Fannie and Freddie have held onto the subprime mortgages they purchased.

Like many financial institutions, Fannie and Freddie suffered losses in 2007 and 2008 as defaults on subprime mortgages rose. It appeared that one or both of the companies might go bankrupt, worsening the financial crisis. To prevent this outcome, the government put Fannie and Freddie under *conservatorship* in September 2008. This action meant that technically the companies remained private, but government regulators took control of their operations. We discuss this episode further in Chapter 19.

Conservatorship was meant to be a temporary arrangement, and as of the writing of this book, the future of the two companies is unclear. They might return to their pre-crisis status, or they might change from private companies into normal government agencies.

Why Securitization Occurs

Securitization occurs because banks want to sell loans and because securities backed by bank loans are attractive to many institutions. In this section we discuss the incentives for securitization, focusing on home mortgages because securitization is most common for that type of loan.

Benefits for Banks Banks sell mortgages because the possibility of default makes it risky to hold them. In addition, the loans made by a particular bank may be poorly diversified, increasing risk. If the bank lends in only one geographic area, for example, a downturn in the local economy can cause a large number of defaults. By selling loans, the bank shifts default risk to the ultimate holders of the loans.

From one point of view, selling loans might seem an odd practice. Why should a bank lend money in the first place if it plans to get rid of the loan? The answer is that the bank still performs its basic function of reducing asymmetric information. It uses its expertise to screen borrowers and design loan covenants (see Section 15-4). Because it does this work, a bank can sell a loan for more than the original amount it gave the borrower. In effect, the institution buying the loan pays the bank for reducing information problems. The bank earns a profit from the sale and avoids the default risk it would face if it held onto the loan.

Many banks both sell mortgage loans and buy mortgage-backed securities. In effect, they trade the relatively few loans they make for small pieces of many loans. They gain diversification, reducing risk. They also gain liquidity, because mortgage-backed securities can be sold more quickly than individual mortgages.

Demand for Mortgage-Backed Securities Many financial institutions buy the securities issued by Fannie Mae and Freddie Mac. Large purchasers include mutual funds and pension funds as well as banks. For these institutions,

Fannie and Freddie's securities are attractive alternatives to bonds. The securities are highly liquid, and they are considered safe because they are backed by prime mortgages and because of Fannie and Freddie's links to the government. At the same time, the securities pay a bit more interest than other safe assets, such as Treasury bonds.

Securities backed by subprime mortgages are a different matter. As we saw in Chapter 17, these securities were purchased before the financial crisis by risk-taking institutions such as investment banks and hedge funds.

The Spread of Securitization

Before the 1990s, there was little securitization of loans beyond the prime mortgage-backed securities created by Fannie Mae and Freddie Mac. Since then, investment banks have extended securitization in two directions. The first innovation was securitization of subprime mortgages. The results were sufficiently disastrous that no new securities backed by subprime mortgages are being issued as of 2010.

The second innovation, securitization of nonmortgage loans, has proven more successful. Today, financial institutions trade securities backed by auto loans, credit-card debt, and student loans. At the end of 2009, 35% of all outstanding bank loans were securitized, compared to only 6% thirty years earlier.

Securitization is sometimes called *shadow banking*, a vaguely ominous term. We've seen the benefits of securitization: it reduces risk and increases liquidity for banks, and it raises the supply of loans. Yet securitization has gained a bad name because it played a role in the financial crisis of 2007–2009, as the following case study discusses.

CASE STUDY

The Subprime Mortgage Fiasco

The crisis that gripped the financial system over 2007–2009 had its roots in a wave of mortgage defaults. This disaster stemmed from the interplay of a housing bubble, the rise of subprime lending, securitization, and gaps in government regulation. Let's review the troubling story.

The Housing Bubble As we discussed in Chapter 16, U.S. housing prices rose 71 percent from 2002 to 2006, and many people believed that prices would continue to rise. In retrospect, however, the rapid price increases were an unsustainable bubble, and prices fell by 33 percent from 2006 to 2009.

Risky Lending A basic cause of the crisis was the behavior of mortgage lenders. Eager to increase business, finance companies made loans to people who were likely to have trouble paying them back. As we've discussed, lenders believed they could measure default risk with credit scores and adjust interest rates to compensate for this risk. The reliance on credit scores led lenders to neglect traditional safeguards against defaults.

Traditional mortgages require substantial down payments. A typical borrower must pay 20 percent of the house price out of her own money to receive a mortgage for 80 percent of the price. Collateral for the mortgage—the total value of the house—exceeds the loan, reducing default risk. During the subprime boom, however, lenders reduced down payments and even offered mortgages with zero money down.

Subprime lenders also loosened rules about borrowers' incomes. For a traditional mortgage, monthly payments cannot exceed a certain percentage of income (often around 30 percent). Formally, subprime lenders adhered to this rule, but often with a "no documentation" policy: borrowers stated their incomes but weren't asked for proof such as pay stubs or past income tax forms. Some people obtained mortgages by exaggerating their incomes.

Finally, lenders tempted borrowers with low introductory interest rates, often called *teaser rates*. In many mortgage contracts, the interest rate was 4 percent or less for the first two years, but then jumped sharply. People took out loans they could afford initially but got into trouble when their payments rose.

Finance companies could engage in risky lending because they receive less attention from government regulators than do banks. Light regulation helped finance companies make loans that now seem imprudent. In 2008, the Federal Reserve banned no-documentation loans, but this was like closing the barn door after the horse had gone.

The Boom Period Risky mortgage lending didn't produce a crisis immediately. Subprime lending was profitable in the late 1990s and early 2000s because default rates were moderate. As shown in Figure 18-3, the percentage of subprime

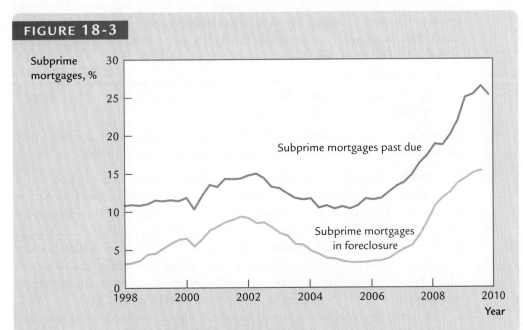

FIGURE 18-3

Subprime mortgages, %

The Subprime Mortgage Crisis Starting in 2006, a rising fraction of subprime mortgage borrowers fell behind on their payments. Foreclosures on subprime mortgages also rose.

Source: Mortgage Bankers Association.

borrowers who were behind on their mortgage payments was about 10 percent in 2000. This delinquency rate rose during the recession of 2001, but it was back down to 10 percent in 2004. In 2005, only 3 percent of subprime mortgages were in foreclosure, meaning the lender had given up on receiving payments from the borrower and moved to seize the borrower's house. This was well above the 0.4 percent foreclosure rate for prime mortgages, but subprime interest rates were high enough to compensate lenders for defaults.

The housing bubble was a key factor behind the subprime boom. Rising housing prices made it easier for homeowners to cope with high mortgage payments. Someone short on cash could take out a second mortgage because the higher value of his home gave him more collateral. Or he could sell the home for more than he paid for it, pay off his mortgage, and earn a capital gain.

The subprime boom fed on itself. Investment banks saw the profits being made on subprime mortgages and wanted to get in on the action. As detailed in Chapter 17, the leading investment banks securitized subprime mortgages and held onto a large share of the securities. Securitization provided more funds for subprime loans. In turn, more subprime lending increased the demand for housing, fueling the rise in housing prices. As a result of these dynamics, subprime mortgages grew from almost nothing in the early 1990s to 14 percent of outstanding mortgages in 2007.

During the boom period, few people—whether investment bankers, regulators, or economists—saw the risks of subprime lending that now seem obvious. The underlying reason is that few anticipated the sharp decline in housing prices that started in 2006. A bursting bubble in Japan had reduced that country's housing prices by nearly half in the 1990s and early 2000s, but most Americans ignored this warning signal. Housing prices had also fallen in some U.S. regions when their economies weakened in the 1980s and 1990s. Yet most observers agreed with Fed chair Alan Greenspan when, in 2005, he said

> Overall, while local economies may experience significant speculative price imbalances, a national severe price distortion [that is, a national housing bubble] seems most unlikely in the United States, given its size and diversity.

Because many policymakers considered a housing bubble "most unlikely," they did not worry about the potential consequences of a bursting bubble.

The Crash When housing prices started falling in 2006, homeowners across the country found themselves with mortgage payments they couldn't afford and no way out. They couldn't borrow more and they couldn't sell their houses for enough to pay off their mortgages. The delinquency rate on subprime mortgages started to rise, reaching 25 percent at the end of 2009. The foreclosure rate was 16 percent, about 5 times the level four years earlier. Eventually, the effects of falling housing prices spread to prime mortgages: the foreclosure rate for prime mortgages rose from 0.4 percent in 2005 to 1.4 percent in late 2009.

The mortgage crisis was a disaster for the millions of people who lost their homes, and it also hurt financial institutions. The first to feel the effects were finance companies that specialized in subprime lending; two large companies, Ameriquest and New Century Financial, went bankrupt in 2007. As we saw in Chapter 17, investment banks, major holders of subprime mortgage–backed

UNCORRECTED PAGES

securities, faced a crisis in 2008. Eventually the crisis affected all parts of the financial system, including stock and bond markets, and it pushed the economy into a deep recession. We discuss the spread of the financial crisis and its macro-economic effects in Chapter 19. ■

18-3 The Business of Banking

Having surveyed the banking industry, we now look at banking from the point of view of a bank manager. We examine the decisions that banks face and how they earn profits. The primary way a bank earns profits is by accepting deposits on which it pays relatively low interest and lending them out at higher rates, then either holding onto the loans or selling them. After analyzing this process, we discuss the risks that banks face, such as loan defaults, and their strategies for containing risk.

The Bank Balance Sheet

We can organize our discussion of the banking business by examining the **balance sheet** of a bank. The balance sheet summarizes a bank's financial condition at a point in time. It lists the bank's assets (what it owns) on the left side and its **liabilities** (what it owes to others) on the right. The right side of the balance sheet also includes the bank's **net worth**, defined as

$$\text{Net Worth} = \text{Assets} - \text{Liabilities}.$$

A bank's net worth is also called its *equity* or *capital*. It is the amount of assets the bank would have if it paid off all its liabilities.

Table 18-2 shows the major items on the balance sheet of Duckworth's Bank, a hypothetical commercial bank. A general way to think about the two sides of the balance sheet is that a bank's liabilities and net worth are its sources of funds and a bank's assets are its uses of funds. Let's review the balance sheet, starting with the right side.[2]

TABLE 18-2

The Balance Sheet of Duckworth's Bank

Assets		Liabilities and Net Worth	
Reserves	$ 10	Deposits	$ 70
Securities	$ 10	Borrowings	$ 20
Loans	$ 80	Net Worth	$ 10
TOTAL	$100	TOTAL	$100

[2] The appendix to Chapter 4 examines a similar balance sheet but ignores some items for simplicity.

Liabilities and Net Worth When banks raise funds, they incur liabilities to the people and firms that provide the funds. The primary type of liability is deposits, which come in several varieties: checking deposits, savings deposits, and certificates of deposit (CDs). CDs require depositors to leave their money in the bank for a fixed amount of time. At the start of 2010, deposits were about 65 percent of the liabilities of U.S. commercial banks.

If a bank wants more funds than it can raise in deposits, it has another source: borrowing. Banks can borrow money from one another, from corporations with spare cash, and from the Federal Reserve. Banks can also borrow in securities markets by issuing bonds.

Net worth, or capital, is the final item on the right side of the balance sheet. Like a bank's liabilities, this item is a source of funds. Initially, a bank acquires capital by issuing stock—savers provide funds to the bank in return for ownership shares. The bank's profits are added to its capital, and losses reduce capital. Capital also falls when the bank pays dividends to its stockholders.

The balance sheet in Table 18-2 shows us that Duckworth's Bank has $70 in deposits and $20 in borrowings, for a total of $90 in liabilities. The bank's net worth is $10.

Assets The asset side of the balance sheet shows how a bank uses the funds it raises. Notice that total assets must equal the sum of liabilities and net worth on the other side of the balance sheet. This equality follows from the definition of net worth as assets minus liabilities.

A bank's primary assets are the loans that it holds. These include loans it has made and not sold as well as any loans it has bought from other banks. These loans produce a flow of interest income. At the beginning of 2010, loans were 55 percent of commercial bank assets.

Banks also hold securities. Regulators restrict these holdings to safe securities, such as Treasury bonds and municipal bonds (bonds issued by state and local governments).

Finally, banks hold **reserves**, funds that are available immediately when depositors make withdrawals. Reserves include cash held in bank branches and ATMs. They also include deposits that banks make to accounts at the Federal Reserve. Every commercial bank has such an account at the Fed, which it uses to clear checks and electronic payments.

The balance sheet in Table 18-2 shows us that Duckworth's Bank has $100 in total assets divided into $10 in reserves, $10 in securities, and $80 in loans.

The primary business decisions facing a bank concern its balance sheet—what liabilities to incur, what assets to hold, and how much capital to raise. We will examine these issues after describing how banks measure profits.

Measuring Profits

For a bank, as for any firm, profits are the difference between revenue and costs. A bank's primary source of revenue is the interest it earns on its assets. Its costs include the interest it pays and the expenses of running its business, such as salaries.

Banks evaluate their profitability with two variables. One is the **return on assets** (ROA). This is the ratio of a bank's profits to its assets:

$$ROA = Profits/Assets.$$

In the example of Duckworth's Bank in Table 18-2, total assets are $100. If profits in the year 2020 are $2, the ROA for that year is $2/100 = 0.02$, or 2 percent.

The second measure of profitability is the **return on equity** (ROE). This variable is the ratio of a bank's profits to its capital:

$$ROE = Profits/Capital.$$

In our example, the bank's capital is $10, so its ROE is $2/10 = 20$ percent.

The ROE is the more important measure of profitability because it shows how much the bank earns for each dollar its stockholders put into the business. Bank managers try to produce high ROEs, just as managers in other businesses try to produce high returns for stockholders.

Figure 18-4 shows the average return on equity for all U.S. commercial banks from 1960 through 2009. In most periods, the ROE has ranged from 10 percent to 15 percent. The two exceptions were the late 1980s and 2007–2009. These two periods saw major banking crises, which we discuss later in this chapter and in Chapter 19.

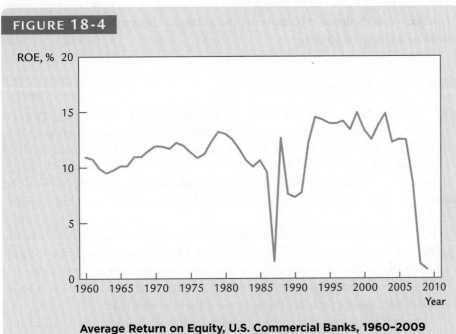

FIGURE 18-4

Average Return on Equity, U.S. Commercial Banks, 1960-2009
U.S. banks earned healthy profits over the period 1960-2009, except during banking crises in the 1980s and in 2007-2009.

Source: Federal Reserve Board.

Liability Management

As a bank seeks profits, one set of decisions it must make concerns its liabilities—the amounts of money it raises through deposits and borrowing. A key factor driving these decisions is the costs of funds.

Deposits are an inexpensive source of funds. Banks pay little or no interest on checking deposits. These deposits create expenses for processing checks and debit payments, but they are still inexpensive overall. Savings deposits and CDs pay more than checking deposits, but their interest rates are low compared to rates on bonds. Deposits are typically held by small savers, who accept low interest rates because they value the liquidity of bank accounts. In addition, some people simply don't know that higher interest rates are available from securities.

Borrowings are a relatively expensive source of funds. Banks borrow partly by issuing bonds, which carry higher interest rates than deposits. Banks also receive loans from other financial institutions, and the rates on these loans are close to bond rates. The lenders demand competitive interest rates because they could buy bonds rather than make a loan. Lenders to banks, such as other banks, are well informed about interest rates and seek the highest available rate.

Because of the varying costs of funds, many banks raise funds in two steps. First, they try to maximize deposits. They attract deposits by establishing convenient branches, providing good service, and advertising. Second, banks choose their level of borrowing. A bank can usually borrow as much as it wants, because other institutions are happy to lend if they receive sufficiently high interest rates.

Banks' choices of borrowings depend on their opportunities for using funds. For example, a bank might have a large number of attractive loan applications but lack enough deposits to make all the loans. In this situation, the bank borrows to increase its lending.

Liquidity Management

We now turn to the asset side of the balance sheet. While banks' primary assets are loans, they also hold reserves and securities. Banks hold these assets primarily to be ready for withdrawals of deposits. Reserves are available immediately if depositors demand money. And the securities held by banks are highly liquid: if banks need additional reserves, they can sell securities quickly in financial markets. For this reason, banks' securities holdings are sometimes called *secondary reserves*.

In contrast, loans are illiquid. Banks sell some types of loans, such as mortgages, but it takes time to negotiate the sales. Other types of loans are difficult to sell at all because of asymmetric information: a bank that has made a loan has gathered information about the borrower, but others have not. If a bank is eager to sell a loan, others fear that the loan has a high default risk.

Although reserves and securities provide liquidity, they also have a disadvantage: they pay low interest rates. A bank's holdings of cash pay no interest, and reserves held in accounts at the Federal Reserve pay very low rates. The safe securities held by banks, such as Treasury bonds, pay more interest than reserves but they pay less than loans.

Banks face a balancing act in choosing their asset allocation. On one hand, they want enough liquid assets to be ready to meet withdrawals. On the other hand, they want to minimize the amount of liquid assets they hold so they can earn the high interest rates paid on loans. A bank's pursuit of these potentially conflicting goals is called **liquidity management**.

Modern banks have developed a tool to ease the liquidity–return tradeoff: short-term borrowing. Although banks can borrow from various sources, they rely primarily on one another. A bank that is running short of liquid assets can borrow reserves from a bank with more liquidity than it needs. These interbank loans (which are usually *overnight loans* with a term of one day) are called **federal funds**. The federal funds market operates throughout every business day, so banks that need reserves can get them quickly.[3]

The availability of federal funds allows banks to operate with low levels of liquid assets and still be ready for withdrawals. In part because of the federal funds market, modern banks face little risk of running out of reserves—except in the extreme case of a bank run, which we discuss later in this chapter.

18-4 Risk Management at Banks

We have discussed how banks manage their assets and liabilities to maximize profits. Banks often succeed in earning healthy profits, yet their business is risky. If things go wrong, a bank can lose money and even be forced out of business. Two big risks that banks face are *credit risk* and *interest rate risk*.

Managing Credit Risk

Credit risk is another name for default risk, the risk that borrowers will not repay their loans. When a borrower defaults, her loan ceases to be an asset for the bank: the loan is worthless if it does not produce payments. When a loan is in default, the bank must *write off* the loan, which means it removes the loan from its balance sheet. A loan write-off reduces the bank's total assets and its net worth (assets minus liabilities), and the bank's stockholders lose money.

As we discussed in Chapter 15, banks seek to reduce credit risk by reducing asymmetric information problems. Screening borrowers reduces adverse selection, and monitoring them reduces moral hazard. For many loans, banks also reduce credit risk by demanding that borrowers put up some collateral before their loans are approved. **Collateral** is an asset of a borrower that the lender can seize if the borrower defaults. For home mortgages, the house serves as collateral. Collateral for business loans often includes a firm's equipment or inventories.

---

[3] Loans between banks are called federal funds because, in the past, borrowers' main motive was to meet requirements for minimum reserves set by the Fed. These requirements still exist, but they do not affect many banks. Most banks choose to hold more than the minimum level of reserves, largely because they need cash to stock their ATMs.

Collateral reduces credit risk in two ways. First, it reduces a bank's loss when a borrower defaults. By seizing collateral and selling it, the bank can recover some or all the money it is owed.

Second, collateral reduces the probability of default because it reduces information problems. Without collateral, borrowers with risky projects are eager to borrow money: they may win big, and they lose nothing if their projects fail and they default. If banks require collateral, high-risk borrowers are less likely to apply for loans because they could lose the collateral; thus, adverse selection decreases. In addition, after a borrower receives a loan, having collateral at stake is an incentive to use the loan prudently; thus, moral hazard decreases.

Banks also reduce credit risk by selling some of their loans. They sell many mortgages to Fannie Mae or Freddie Mac. When banks make very large loans, they often agree in advance to sell pieces of the loans to other banks. This arrangement is called *loan syndication*. When a loan is split among banks, no single bank loses too much from a default.

Managing Interest Rate Risk

Banks' profits are affected by short-term interest rates in financial markets, such as the Treasury bill rate. Increases in interest rates tend to reduce profits, and decreases raise profits. The resulting instability in profits is called **interest rate risk**.

Maturity Mismatch The explanation for interest rate risk involves the maturities of banks' assets and liabilities. Most liabilities have short maturities, meaning funds are not committed to the bank for long. Checking and savings deposits have zero maturities: they can be withdrawn at any moment. CDs typically mature after a year or two. Most borrowings by banks are also liabilities with short maturities. Federal funds, for example, are usually borrowed for one day at a time.

Because of these short maturities, interest rates on bank liabilities must compete with rates on securities offered for sale in financial markets. Suppose the Treasury bill rate rises. Rates on banks' borrowings rise immediately. Rates on deposits react more slowly, but they must rise before long or a substantial fraction of depositors will withdraw their money to earn higher rates on Treasury bills or other securities. Because banks must adjust the interest rates they pay when rates on securities change, bankers say their liabilities are *rate sensitive*.

In contrast, bank assets typically have long maturities. Many business loans have terms of 10 years. Traditional home mortgages have 30-year terms. If the Treasury bill rate rises, banks can charge higher rates on future loans, but the loans they hold currently have lower rates locked in for long periods. These loans are *not* rate sensitive.

To summarize, a bank's liabilities are mainly rate-sensitive and its assets are not. This *rate-sensitivity gap* means that a rise in short-term interest rates raises the interest that banks pay by more than the interest they earn. The net result is a decrease in bank profits.

Reducing Risk Banks use several techniques to reduce interest rate risk: loan sales, floating interest rates, and derivatives.

- *Loan sales.* We saw earlier that loan sales reduce credit risk. They can also reduce interest rate risk. If a bank sells long-term loans, it has fewer assets with fixed interest rates. It can use the proceeds from the loan sales to acquire assets with shorter maturities, such as Treasury bills and short-term loans, which are rate sensitive. This shift in the bank's assets reduces the rate-sensitivity gap between liabilities and assets. The smaller gap means that changes in interest rates have smaller effects on profits.

- *Floating rates.* A bank can also use **floating interest rates** for its long-term loans. A floating rate is an interest rate tied to a short-term rate. For example, the rate on a 10-year business loan might be the Treasury bill rate plus 2 percent. If Treasury bills pay 4 percent, the bank receives 6 percent on the loan. If the Treasury bill rate rises to 7 percent, the loan rate rises to 9 percent.

  Floating rates turn long-term loans into rate-sensitive assets. The loans themselves are committed for long periods, but the interest rates respond to short-term rates. Like loan sales, floating rates reduce a bank's rate-sensitivity gap. For this reason, banks charge floating rates on most business loans. Some home mortgages, called *adjustable-rate mortgages (ARMs)*, also have floating rates.

- *Derivatives.* Finally, banks can hedge interest rate risk with derivatives. For example, a bank can sell futures contracts for Treasury bonds, a transaction that yields profits if bond prices fall (see Section 17.6). Bond prices fall when interest rates rise, so higher rates produce profits for the bank. These profits offset the loss arising from the rate-sensitivity gap.

Equity and Insolvency Risk

We've seen how banks can lose money if borrowers default on loans or interest rates rise. Sometimes such losses mean only a year or two of low profits. If losses are large enough, however, a bank can face **insolvency**. This means its total assets fall below its liabilities and its net worth becomes negative.

Table 18-3 gives an example. Initially, Duckworth's Bank has the balance sheet in panel (a). It has $100 in assets, $90 in liabilities, and $10 in net worth (capital). Then disaster strikes: borrowers default on $20 of loans. The bank writes off these loans, reducing its total assets to $80, as shown in panel (b). Now the bank's net worth is -$10: the bank is insolvent.

An insolvent bank cannot stay in business. With negative net worth, it cannot pay off all its deposits and borrowings. In this situation, government regulators step in and force the bank to close. This outcome hurts the banks' stockholders because their stock becomes worthless. It also hurts bank managers, who are likely to lose their jobs. For these reasons, banks seek to avoid insolvency.

The Equity Ratio Banks can reduce their insolvency risk by holding more capital. Suppose Duckworth's Bank had started with $30 in capital rather than $10. Then capital would have stayed positive even after the bank wrote off $20 in loans. Higher capital means a deeper cushion against losses.

To be more precise, a bank's insolvency risk depends on its level of capital relative to its assets. This is measured by its **equity ratio** (ER):

$$\text{Equity Ratio} = \text{Capital}/\text{Assets}.$$

TABLE 18-3

Duckworth's Bank Becomes Insolvent

(a) Initial Balance Sheet

Assets		Liabilities and Net Worth	
Reserves	$ 10	Deposits	$ 70
Securities	$ 10	Borrowings	$ 20
Loans	$ 80	Net Worth	$ 10
TOTAL	$100	TOTAL	$100

(b) Balance Sheet After Loan Defaults

Assets		Liabilities and Net Worth	
Reserves	$10	Deposits	$ 70
Securities	$10	Borrowings	$ 20
Loans	$60	Net Worth	$−10
TOTAL	$80	TOTAL	$ 80

The equity ratio shows what percent of assets a bank would have to lose to become insolvent. In Table 18-3, the initial equity ratio for Duckworth's Bank was $10/$100 = 10 percent. Any loss exceeding 10 percent of assets was enough to make the bank insolvent. If the bank had had the same assets but $30 in capital, its equity ratio would have been a safer 30 percent.

A bank can raise its equity ratio either by raising capital (the numerator) or by reducing assets (the denominator). The bank can raise capital by issuing new stock or by reducing dividends to stockholders. It can reduce assets by making fewer loans or purchasing fewer securities. Any of these actions reduces insolvency risk.

The Equity Ratio and the Return on Equity Raising the equity ratio also has a big disadvantage: it makes a bank less profitable. Recall that profitability is measured by the return on equity (ROE), the ratio of profits to capital. This variable falls when the equity ratio rises.

We can see this effect with a little algebra. We take the formula for ROE and divide both the numerator and denominator by assets:

$$\text{ROE} = \text{Profits/Capital} = (\text{Profits/Assets})/(\text{Capital/Assets}).$$

In this formula, profits/assets is the return on assets (ROA). Capital/assets is the equity ratio (ER). So we can simplify to

$$\text{ROE} = \text{ROA/ER}.$$

The return on equity depends on the return on assets and the equity ratio. For a given ROA, raising the equity ratio reduces the ROE.

To understand this effect, suppose a bank raises its equity ratio by issuing new stock. It keeps its assets the same. With the same assets, the bank gets the same flow of profits, but now these profits are split among more stockholders. Each share of stock earns less.

To summarize, a bank faces a tradeoff when it chooses its equity ratio. A higher ratio reduces insolvency risk but also reduces the return on equity. A bank would like a ratio that is high enough to make insolvency unlikely but low enough to produce good returns for its stockholders.

The Banking Crisis of the 1980s

Figure 18-5 shows the number of U.S. bank failures from 1960 through 2009. In most years, fewer than 10 banks fail. Failures were higher in 2008 and 2009, reflecting the financial crisis and recession of those years. Yet the largest surge in failures occurred in the 1980s. Failures rose rapidly over that decade, peaking at 534 in 1989. Some of the failed institutions were commercial banks, but the majority were savings and loan associations (a type of bank discussed in Section 18-1). The episode is often called the *S&L crisis*.

Two causes of the crisis were rising interest rates and loan defaults. Examining the episode yields a deeper understanding of interest rate risk and credit risk.

Rising Interest Rates In the 1980s, banks, especially S&Ls, had large rate-sensitivity gaps. Most liabilities of S&Ls were deposits with zero maturities, and most assets were long-term, fixed-rate mortgages. Many of these loans had been made in the 1960s, when interest rates were low. In 1965, the Treasury bill rate was about 4 percent and the 30-year mortgage rate was about 6 percent.

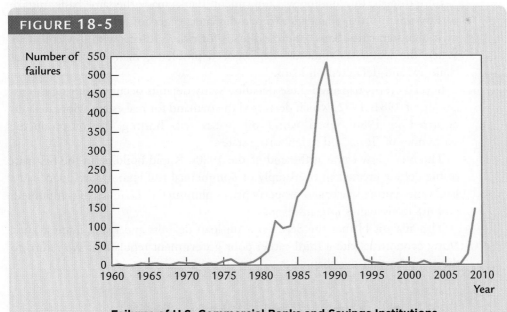

FIGURE 18-5

Failures of U.S. Commercial Banks and Savings Institutions, 1960–2009 The number of bank failures rose during the financial crisis of 2007–2009, but it was even higher during the savings and loan crisis of the 1980s.

Source: Federal Deposit Insurance Corporation.

Interest rates rose rapidly in the 1970s and early 1980s. Recall that the nominal interest rate is the sum of the real rate and inflation. In the 1970s real rates were low, but inflation pushed up nominal rates. At the end of the decade, the Fed raised real rates to fight inflation. It took time for inflation to respond, so both real rates *and* inflation were high in the early 80s. The nominal rate on Treasury bills peaked at 14 percent in 1981.

You can guess what happened from our earlier discussion of interest rate risk. Banks were forced to raise interest rates on deposits along with the Treasury bill rate. In the early 1980s, they paid higher rates on deposits than they received on many mortgages. So they suffered large losses.

The Commercial Real Estate Bust In the early 1980s, banks sharply raised their lending for commercial real estate projects, such as office buildings and shopping centers. This lending rose for several reasons:

- Real estate prices were high, spurring new construction. So there was a large demand for real estate loans.

- Bank loans to corporations were declining as more and more companies raised funds by issuing bonds. Banks sought new loan opportunities to offset the business they were losing.

- Regulations changed. Traditionally, S&Ls specialized in home mortgages and were forbidden to lend for commercial real estate. Congress lifted this ban in 1980, so S&Ls joined commercial banks in lending to commercial real estate developers.

In retrospect, this lending was imprudent. Banks made the same basic mistake as subprime mortgage lenders two decades later: eager for business, they relaxed their loan standards. Banks approved loans for risky projects with low collateral. When the real estate industry experienced problems, many developers went bankrupt and defaulted on loans.

Several events triggered these defaults. Many defaults occurred during the recession of 1981–1982, which decreased the demand for real estate. More defaults occurred in 1986, when world oil prices fell, hurting the oil-producing economies of Texas and neighboring states.

The final blow came at the end of the 1980s. Rapid building in the first part of the decade created an oversupply of commercial real estate. Developers had a hard time renting space, and property prices plummeted. Loan defaults mounted, pushing many banks into insolvency.

This analysis blames the S&L crisis on loan defaults and rising interest rates. Many economists cite a third cause: poor government regulation. We return to this point later in the chapter. ■

18-5 Bank Runs, Deposit Insurance, and Moral Hazard

In any industry, a firm can fail. It can lose money, run out of funds, and be forced out of business. Often, economists think this outcome is efficient. If a firm is not profitable, its resources should be freed up for more productive uses.

When it comes to banks, however, economists have a less benign view of failure. One reason is the risk of a **bank run**, in which depositors lose confidence in a bank and make sudden, large withdrawals. A run can push a healthy bank into insolvency and cause it to fail. When that happens, both the bank's owners and its depositors suffer needless losses.

How Bank Runs Happen

The risk of a bank run is an extreme form of liquidity risk, the risk that a bank will have trouble meeting demands for withdrawals. As we saw earlier, banks manage liquidity risk by holding reserves and secondary reserves, such as Treasury bills. If they are short on reserves, they borrow federal funds from other banks. Normally these methods are sufficient to contain liquidity risk.

However, things are different when a bank experiences a run. A sudden surge in withdrawals overwhelms the bank. It runs out of liquid assets and cannot borrow enough to cover all the withdrawals.

At this point, the bank can raise additional funds by selling loans. But recall that loans are illiquid: because of asymmetric information, it is hard to sell them quickly. To quickly find buyers, the bank will likely have to accept low prices—less than the loans are really worth. In financial jargon, the bank is forced into a *fire sale* of loans.[4] Selling loans for less than their true value reduces the bank's total assets. If it loses enough, capital falls below zero and the run causes insolvency.

What causes runs? Some occur because a bank is insolvent even before the run: the bank does not have enough assets to pay off its liabilities and will likely close. In this situation, depositors fear they will lose their money. These fears are compounded by the first-come, first-served nature of deposit withdrawals. The first people to withdraw get their money back, but those who act slowly may find that no funds are left. So depositors rush to withdraw before it's too late, and a run occurs.

A run can also occur at a bank that is initially solvent. This happens if depositors lose confidence in the bank, which can happen suddenly and without good reason. Suppose someone starts a rumor that a bank has lost money and become insolvent. This rumor is totally false. However, depositors hear the rumor and worry that it might be true. Some decide to play it safe and withdraw their funds.

Seeing these withdrawals, other depositors begin to fear that a run is starting. They decide to get their money out before everyone else does and the bank fails. Suddenly there are lots of withdrawals: a run *does* occur. Ultimately, the bank is forced into a fire sale of assets, and its capital is driven below zero.

Section 16-5 discussed the phenomenon of self-fulfilling expectations. We saw there how expectations can influence asset prices. If people expect stock prices to fall, then they sell stocks, causing prices to fall. Bank runs are the same kind of event: if people expect a run, then a run occurs. This can happen even if nothing is wrong at the bank before the run.

---

[4] The metaphor behind "fire sale" is a company whose warehouse has burned down, forcing it to sell goods quickly before they are stolen or damaged by the elements.

An Example

Suppose Duckworth's Bank has the balance sheet shown in Table 18-4(a). The bank has a positive level of capital, or net worth. It also has enough reserves and securities to meet normal demands for withdrawals. There is no good reason for Duckworth's Bank to go out of business.

Then a negative rumor about the bank starts circulating. Worried depositors decide to withdraw their funds. We'll assume they want to withdraw all $70 of deposits in the bank.

To pay depositors, Duckworth's Bank first uses its reserves and securities, a total of $20. Then, with its liquid assets exhausted, the bank must quickly sell its loans. We'll assume this fire sale produces only 50 cents per dollar of loans. The bank sells its $80 in loans, receives $40, and gives this money to depositors. At this point, the bank has paid off a total of $60 in deposits.

The bank's new balance sheet is shown in Table 18-4(b). The bank now has no assets. It still has $30 in liabilities, consisting of its $20 in borrowings and $10 in deposits (since it paid off only $60 of its initial $70 in deposits). The bank's net worth is negative, meaning it is insolvent. It cannot pay the $10 demanded by depositors, and it also has no funds to pay back its $20 in borrowings. As a result, Duckworth's bank goes out of business.

This example assumes that Duckworth's Bank *cannot* borrow federal funds to pay depositors. If it could, its borrowings would rise by the amount its deposits fell, and this one-for-one trade would not change its total liabilities or reduce its net worth. It is likely, however, that a bank facing a run will not be able to increase its borrowings. Other banks see the run on Duckworth's and recognize that it threatens Duckworth's solvency. They won't lend federal funds because they, along with some depositors, won't be repaid if Duckworth's is forced to close.

TABLE 18-4

A Run at Duckworth's Bank

(a) Initial Balance Sheet

Assets		Liabilities and Net Worth	
Reserves	$ 10	Deposits	$ 70
Securities	$ 10	Borrowings	$ 20
Loans	$ 80	Net Worth	$ 10
TOTAL	$100	TOTAL	$100

(b) Balance Sheet After Run

Assets		Liabilities and Net Worth	
Reserves	$0	Deposits	$ 10
Securities	$0	Borrowings	$ 20
Loans	$0	Net Worth	$−30
TOTAL	$0	TOTAL	$ 0

The run on and closure of Duckworth's Bank hurts the owners of the bank: they lose the $10 in capital that they had before the run. It also hurts the holders of the last $10 in deposits, which become worthless, and the institutions that provided Duckworth's initial $20 in borrowings, which are not repaid.

CASE STUDY

The Run on Northern Rock Bank

Since World War II, bank runs have been rare in advanced economies. Before September 2007, the United Kingdom had not experienced a run for 140 years. But suddenly, on September 14, long lines of worried depositors formed at branches of Northern Rock Bank. Depositors also jammed the banks' phone lines and crashed its Web site. Between September 14 and September 17, depositors managed to withdraw 2 billion pounds (roughly $4 billion) from Northern Rock.

Northern Rock Bank is headquartered in northern England (hence the name), and it lends primarily for home mortgages. Before the run, Northern Rock was the fifth-largest mortgage lender in the United Kingdom, and growing rapidly. The bank's lending far exceeded its deposits, so it used borrowing to finance much of the lending. A major source of funds was short-term loans from other banks (the equivalent of federal funds in the United States).

Northern Rock's problems began across the Atlantic, with the subprime mortgage crisis in the United States. In the summer of 2007, people started to realize that the U.S. crisis might spread, threatening the solvency of other countries' financial institutions. With this idea in the air, banks became wary of lending to each other—and especially wary of lending to banks that specialized in mortgages. As a result, Northern Rock had trouble raising funds as it had in the past. Other banks either refused to lend to Northern Rock or demanded high interest rates.

In a bind, Northern Rock turned to the United Kingdom's central bank, the Bank of England, asking for an emergency loan. The Bank of England approved a loan to Northern Rock and planned an announcement, but the news leaked out prematurely. On September 13, a well-known business reporter said on television that Northern Rock "has had to go cap in hand" to the Bank of England. Hearing that their bank had a problem, Northern Rock's depositors had the typical reaction: they rushed to withdraw their funds.

Deposits flowed out of Northern Rock for three days, until the British government intervened. On September 17, the government announced it would guarantee Northern Rock's deposits: if the bank failed, the government would compensate depositors. This action restored confidence enough to end the run.

Yet Northern Rock's problems were not over. The run damaged the bank's reputation, and it continued to have trouble raising funds. With fears growing about Northern Rock's solvency, the British government took over the bank in February 2008, with compensation for the bank's shareholders. As of 2010, the bank was still owned by the government. ∎

Bank Panics

Sometimes runs occur simultaneously at many individual banks. People lose confidence in the whole banking system, and depositors everywhere try to withdraw their money. Such an event is called a **bank panic**.

Nationwide bank panics were once common in the United States. Between 1873 and 1933, the country experienced an average of three panics per decade. Bank panics occur because a loss of confidence is contagious. A run at one bank causes depositors at other banks to wonder whether their money is safe. This uncertainty triggers runs at those banks, which shakes confidence further, which causes more runs, and so on.

In the United States, a typical bank panic started with runs on New York banks. These triggered runs in other parts of the East, and then the panic spread westward. The following case study discusses the last and most severe bank panics in U.S. history.

CASE STUDY

Bank Panics in the 1930s

Chapter 11 discussed the Great Depression of the 1930s, when the unemployment rate reached 25 percent. One cause of the Depression was bank failures, which disrupted the flow of funds from savers to investors. These failures were caused by a series of bank panics.

Figure 18-6 shows the percentage of all U.S. banks that failed in each year from 1876 through 1935. It shows that bank failures rose moderately in the

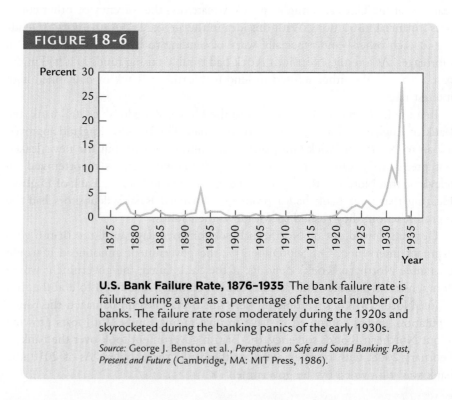

FIGURE 18-6

U.S. Bank Failure Rate, 1876–1935 The bank failure rate is failures during a year as a percentage of the total number of banks. The failure rate rose moderately during the 1920s and skyrocketed during the banking panics of the early 1930s.

Source: George J. Benston et al., *Perspectives on Safe and Sound Banking: Past, Present and Future* (Cambridge, MA: MIT Press, 1986).

1920s. Most failures occurred at small, rural banks. These banks made loans to farmers, and falling agricultural prices during the 1920s led to defaults. These failures were isolated, however; most banks appeared healthy.

Major trouble began in 1930. Failures rose at rural banks in the Midwest, and this made depositors nervous about other banks in the region. These worries were exacerbated by general unease about the economy, a result of the 1929 stock market crash. Bank runs started in the Midwest, and this time they spread eastward.

A psychological milestone was the failure of the Bank of the United States, located in New York, in December 1930. It was one of the country's largest banks, and the largest ever to fail. In addition, while it was an ordinary commercial bank, its name suggested some link to the government. Its failure shook confidence in the whole banking system.

Other events eroded confidence further. Some well-known European banks failed in 1931. In the 1932 election campaign, Democrats publicized banking problems to criticize the Republican administration. The stream of worrisome news produced a nationwide panic.

When Democrat Franklin Roosevelt became president on March 4, 1933, he quickly took charge of the banking crisis. On March 6, Roosevelt announced a *bank holiday*: across the country, all banks were required to shut down temporarily. Starting on March 13, banks were allowed to reopen, but only if the Secretary of the Treasury certified they were solvent. A quarter of all U.S. banks failed in 1933, but Roosevelt's policies ended the panic.

President Roosevelt understood the psychology of panics. His famous statement that "we have nothing to fear but fear itself" referred partly to banking and captures the fact that panics result from self-fulfilling expectations.[5] ∎

Deposit Insurance

No bank panics have occurred in the United States since 1933. Runs have occurred at individual banks, but they are rare because the government figured out how to solve the problem: **deposit insurance**.

Deposit insurance is a government's promise to compensate depositors for their losses when a bank fails. In our example of Duckworth's Bank (Table 18-4), insurance would pay off the last $10 in deposits after Duckworth's runs out of assets. In addition to protecting depositors when bank failures occur, insurance makes failures less likely. This effect arises because insurance eliminates bank runs, a major cause of failures.

The reason is simple. A run occurs when depositors start worrying about the safety of their deposits and try to withdraw them. Deposit insurance eliminates the worry because depositors know they will be paid back if their bank fails. They have no reason to start a run, even if they hear bad rumors about the bank.

---

[5] For more on the bank panics of the 1930s, see Chapter 7 of Milton Friedman and Anna Schwartz, *A Monetary History of the United States, 1867–1960* (Princeton, N.J.: Princeton University Press, 1963).

In the United States, deposit insurance is provided primarily by the **Federal Deposit Insurance Corporation** (FDIC), a U.S. government agency. Congress created the FDIC in 1933 in response to the bank panics of the early 1930s. If a bank fails and depositors lose money, the FDIC compensates them up to a limit, which is currently $250,000 per bank account. In 2008 during the financial crisis, the limit was raised from $100,000 in an effort to boost confidence in the banking system.

Many countries have more limited deposit insurance than the United States. At the time of the Northern Rock bank run, the United Kingdom had deposit insurance but paid only 90 percent of losses. Northern Rock's customers ran to the bank because they stood to lose 10 percent of their deposits if the bank failed (until the fourth day of the run, when the government guaranteed deposits fully).

Moral Hazard in Banking

Deposit insurance fixes the problem of bank runs. Unfortunately, it makes another problem worse. This problem is one of moral hazard: because they do not bear the full risk of becoming insolvent, bankers have incentives to misuse deposits.

One of the basic purposes of banks is to reduce the problem of moral hazard in loan markets. Borrowers have incentives to misuse the funds they receive from lenders. Banks reduce this problem through monitoring, loan covenants, and collateral. Unfortunately, banking itself creates new moral hazard problems in which bankers are the parties with incentives to misuse funds. They can use deposits in ways that benefit themselves but hurt depositors.

One way that bankers can exploit depositors is by taking on excessive risk. Suppose a bank lends to borrowers with risky projects who are willing to pay high interest rates. If the projects succeed, the interest income produces high profits for the bank's owners. If the projects fail, the borrowers default and the bank may become insolvent.

However, not all the losses from insolvency fall on the bank. In the absence of deposit insurance, depositors also lose when the bank can't pay them back. With insurance, the government bears the cost of lost deposits. Either way, bankers have incentives to gamble because someone else pays part of the costs if their gambles fail.

We can see this point from our earlier example of insolvency (Table 18-3). In that example, Duckworth's Bank lost $20 from writing off loans. Only part of the cost was borne by the banks' owners: they lost their $10 in capital. The rest of the cost—$10 in lost deposits—fell on depositors or the government.

In addition to excessive risk taking, bankers can exploit depositors in a less subtle way: by stealing their money. The famous robber Willie Sutton was once asked why he chose to hold up banks. His response was, "That's where the money is." The same reasoning applies to white-collar crime when a bank's management is unscrupulous. Large amounts of money flow in and out of banks, creating opportunities for fraud and embezzlement. History provides many examples of bank failures caused by dishonesty.

As usual, the root of moral hazard is asymmetric information. If depositors could see what bankers do with their money, they could forbid gambling and stealing. But it isn't easy to observe what happens inside banks.

The Problem With Deposit Insurance

We can now see a drawback of deposit insurance: it exacerbates the problem of moral hazard. To see this, think about a world without deposit insurance. Depositors worry that banks may fail, costing them money. As a result, they have incentives to monitor banks. Before depositing money, prudent people will investigate a bank's safety. For example, they might check the bank's balance sheet to be sure that insolvency risk is low. After making deposits, people will watch the bank and withdraw their money if there are signs of trouble.

We saw that nervous depositors can cause bank runs. But they also have a positive effect: they discourage banks from misusing deposits. If a bank takes excessive risks or money disappears mysteriously, depositors are likely to notice and withdraw their funds. And the bank will have trouble attracting new deposits. This threat gives banks a reason to keep deposits safe.

Insurance eliminates depositors' incentives to monitor banks. Depositors know they will be compensated if banks fail, so they don't care much if bankers take risks or embezzle their money. They don't bother to check balance sheets for danger signs. This inattention gives bankers greater freedom to misuse deposits: they don't fear that bad behavior will be punished by withdrawals.

Governments recognize the problem with deposit insurance and try to reduce it by limiting the protection they provide. Recall that the FDIC limits its payments to $250,000 per account. Some deposits exceed this level, such as accounts of large corporations or state governments. Large depositors have incentives to monitor banks and withdraw their funds if banks misuse them. Yet moral hazard is still severe, given insurance for most deposits and banks' incentives to misuse funds.

18-6 Bank Regulation

Governments are keenly aware of the moral hazard problem in banking. They could reduce this problem by eliminating deposit insurance, but that might lead to bank runs. To maintain insurance and combat moral hazard, many governments heavily regulate the banking industry. Regulators do the job that depositors neglect when they are insured: they monitor banks' activities and try to prevent them from misusing depositors' funds.

The rest of this chapter surveys bank regulation. We will focus on the regulation of U.S. commercial banks as of 2010. Regulations for banks and other financial institutions are in the process of changing as a result of the recent financial crisis, as we discuss in Chapter 19.

Who Regulates Banks?

A number of government agencies regulate U.S. banks. A bank first meets regulators when it applies for a *charter*—a license to operate. Commercial banks can be chartered either by a federal agency called the Office of the Comptroller of the Currency (OCC) or a state agency such as Maryland's Office of Financial Regulation. Banks chartered by the OCC are called *national banks* and those chartered by state agencies are *state banks*.

Chartering is the first step in bank regulation. A prospective bank submits an application that describes its business plan, its expected earnings, its initial level of capital, and its top management. Regulators review the application and judge the soundness of the bank's plans. If the risk of failure appears too high, the application is denied. In the same way that banks study loan applicants' business plans to screen out borrowers who will misuse loans, regulators try to screen out banks that will misuse deposits.

After a bank is chartered, its operations are overseen by one or more regulators. Commercial banks chartered by the OCC are regulated by the OCC. Most commercial banks chartered by state agencies are regulated by those agencies *and* the Federal Reserve. A few small banks that are not members of the Federal Reserve system are regulated primarily by the Federal Deposit Insurance Corporation. The FDIC becomes involved with any bank that is near insolvency.

This complex system is not based on any logical design. Instead, it reflects the historical development of bank regulation. For example, before the Civil War, only state governments chartered and regulated banks. Concerns about corruption at those banks led to the National Bank Act of 1863, which created the OCC and national banks.

Periodically, the government has considered proposals to streamline bank regulation. In 1993, the Clinton administration proposed the creation of a Federal Banking Commission, which would have been the primary regulator of all banks. Such proposals have not been enacted, in part because of opposition from the Federal Reserve, which has not wanted to relinquish its regulatory role. However, the financial crisis of 2007–2009 rekindled interest in a simplified regulatory system, as we discuss in Chapter 19.

Restrictions on Balance Sheets

Once a bank is chartered and in business, regulators try to contain risk taking by putting restrictions on the bank's balance sheet. Regulations limit the assets that a bank can hold and mandate minimum levels of capital.

Restrictions on Assets Banks can choose among a variety of assets, including safe assets with relatively low returns and riskier assets with higher returns. As we've discussed, moral hazard distorts this choice. Banks have incentives to take on too much risk because the costs that might result are paid partly by depositors or the deposit insurance fund.

To address this problem, regulators restrict the assets that banks can hold. In the United States, there are strict limits on securities holdings. Banks can hold only the safest securities, such as government bonds and bonds issued by corporations with low default risk (as measured by bond-rating agencies). Banks cannot hold risky corporate bonds or stock in any company.

Regulators also restrict the loans that banks make. Each bank's lending must be diversified: no single loan can be too large. At national banks, loans to any one borrower cannot exceed 15 percent of the bank's capital. Loan limits at state banks vary by state. Regulators also set minimum levels of collateral for some kinds of loans, such as loans for commercial real estate.

Capital Requirements We learned earlier that when a bank chooses its level of capital, it faces a tradeoff. Lower capital raises the return on equity but it also raises the bank's insolvency risk, a tradeoff that creates moral hazard: Bank owners benefit from the higher return on equity but do not bear the full cost of insolvency. As a result, banks have incentives to choose low levels of capital, thus creating excessive risk.

Regulators address this problem by imposing **capital requirements**, rules that mandate minimum levels of capital that banks must hold. Required capital is set at levels that regulators think will keep insolvency risk low.

In the United States, capital requirements have two parts. The first is a minimum level for a bank's equity ratio (the ratio of capital to assets). Currently, this minimum is 5 percent: a bank's capital must equal at least 5 percent of its assets for regulators to consider it "well capitalized."

The second requirement is based on an international agreement about capital requirements, the 1988 *Basel Accord*. This rule takes into account the riskiness of different kinds of assets. Among the assets that banks hold, some are very safe and others are relatively risky. The riskier a bank's assets, the more capital it is required to hold. Having more capital protects banks from insolvency if risky assets lose value.

Specifically, the Basel Accord requires banks to hold capital that equals at least 8 percent of their *risk-adjusted assets*. This variable is a weighted sum of different groups of assets, with higher weights given to assets with higher risk. The safest assets, such as reserves and Treasury bonds, have weights of zero. Loans to other banks have weights of 20 percent. A number of assets have 50 percent weights, including municipal bonds and home mortgages (which were considered fairly safe when the Basel Accord was signed). The weights on most other loans are 100 percent.

Capital requirements are controversial. Banks have long complained that the rules are too restrictive. Before the recent financial crisis, the U.S. government was considering changes that would have given banks more flexibility in judging how much capital they need. In the wake of the crisis, which produced a rise in bank failures, it is likely that capital requirements will become more rather than less strict.

Supervision

Another element of government regulation is **bank supervision**, the monitoring of banks' activities. The agency that regulates a bank checks that the bank is meeting capital requirements and obeying restrictions on asset holdings. Regulators also make more subjective assessments of the bank's insolvency risk. If they perceive too much risk, they demand changes in the bank's operations.

A bank's supervisors gather information in two ways. First, they require the bank to report on its activities. The most important of these reports is the *call report*, which contains detailed information on the bank's finances, including a balance sheet and a statement of earnings and losses. A bank must submit a call report every quarter. Regulators examine call reports for signs of trouble, such as declining capital, increases in risky assets, or rising loan delinquencies.

Second, regulators gather information through *bank examinations*, in which a team of regulators visits a bank's headquarters. Every bank is visited at least once a year, more often if regulators suspect problems. Examiners sometimes arrive without warning, making it harder for banks to hide questionable activities.

Examiners review a bank's detailed financial records, study internal memos and minutes of meetings to better understand the bank's business, and interview managers about various policies, such as the criteria for approving loans. Examiners also check outside sources to verify information provided by the bank. For example, they contact some of the bank's loan customers to ensure that the loans really exist and that borrowers have the collateral reported by the bank.

After examiners visit, a bank receives a grade that summarizes its risks to solvency. The grade is based on a range of factors, including the bank's level of capital, the riskiness of its loans, its recent earnings, and the examiners' judgment of the competence of bank managers. Examination grades range from 1 to 5; a rating of 1 means a bank is "fundamentally sound," while a 5 means "imminent risk of failure."

If a bank's grade is 1 or 2, regulators leave it alone until its next examination. If the rating is 3 or worse, regulators require the bank to take action to reduce risk. This could mean tightening the loan approval process, slowing the growth of assets, cutting dividends to shareholders, or firing bad managers. Regulators can either negotiate an agreement with the bank or issue a unilateral order. If the bank's problems are severe, regulators impose fines. If they find evidence of criminal activity, such as embezzlement, they turn the case over to the FBI.

Closing Insolvent Banks

Regulators try to prevent banks from becoming insolvent, but sometimes it happens. Consequently, another task of regulators is to deal with insolvent banks. Today, U.S. regulators force these banks to close quickly. This policy reflects past experiences, such as the S&L crisis of the 1980s, in which delays in closing banks proved costly.

The Need for Government Action In most industries, an unprofitable firm cannot survive for long. If it loses enough money, it becomes insolvent: its debts to banks and bondholders exceed its assets. In this situation, the firm has trouble making debt payments, and lenders won't provide additional funds. The firm runs out of money to operate its business and is forced into bankruptcy.

However, this process may *not* occur for an insolvent bank. The reason is that the bulk of bank liabilities are insured deposits, and insurance makes depositors indifferent to their banks' fates. An insolvent bank is likely to fail eventually, but its depositors don't suffer. Indeed, the bank may be able to attract deposits and stay in business for a long time.

This outcome is dangerous for two reasons. First, the bank may continue practices that led it to insolvency, such as lax procedures for approving loans. These practices are likely to produce further losses, so the bank's net worth becomes more and more negative. Eventually the bank collapses at a high cost to the insurance fund.

Second, the bank may do risky things that it *didn't* do in the past because the moral hazard problem, which exists for all banks, is particularly severe for insolvent ones. If a bank's capital is negative, its owners have nothing left to lose if they take risks. And they have much to gain: if their gambles succeed, they may earn enough to push the bank's capital above zero. In that case, the bank stays in business and managers keep their jobs.

Forbearance Despite the dangers posed by insolvent banks, regulators have sometimes chosen *not* to shut them down. Banks have continued to operate with negative capital. A regulator's decision not to close an insolvent bank is called **forbearance**.

Forbearance occurs because bank closures are painful. Bank owners lose any chance for future profits, managers lose their jobs, and depositors lose their uninsured funds. Closures are costly for the FDIC, which must compensate insured depositors. Closures can also be embarrassing for regulators, because they suggest that bank supervision has been inadequate. For all these reasons, regulators are tempted to let insolvent banks stay open.

Forbearance is a gamble on the part of regulators. As we've discussed, an insolvent bank may start earning profits and become solvent. If that happens, everyone avoids the pain of closure. On the other hand, if the bank continues to lose money, closure is more costly when it finally occurs.

Forbearance exacerbated the savings and loan crisis of the 1980s. Many S&Ls were insolvent by the early 1980s, when interest rates peaked. In retrospect, regulators should have closed these banks promptly, but they did not. Instead, the Federal Home Loan Bank Board, which regulated S&Ls at the time, loosened regulations to help banks stay open. It reduced capital requirements in 1980 and 1982. It also changed accounting rules to allow S&Ls to report higher levels of assets, and hence higher capital. For example, it allowed banks to write off bad loans over a 10-year period rather than all at once.

This policy was unsuccessful: as we've seen, bank failures surged in the late 1980s. Ultimately the government paid $150 billion (at the time, about 3 percent of a year's GDP) to compensate depositors at failed banks. This episode motivated Congress to pass the FDIC Improvement Act of 1991, which established stringent rules for closing banks. These rules govern bank closures today.

The Closure Process Regulators monitor bank capital as part of the supervision process. Under the rules established in 1991, regulators can close a bank immediately if its capital falls below 2 percent of its assets. Note that closure can occur while the bank is still barely solvent—capital can be low but positive. Regulators try to act before capital becomes negative, a situation that creates severe moral hazard.

Regulators have a second option when capital falls below 2 percent of assets: they can give the bank a final chance to increase its capital. The bank can try to add capital by issuing new stock, which people will buy if they think the bank will be profitable in the future. Usually the bank is given three to nine months to increase capital substantially. If it can't, then it must close.

The decision to close a bank is made by the agency that granted the bank's charter (for a commercial bank, either the OCC or a state agency). This agency calls in the FDIC, which takes over the bank. In most cases, the FDIC does not simply shut down the bank; instead, it sells most of the bank's assets and liabilities to another, healthier bank. Depositors keep their deposits and bank branches stay open under new ownership.

An example is the September 2008 failure of Washington Mutual (WaMu), a victim of the subprime mortgage crisis. Before failing, WaMu was the sixth-largest bank in the country. When the FDIC took it over, its stockholders lost their money. So did financial institutions from which WaMu had borrowed—unlike deposits, loans to a bank are not insured. The FDIC sold WaMu's assets and deposits to JP Morgan Chase for $1.9 billion, a tiny amount considering that WaMu had $300 billion of assets in 2007. The day after this deal, WaMu's branches reopened as branches of JP Morgan Chase.

18-7 Conclusion

This chapter has surveyed several aspects of the financial system: the diverse banking industry, the subprime lenders that attract customers who can't borrow from banks, and the securitization of bank loans by government-sponsored enterprises and investment banks. We have seen how banks and subprime lenders earn profits and learned about the risks they face, ranging from credit risk to bank runs. We have also discussed how the government tries to prevent bank failures through deposit insurance and restrictions on risk taking by banks.

As this book is being written, the banking industry is in a state of flux as a result of the financial crisis of 2007-2009. Subprime lending has fallen drastically; the giant mortgage agencies, Fannie Mae and Freddie Mac, are temporarily under government conservatorship; and political leaders are debating a host of proposed regulatory changes to prevent future financial crises. Chapter 19 discusses where the banking industry might be headed.

Summary

1. Types of banks—institutions that make loans and accept deposits—include commercial banks, savings institutions, and credit unions. Finance companies make loans but do not accept deposits.

2. People with low incomes or poor credit histories borrow from subprime lenders, including subprime finance companies, payday lenders, pawnshops, and illegal loan sharks.

3. Many bank loans, especially home mortgages, are securitized. Securitization increases the funds available for loans and allows banks to eliminate default risk on their loans.

4. The left side of a bank's balance sheet shows its assets, including reserves, securities, and loans. The right side shows the bank's liabilities, including deposits and borrowings, and its net worth.

5. Banks face credit risk, which they seek to reduce by screening and monitoring borrowers and by demanding collateral. They also face interest rate risk, which they limit through loan sales, floating interest rates, and the trading of derivatives.

6. A bank run occurs when depositors lose confidence in a bank and make sudden, large withdrawals. A run can cause a previously healthy bank to fail. It can result from self-fulfilling expectations: people withdraw money because they expect withdrawals by others.

7. Deposit insurance, a promise by the government to compensate depositors if a bank fails, prevents bank runs because it makes depositors confident that their money is safe.

8. Bankers have incentives to misuse deposits by taking on excessive risk or by looting. Deposit insurance exacerbates this moral hazard problem because it reduces depositors' incentives to monitor banks.

9. U.S. banks are heavily regulated by a variety of federal and state agencies. Regulators seek to reduce the risk of bank failure by restricting the riskiness of banks' assets and by requiring minimum levels of capital.

10. One part of bank regulation is supervision and monitoring of banks' activities. Banks must file quarterly call reports on their finances and submit to on-site examinations at least once a year.

KEY CONCEPTS

Commercial bank
Savings institution
Credit union
Finance company
Community bank
Subprime lender
Payday lender
Pawnshop
Loan shark
Securitization
Mortgage-backed securities

Balance sheet
Liabilities
Net worth
Reserves
Return on assets
Return on equity
Liquidity management
Federal funds
Credit risk
Collateral
Interest rate risk

Floating interest rate
Insolvency
Equity ratio
Bank run
Bank panic
Deposit insurance
Federal Deposit Insurance Corporation
Capital requirements
Bank supervision
Forbearance

QUESTIONS FOR REVIEW

1. Describe the similarities and differences between commercial banks and savings institutions.

2. Identify the four types of subprime lenders and explain how each one deals with the higher default risk of subprime loans.

3. Explain the process of how loans undergo securitization.

4. What are Fannie Mae and Freddie Mac? What are their links to the government in the past and at present?

5. Define the major items on the assets and liabilities sides of a bank's balance sheet.

6. If a bank has $100 million in assets and $80 million in liabilities, what is the bank's net worth?

7. What is credit risk? How does a bank limit its exposure to credit risk?

8. What is interest rate risk? How does a bank limit its exposure to interest rate risk?

9. Explain how deposit insurance works, the reasons that governments provide deposit insurance, and the problems that deposit insurance can create.

10. What are the main ways in which regulators try to prevent banks from misusing depositors' funds?

PROBLEMS AND APPLICATIONS

1. HSBC has $1 trillion in assets and operates in about 100 countries. It calls itself "the world's local bank." What business strategies does this phrase suggest? Why might these strategies be successful?

2. Securitization has spread from mortgages to student loans, auto loans, and credit-card debt. However, few loans to businesses have been securitized, except for loans guaranteed by the government's Small Business Administration. Explain why.

3. Suppose that loan sharks propose legislation to promote their industry. They want a legal right to break the kneecaps of loan defaulters.

   a. Suppose you were hired as a lobbyist for the loan sharks. What arguments could you make to support their proposal?

   b. How would you respond to these arguments if you oppose kneecap breaking?

4. Suppose that Duckworth's Bank starts with the balance sheet in Table 18-2. Then the bank sells $10 of loans for $10 of cash.

   a. What is the immediate effect on the balance sheet?

   b. After the loan sale, what additional transactions is the bank likely to make? What will the balance sheet look like after these transactions?

5. Suppose Hibbard's Finance Company raises most of its funds by issuing long-term bonds. It uses these funds for floating-rate loans.

   a. How does the company's rate-sensitivity gap differ from those of most banks?

   b. What deal could the company make with a bank to reduce interest rate risk for both parties?

6. Canada does not have institutions like Fannie Mae and Freddie Mac that securitize mortgages. How do you think this fact affects the types of mortgages offered by Canadian banks? (*Hint:* Think about interest rate risk.)

7. Suppose a bank has $200 million in assets, $10 million in profits, and $40 million in capital.

   a. What is the bank's return on assets?

   b. What is the bank's return on equity?

8. Suppose you are a depositor at Duckworth's Bank, which has the balance sheet shown in Table 18-2. Deposit insurance does not exist. You originally deposited your money in Duckworth's because its branch locations are more convenient than those of other banks.

   a. Suppose you know that Duckworth's other depositors plan to keep their money there. Should you do the same or withdraw your money and deposit it elsewhere?

b. Suppose you know that other depositors plan to make large withdrawals from Duckworth's. What should you do?

c. What do your answers to parts (a) and (b) tell you about the likelihood and causes of bank runs?

9. Suppose an economy has a high level of loans from one bank to another. How might this fact affect the likelihood of a bank panic?

10. Some economists suggest that banks should be charged premiums for deposit insurance based on their levels of capital. Premiums should be higher if capital is lower. What is the rationale for this proposal? Are there any drawbacks to the idea?

11. Consider an analogy (the type on the SATs): "A bank regulator is to a bank as a bank is to a borrower." In what ways is this analogy true?

12. Consider two possibilities: (i) A bank is forced to close even though there is no good reason for it to close; (ii) A bank remains open even though there *are* good reasons for it to close.

a. Explain why (i) and (ii) are possible and what regulations affect the likelihood of these outcomes.

b. Can some combination of regulations make both (i) and (ii) unlikely?

13. Many states allow payday lending but impose restrictions on the practice. For example, a state may limit the amount someone can borrow or the number of times a loan can be rolled over. Find out whether payday lending is legal in your state and, if so, what restrictions exist. How stringent are these restrictions compared to those in other states?

14. Go to the Web site of the Office of the Comptroller of the Currency and look up "enforcement actions." Find an example of a specific enforcement action against a bank. Explain what the OCC did and what problem it was trying to rectify.

UNCORRECTED PAGES

Financial Crises

There was a time when the credit markets had essentially frozen and when blue chip industrial companies were having trouble raising money. I knew then we were on the brink...We easily could have had unemployment of 25 percent."

—Henry M. Paulson (former Treasury Secretary),
commenting on the state of the U.S. economy in 2008

Throughout this book, we have seen that many kinds of shocks can decrease an economy's output in the short run. Examples include increases in taxes, decreases in consumer confidence, and increases in oil prices. However, one kind of shock is especially devastating to an economy: a **financial crisis**. Such a major disruption of the financial system typically involves sharp falls in asset prices and failures of financial institutions. In the United States, a financial crisis in the early 1930s triggered the Great Depression. A U.S. crisis that started in 2007 produced a recession that by many measures was the worst since the Depression. Financial crises have also damaged economies around the world, such as those of Argentina in 2001 and Greece in 2009–2010.

Regardless of where or when they occur, financial crises are complex events; the feedbacks among different parts of the financial system and the economy make them dangerous and difficult to stop. To understand crises, we must understand the workings of financial markets and the banking system (the topics of Chapters 15–18), the short-run behavior of the aggregate economy (Chapters 9–12), and the effects of macroeconomic policies (Chapters 13–14).

In this chapter, we first look at the events in a typical financial crisis and the various ways in which governments and central banks respond to them. We then use this background to examine what happened to the United States starting in 2007 and discuss some of the reforms that have been proposed in the wake of this crisis to make future financial crises less likely or less severe. Finally, we explore financial crises in emerging economies and what makes them different from those in advanced economies, including the role of the International Monetary Fund in combating crises.

19-1 The Mechanics of Financial Crises

No two financial crises are exactly alike, but most share a few basic features. We first discuss what happens to the financial system in a crisis and then look at how a crisis affects the rest of the economy.

Events in the Financial System

At the center of most crises are declines in asset prices, failures of financial institutions caused by insolvency or liquidity crises, or some combination of these events.

Asset-Price Declines A crisis may be triggered by large decreases in the prices of stocks, real estate, or other assets. Many economists interpret these decreases as the ends of asset-price bubbles. Recall from Chapter 16 that a bubble occurs when asset prices rise far above the present value of the expected income from the assets. Then, at some point, sentiment shifts: people begin to worry that asset prices are too high and start selling the assets, pushing prices down. Falling prices shake confidence further, leading to more selling, and so on. Asset prices may fall over periods of months or years, or a crash may occur in the course of a single day.

Insolvencies In a typical crisis, decreases in asset prices are accompanied by failures of financial institutions. An institution may fail because it becomes insolvent; that is, its assets fall below its liabilities and its net worth (capital) becomes negative. A commercial bank can become insolvent because of loan defaults, increases in interest rates, and other events. When a bank becomes insolvent, regulators are likely to force its closure.

Other kinds of financial institutions can also become insolvent. Hedge funds, for example, borrow money from banks to purchase risky assets. If the prices of these assets decline, a fund's net worth can become negative. When this happens, the fund is likely to default on its debts and go out of business.

Insolvencies can spread from one institution to many others because financial institutions have debts to one another. Banks have deposits at other banks, lend to one another in the federal funds market, and lend to hedge funds and investment banks. If one institution fails, its depositors and lenders suffer losses, and they, in turn, may become insolvent.

Liquidity Crises Even if a financial institution is initially solvent, it can fail because it doesn't have enough liquid assets to make payments it has promised. The classic example of a liquidity crisis is a bank run. Depositors lose confidence in a bank, try to withdraw large amounts from their accounts, and exhaust the bank's reserves and liquid securities. To make the payments it has promised its depositors, the bank must sell its illiquid assets at fire-sale prices (less than the assets' true value), and losses on these transactions can push it into insolvency.

Liquidity crises can also occur at nondepository institutions, such as hedge funds and investment banks. These institutions often raise funds by making short-term loans and issuing *commercial paper* (short-term bonds). To stay in business, they must raise new funds continuously to pay off maturing debts. If creditors lose confidence and cut off funding, an institution can be forced into a fire sale of its illiquid assets, leading to insolvency.

Liquidity crises can spread from one financial institution to another largely for psychological reasons. If a bank experiences a run, for example, depositors at other banks start worrying about the safety of their own funds. They may start making withdrawals, thus triggering an economy-wide bank panic and widespread failures.

Financial Crises and the Economy

Financial crises have both direct and indirect costs. The direct costs include losses to asset holders when asset prices fall. They also include losses from financial institution failures. Owners of a failed institution lose their equity, and the institution's creditors lose funds they have lent. When a failed institution is a bank, losses also fall on uninsured depositors and the Federal Deposit Insurance Corporation (FDIC).

Although these direct costs can be large, the greatest costs from financial crises come from their indirect effects. A crisis can set off a chain of events that plunges the whole economy into a recession. Figure 19-1 summarizes the key parts of this process.

Lending and Spending A fall in asset prices can cause a sharp fall in aggregate demand. One reason is that asset holders suffer a loss of wealth, which leads them to reduce their consumption. Falling asset prices also shake the confidence of firms and consumers, who may interpret them as signs that the overall economy is in trouble. Uncertain of the future, they put off major decisions about spending until things settle down, and investment and consumption fall.

A fall in asset prices also makes it harder for individuals and firms to borrow. Lower prices decrease the value of borrowers' collateral, which is required to overcome adverse selection and moral hazard in loan markets. The result is a **credit crunch**, a sharp decrease in bank lending. Some borrowers are cut off from loans or face higher interest rates.

Failures of financial institutions also cause a credit crunch. When commercial banks fail, they stop lending. Surviving banks may fear failure and become more conservative in approving loans. They may also reduce loans in order to increase their liquid assets and guard against runs. When investment banks fail, securitization falls, which reduces the funds available for bank loans.

A credit crunch means less spending by firms and individuals who rely on credit. This decrease in investment and consumption reduces aggregate demand, adding to the direct effect of asset-price declines. In the short run, a fall in aggregate demand reduces output. In this way, a crisis can cause a deep recession.

A Vicious Circle Unfortunately, that's not the end of the story. If a financial crisis causes a recession, the recession can then exacerbate the crisis. Asset prices are likely to fall further. For example, stock prices fall because the recession reduces firms' expected profits, and real estate prices fall because of lower demand for real estate.

FIGURE 19-1

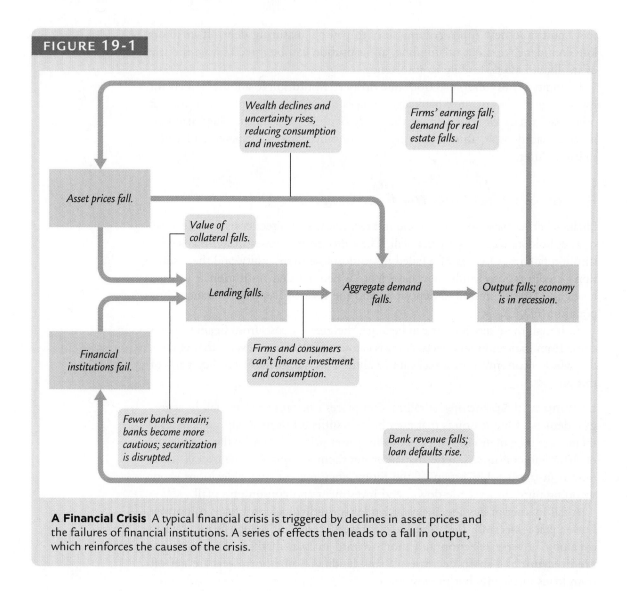

A Financial Crisis A typical financial crisis is triggered by declines in asset prices and the failures of financial institutions. A series of effects then leads to a fall in output, which reinforces the causes of the crisis.

A recession also worsens the problems of financial institutions. Banks lose revenue because a recession reduces the demand for loans. Firms go bankrupt, increasing loan defaults. Worries about these problems make bank panics more likely. For all these reasons, bank failures rise during a recession.

Because of these feedbacks, a financial crisis can trigger a vicious circle of falling output and worsening financial problems. Once a crisis starts, it can sustain itself for a long time.

So far we've discussed the most common elements of crises. Crises often have additional wrinkles—other ways they hurt the economy and build on themselves. To see how much can go wrong, let's examine the Great Depression of the 1930s. Chapter 11 analyzed that disaster using the *IS–LM* model; here, we see that our model of financial crises can shed further light on this historic event.

Disaster in the 1930s

The Depression began in the early 1930s with a financial crisis that had the classic ingredients of falling asset prices and failures of financial institutions. The fall in asset prices started with a stock market crash: on October 28, 1929, the Dow Jones Index fell 13 percent. After the crash, stock prices kept falling: the Dow Index fell from 365 before the crash to 41 in 1932, a decrease of 89 percent.

The stock market crash created great uncertainty about the economy because a crash of this size was an unprecedented event. Uncertainty led firms and consumers to postpone major purchases, such as automobiles, so aggregate demand fell.

A wave of bank failures then rolled across the country from 1930 to 1933. Midwestern banks failed when farmers defaulted on loans, and these failures made people nervous about other banks. Eventually a series of panics swept the country as depositors lost confidence and, with no deposit insurance to protect them, rushed to withdraw funds. President Franklin Roosevelt eventually ended the panics with the bank holiday of March 1933, but more than a third of all U.S. banks failed.

Falling stock prices and massive bank failures reduced bank lending dramatically, resulting in a credit crunch. Because firms and individuals couldn't borrow, investment and consumption fell, causing a decrease in aggregate demand.

As usual in crises, falling aggregate demand and hence falling output magnified the problems of the financial system, especially the stock market. With the economy depressed, firms' earnings prospects were bleak. Stock prices stayed low: it took until 1954 for the Dow Index to climb back to its 1929 level.

As we discussed in Chapter 11, a special twist in this episode was a sharp fall in the money supply, a result of the Federal Reserve's passive response to the bank panics. This development led to deflation: the aggregate price level fell by 22 percent from 1929 to 1933. Deflation in turn increased the real burden of debts, causing many borrowers, especially farmers, to default on bank loans. These defaults further weakened banks and prolonged the severe credit crunch. The Depression was made "Great" because so many problems occurred at the same time. ■

19-2 Financial Rescues

A financial crisis is a vicious circle in which problems in the financial system and falling aggregate demand reinforce one another. Governments and central banks seek to break this cycle. They do so partly with expansionary fiscal and monetary policies, which boost demand. In crises, however, policy actions are typically not limited to these standard macroeconomic tools. Policymakers also take a range of actions aimed directly at reducing the problems of the financial system, especially the failures of financial institutions.

Generally these policies involve the use of government or central-bank funds to prevent institutions from failing or to compensate individuals or firms that are hurt by failures. In popular discussion, such policies are often called *bailouts*. This umbrella term is imprecise, however, because it is used for policies that vary widely. Bailouts range from giveaways of government money to loans or asset purchases that are costless or even profitable for taxpayers. This section explores some policy actions aimed at ending a financial crisis and looks at the debate about their benefits and costs.

Liquidity Crises and the Lender of Last Resort

Liquidity crises at financial institutions, such as bank panics, are one cause of broader financial crises. A liquidity crisis can push a solvent institution into insolvency, causing it to fail for no good reason. Most economists think policymakers should try to prevent such occurrences.

Fortunately, a central bank has a simple solution for liquidity crises. It can make emergency loans to institutions that are running out of liquid assets, allowing them to avoid fire sales of their illiquid assets. A borrowing institution remains solvent and repays the central bank when its liquidity crisis subsides. To ensure repayment, the central bank requires the borrower to pledge some of its assets as collateral for the loan.

A financial institution facing a liquidity crisis needs help from the central bank because it has trouble borrowing from other private institutions. Potential lenders are wary of an institution that could be driven into insolvency and default on its debts. When the central bank steps in, it acts as **lender of last resort** to an institution with no other source of funds.

When Congress established the Federal Reserve in 1913, the main purpose was to create a lender of last resort for U.S. banks. Unfortunately, during the bank panics of the early 1930s, the Fed underestimated the danger to the banking system and the economy and therefore did not lend to many banks. The Fed learned from this mistake and has acted quickly in more recent liquidity crises.

Deposit insurance helps prevent bank runs, thus reducing the need for a lender of last resort, but it does not eliminate the need entirely. Some banks raise most of their funds through borrowing and deposits that exceed the limit on insurance. These uninsured funds disappear quickly if depositors and lenders lose confidence in a bank. A lender of last resort is needed for such an emergency.

In the United States, a loan from the Federal Reserve to a bank is called a **discount loan**. A bank facing a liquidity crisis can apply for such a loan, which the Fed approves if it judges that the bank is solvent and can post sufficient collateral. The Fed sets the interest rate on discount loans, the *discount rate*, at a level higher than the federal funds rate, the rate on overnight loans between banks. This policy encourages banks to borrow from one another in normal times and to approach the Fed only in emergencies when they can't borrow elsewhere.

Discount loans are available only to commercial banks and savings institutions, financial institutions that fit the definition of "bank": they accept deposits and make loans. At times, however, the Fed has stretched its role as lender of last resort by providing liquidity to other financial institutions. After the terrorist attacks of September 11, 2001, for example, the Fed encouraged banks to lend to securities firms facing liquidity crises; in turn, the Fed promised to lend any necessary funds to the banks. As we discuss later in this chapter, the Fed lent money directly to securities firms during the financial crisis of 2007–2009.

Giveaways of Government Funds

When a central bank acts as lender of last resort, it helps a solvent institution facing a liquidity crisis. The loan prevents the institution from failing, and it is repaid with interest. Ultimately, there is no cost to the central bank, the government, or taxpayers.

Not all failures of financial institutions are caused by liquidity crises. Sometimes an institution simply loses money, so its assets fall below its liabilities and it becomes insolvent. Normally, this causes the institution to fail and default on its debts. In some cases, however, policymakers intervene to prevent this outcome. Instead of lending to an institution, the government or central bank gives money away. It may give funds to the failing institution to restore its solvency and keep it in business. Alternatively, it may let the institution fail but compensate other individuals and institutions that are hurt by the failure.

Deposit insurance commits the government to paying part of the costs of bank failures. The FDIC compensates depositors for their losses up to some limit. Today, few economists question the desirability of deposit insurance, at least in countries with effective bank regulation. The controversial issue is whether compensation should extend beyond promised insurance payments. When a bank fails, should the government protect uninsured depositors and creditors? Should it aid institutions with no insurance guarantees, such as investment banks and hedge funds? Let's discuss the debate over these questions.

The Pros and Cons of Giveaways When the government gives away funds beyond required insurance payments, its purpose is to prevent the problems of an insolvent financial institution from spreading. As we've discussed, banks and other institutions deposit money and lend to one another. If one institution fails, it defaults on debts to other institutions, and their losses can cause them to fail. A rash of failures can produce a financial crisis and push the economy into a recession. The government can prevent this outcome by preventing the first institution from failing or by compensating other institutions for losses from the initial failure.

Such government intervention has two kinds of costs. The first is the direct costs of payments from the government. These costs are ultimately borne by taxpayers. The second cost is a worsening of moral hazard, the problem that financial institutions may misuse the funds they raise.

In particular, the prospect of government aid makes it more likely that institutions will take excessive risks, lose money, and become insolvent. Normally, an institution's creditors and uninsured depositors monitor what happens to their money and cut off funds if the institution misuses them. But if the government intervenes when institutions face failure, everyone comes to expect protection from losses. Nobody has incentives to monitor, so institutions can easily raise funds to finance gambles. These institutions earn a lot if the gambles succeed, and if they lose, the losses fall largely on taxpayers.

When any given institution is in danger of failing, it's hard to know how badly the failure would damage the financial system. It's also hard to gauge how much a government rescue will increase moral hazard in the future. Because of these uncertainties, economists differ sharply on the desirability of government intervention.

Too Big to Fail Historically, decisions about whether to rescue an insolvent financial institution have been influenced strongly by the institution's size. A large institution has more links to other institutions than a small one does. It is likely to borrow heavily, and if it is a bank, it is likely to hold deposits from other banks. Consequently, regulators fear that the failure of a large institution threatens the financial system, whereas the failure of a small institution is relatively harmless. In other words, some financial institutions are deemed **too big to fail (TBTF)**.

This term was coined by a congressman after the rescue of Continental Illinois Bank in 1984, an episode discussed in the following case study.

CASE STUDY

The Continental Illinois Rescue

Before 1984, the U.S. government had never extended significant aid to an insolvent financial institution beyond promised payments on deposit insurance. That changed when Continental Illinois, then the nation's seventh-largest commercial bank, ran into trouble. Continental had lent heavily to energy companies and to the governments of developing countries, and both groups defaulted during a worldwide recession in the early 1980s. In May 1984, Continental was on the brink of failure.

Regulators feared that the failure of Continental Illinois would have widespread effects. Over 2,000 smaller banks had accounts at Continental. For 66 of these banks, deposits at Continental exceeded their total capital; for another 113, the deposits were more than half of their capital. Regulators feared that many of these banks would fail if they lost their deposits, shaking confidence in the financial system. The comptroller of the currency, the head regulator of national banks, said after the crisis that Continental's failure would have caused "a national, if not international, financial crisis the dimensions of which were difficult to imagine."[1]

Policymakers acted aggressively to save Continental. Despite the bank's insolvency, the Fed lent it $3.6 billion to keep it in operation. The FDIC promised to protect all of Continental's creditors and depositors, waiving the usual limit on insurance. Eventually, the FDIC bought Continental from its shareholders, added capital, and sold it to Bank of America. In the process, the FDIC lost about $1 billion.

These actions were controversial at the time, and they remain so. Critics stress the moral hazard problem and argue that policymakers overstated the risks from

---

[1] Todd Conover, testimony before House Banking Committee, September 19, 1984.

a failure of Continental. The debate over treating some institutions as too big to fail continued in the years after the Continental rescue and intensified during the financial crisis of 2007–2009. ■

Risky Rescues

The potential failure of a large financial institution creates a dilemma for policymakers. Letting the institution fail and default on its debts can damage the financial system, but preventing this outcome is costly for taxpayers and creates moral hazard. Policymakers wrestled with this dilemma repeatedly during the financial crisis of 2007–2009. Looking for a compromise between inaction and giveaways of government funds, they developed two new ways to aid troubled financial institutions: risky loans and equity injections. Unlike loans to solvent institutions facing liquidity crises, these policies expose taxpayers to a risk of losing money. On the other hand, unlike traditional giveaways of government funds, risky loans and equity injections *may not* cost the government anything and might even earn money. Let's discuss these policies and the rationale for using them.

Risky Loans In this type of rescue, the central bank moves beyond its traditional role as lender of last resort, in which it makes *riskless* loans to solvent institutions. When the central bank makes risky loans to prevent failures of financial institutions, it is not certain the loans will be paid back.

Chapter 17 touched on examples of risky loans by the Federal Reserve. In some cases, the Fed has taken on risk by lending to institutions that might fail. In September 2008, for example, it lent $85 billion to the insurance conglomerate AIG, which was near bankruptcy because of losses on credit default swaps. This loan prevented AIG from defaulting immediately on debts to other institutions, but it meant the Fed was on the hook for $85 billion if, as many feared, AIG declared bankruptcy later.

In other cases, the Fed has taken on risk by lending against collateral of uncertain value. In March 2008, it lent $29 billion to JP Morgan Chase to finance the takeover of the investment bank Bear Stearns. The collateral was some of Bear's holdings of subprime mortgage backed securities—the securities whose decline in value had pushed Bear to the brink of bankruptcy. Crucially, the loan to JP Morgan was made *without recourse*: if the value of the collateral declined further, the Fed would be entitled only to the collateral, not the $29 billion it had lent. The Fed stood to lose if the subprime crisis worsened.

During the crisis of 2007–2009, many economists and politicians criticized the Fed for risking money on troubled financial institutions. Fed officials argued, however, that the risks were modest. Part of their rationale was that the Fed's actions would ease the financial crisis, which in turn would reduce the risk that its debtors would default or that the value of their collateral would fall. That is, by agreeing to accept some of the potential losses from the financial crisis, the Fed hoped to prevent these losses from occurring. This strategy was similar to the logic of deposit insurance: by agreeing to bear the costs of a harmful event (bank runs), the government makes the event less likely.

Equity Injections A financial institution becomes insolvent when its capital or equity falls below zero. It can restore solvency and stay in business if it raises new capital by issuing stock. If an institution is troubled, however, individuals and private firms may not be willing to buy its stock. This problem is the rationale for **equity injections**, or purchases of stock, by the government. The U.S. Treasury Department pioneered this rescue policy in 2008 and 2009.

In buying the stock of a financial institution, the government provides the institution with capital to ensure its solvency. Like any purchaser of stock, the government receives an ownership share in the institution and it takes on risk. If the institution ultimately fails, or if it requires further assistance to survive, the government can lose money. On the other hand, the government can earn a profit on behalf of taxpayers if the institution recovers and its stock price rises. Equity injections are controversial because opinions vary on the government's likely gains or losses.

Government purchases of stock are also controversial because they deviate from a financial system based on free markets. Critics argue that the behavior of government-owned institutions may be influenced by politics. In 2008, for example, the Treasury imposed restrictions on executive pay as a condition for purchasing stock. Many voters supported such restrictions, believing that executives who had played a role in the financial crisis should not receive huge salaries and bonuses. Critics argued that high pay was needed to retain the most talented executives and that the government should not interfere with the market forces determining salaries.

19-3 The U.S. Financial Crisis of 2007–2009

The Great Depression of the 1930s showed how a financial crisis can have devastating macroeconomic repercussions. For many years after World War II, however, no such crisis caused an economic upheaval in the United States. Bank failures during the savings-and-loan crisis of the 1980s cost the government $124 billion and embarrassed regulators, but the episode had modest effects on the overall economy. In the 1990s and into the 2000s, failures of financial institutions were rare. Many economists credited the bank regulation described in Chapter 18 for keeping the financial system safe.

More generally, the 1990s and early 2000s were a period of stability in the U.S. economy. The high inflation of the 1970s and the deep recession caused by the disinflation of the 1980s joined the Great Depression in the history books. Economists often referred to the 1990s and 2000s as the "Great Moderation" because of its low inflation and steady output growth.

Over 2007–2009, everything changed. The United States experienced a 55 percent fall in the stock market, the failures of some of the country's most prestigious financial institutions, and a disruption in lending throughout the economy. The worst recession since the 1930s pushed the unemployment rate from under 5 percent in 2007 to over 10 percent in late 2009.

As with any disaster, controversy abounds about what events were critical and who deserves the blame. With hindsight, however, we can see that a series of adverse events had central roles in the financial crisis. The timeline in Figure 19-2 summarizes these events and also shows the unprecedented responses of the government and Federal Reserve to the crisis. Some economists have bitterly criticized these actions, although others think they saved the economy from an even worse fate—a collapse that could have rivaled the 1930s for the worst economic disaster in U.S. history.

2006-2007

The Subprime Crisis and the First Signs of Panic

In 2006 and 2007, as housing prices fell and defaults on subprime mortgages rose, it became increasingly clear that institutions that had made subprime loans would suffer large losses. Two large finance companies that specialized in subprime mortgages, New Century Financial and Ameriquest, declared bankruptcy in April and August 2007, respectively. Other financial institutions that held securities backed by subprime mortgages suffered billions of dollars of losses, leading firms such as Citigroup and Morgan Stanley to fire their chief executives in 2007.

Yet few saw the subprime crisis as a threat to the entire financial system or economy. In mid-2007, economists estimated that financial institutions might lose a total of $150 billion on subprime mortgages—not pocket change, but not a lot compared to the U.S. annual GDP of $14 trillion.

The Liquidity Crisis of August 2007 Warning signs of the economic disaster to come showed up in the summer of 2007. As losses on subprime mortgages rose, banks started to worry about one another. Could losses grow to the point that they pushed major institutions into insolvency? On August 9, the huge French investment bank BNP Paribus announced large losses on subprime mortgages, news that ratcheted up the fears of U.S. bankers. These fears showed up in the federal funds market, in which banks lend to one another. Lenders suddenly became scarce because banks questioned whether borrowers would be able to repay their loans.

On August 9 and 10, the scarcity of lenders pushed the federal funds rate far above the Federal Reserve's target of 5.25 percent. The Fed responded to this development with *open-market operations* in which it purchased large amounts of government bonds, pushing cash into the banking system and reducing interest rates.

Banks around the world remained worried about one another's solvency for the rest of 2007 and into 2008, causing some banks to have trouble raising funds. In September 2007, Northern Rock Bank in the United Kingdom ran short of liquid assets and asked the Bank of England, the nation's central bank, for a loan. News of this request caused depositors to lose confidence in Northern Rock, producing the United Kingdom's first bank run in over a century (see Chapter 18).

The Fed's Response In the United States, the Federal Reserve responded to the disruption of interbank lending by vigorously playing its role as lender of last

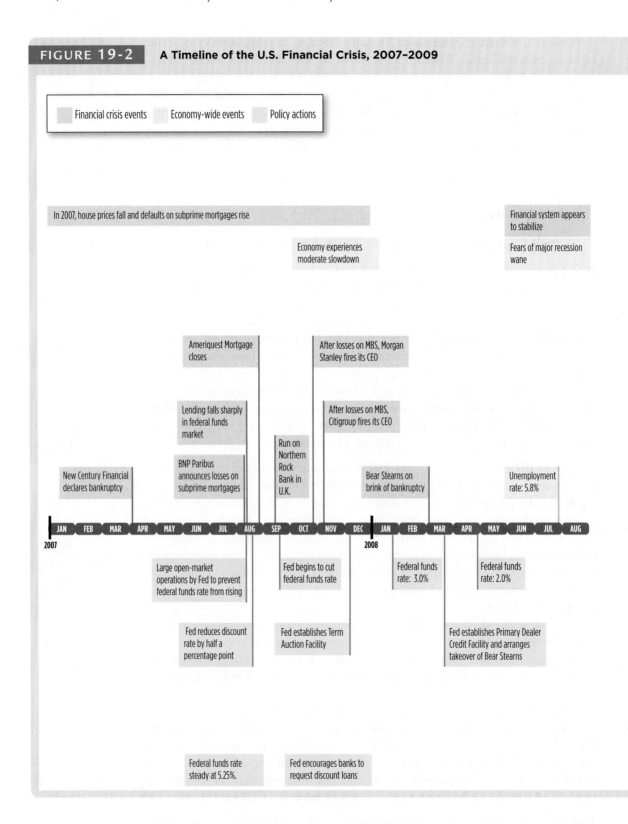

FIGURE 19-2 A Timeline of the U.S. Financial Crisis, 2007–2009

UNCORRECTED PAGES

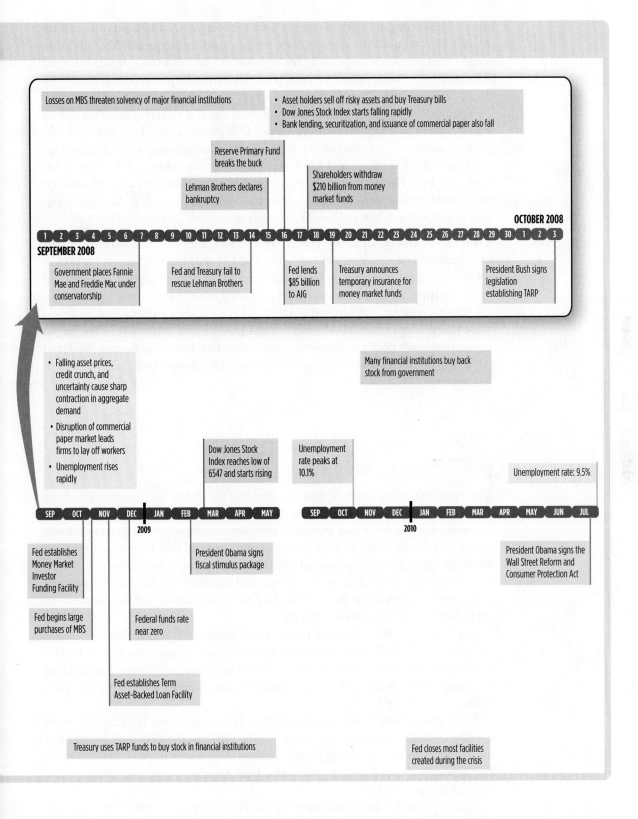

Losses on MBS threaten solvency of major financial institutions

- Asset holders sell off risky assets and buy Treasury bills
- Dow Jones Stock Index starts falling rapidly
- Bank lending, securitization, and issuance of commercial paper also fall

Reserve Primary Fund breaks the buck

Lehman Brothers declares bankruptcy

Shareholders withdraw $210 billion from money market funds

OCTOBER 2008

SEPTEMBER 2008

Government places Fannie Mae and Freddie Mac under conservatorship

Fed and Treasury fail to rescue Lehman Brothers

Fed lends $85 billion to AIG

Treasury announces temporary insurance for money market funds

President Bush signs legislation establishing TARP

- Falling asset prices, credit crunch, and uncertainty cause sharp contraction in aggregate demand
- Disruption of commercial paper market leads firms to lay off workers
- Unemployment rises rapidly

Many financial institutions buy back stock from government

Dow Jones Stock Index reaches low of 6547 and starts rising

Unemployment rate peaks at 10.1%

Unemployment rate: 9.5%

SEP OCT NOV DEC JAN FEB MAR APR MAY   SEP OCT NOV DEC JAN FEB MAR APR MAY JUN JUL

2009   **2010**

Fed establishes Money Market Investor Funding Facility

President Obama signs fiscal stimulus package

President Obama signs the Wall Street Reform and Consumer Protection Act

Fed begins large purchases of MBS

Federal funds rate near zero

Fed establishes Term Asset-Backed Loan Facility

Treasury uses TARP funds to buy stock in financial institutions

Fed closes most facilities created during the crisis

resort. It encouraged banks to request discount loans if they needed cash, and on August 16 it reduced the discount rate by half a percentage point. Yet few banks sought discount loans, apparently fearing that this action would signal weakness. The Northern Rock episode showed that requesting help from the central bank could backfire.

The low level of discount lending prompted the Fed to create the *Term Auction Facility (TAF)* in December 2007. Under this program, the Fed lent to banks through auctions. Every two weeks, it provided a predetermined level of loans (typically between $25 billion and $75 billion) to banks that submitted the highest interest rate bids. Banks were more eager to bid in these auctions than to take out traditional discount loans because the Fed took the lead in lending. Also, participation in auctions was not publicized as widely as requests for discount loans were.

Effects on the Economy Late 2007 also saw a moderate slowdown in the U.S. economy. Housing prices had started to fall, and the resulting reduction in wealth reduced consumption. Consumption and investment were also dampened by uncertainty about the economy, which partly reflected the signs of trouble in the financial system and partly the unfortunate coincidence that world oil prices were rising. Concerned about these developments, the Federal Reserve began easing monetary policy to boost aggregate demand. Between August 2007 and January 2008, it reduced its target for the federal funds rate from 5.25 percent to 3.0 percent.

2008

Bear Stearns and the Calm Before the Storm

The next unpleasant surprise was the near-failure of the investment bank Bear Stearns. As we discussed in Chapter 17, Bear held large quantities of subprime mortgage–backed securities and suffered mounting losses as the prices of these securities fell over 2007. In March 2008, rumors spread that Bear might become insolvent, and these fears produced a liquidity crisis. Bear relied heavily on short-term borrowing to fund its asset holdings, and much of this funding disappeared as lenders lost confidence in the firm. As Bear Stearns ran out of liquid assets, its lawyers prepared to file for bankruptcy.

On March 16, Bear Stearns's predicament produced the first financial rescue of the crisis: the Fed's risky loan to JP Morgan Chase to purchase Bear. The Fed acted out of fear that a failure of Bear would hurt other institutions that had lent it money. It also feared a blow to confidence that would trigger liquidity crises at other investment banks.

Some economists, however, thought the Fed's fears about Bear Stearns were overblown. They criticized the rescue for the risk that the Fed took on and the moral hazard created by saving Bear's creditors from losses. In April 2008, former Fed official Vincent Reinhart called the Bear Stearns rescue "the worst policy mistake in a generation."

Shortly after the Bear Stearns deal, the Fed made other efforts to head off problems in the financial system and economy. It once again reduced its target for the federal funds rate, taking it down to 2.0 percent at the end of March 2008. In the same month, the Fed sought to prevent liquidity crises by expanding its role as lender of last resort. It established the *Primary Dealer Credit Facility (PDCF)*, which offered loans to *primary dealers* in the government securities market—the institutions that trade with the Fed when it performs open-market operations. Primary dealers include the largest investment banks as well as commercial banks, so investment banks also became eligible for emergency loans from the Fed.

After the Bearn Stearns rescue, no major shocks hit the financial system for six months. Over the summer of 2008, fears about the solvency of financial institutions receded, and policymakers became hopeful that the economic damage from the financial drama would be modest. In June, Fed Chair Ben Bernanke said, "The risk that the economy has entered a substantial downturn appears to have diminished over the last month or so."

Disaster Strikes: September 7–19, 2008

Over two weeks in September 2008, optimism about the economy vanished as the financial crisis exploded. Bad news arrived at a dizzying pace.

Fannie and Freddie Face Insolvency Mounting losses on mortgage-backed securities threatened the solvency of Fannie Mae and Freddie Mac, the government-sponsored enterprises that securitize a large share of U.S. mortgages. On September 7, the government took Fannie and Freddie into conservatorship. Under this arrangement, the Treasury promised to cover Fannie and Freddie's losses with public funds so they wouldn't default on bonds they had issued. Default would have caused catastrophic losses to commercial banks and other financial institutions that held trillions of dollars of Fannie's and Freddie's bonds. A bankruptcy of Fannie or Freddie would also have disrupted mortgage lending, because many banks made loans with the expectation of selling them to Fannie or Freddie.

The government received stock that gave it 80 percent ownership stakes in Fannie and Freddie. Nonetheless, its action was in essence a pure giveaway of government funds. It was clear that Fannie and Freddie were insolvent and that the government would be giving them more money than their stock was worth. As of 2010, the Fannie and Freddie rescues had cost the government more than $200 billion.

Lehman Brothers' Bankruptcy Then came what many now consider the key blow to the financial system: the declaration of bankruptcy by the investment bank Lehman Brothers on September 15. Like Bear Stearns, Lehman had had large losses on mortgage-backed securities, taking it to the brink of failure. And once again, the Federal Reserve sought to arrange a takeover, in this case by the British bank Barclay's. But the deal fell through at the last minute, in part because of objections from British bank regulators.

It is unclear whether the Fed or the Treasury could still have saved Lehman. Ben Bernanke and Henry Paulson, the Secretary of the Treasury at the time, have said they did not have the legal authority to provide funds to Lehman after the Barclay's deal fell through. Critics contend that policymakers could have done something and that they misjudged the harm of letting Lehman fail. The Fed and the Treasury may have hesitated about acting aggressively because of the earlier negative reaction to the Bear Stearns rescue. A new rescue would have sparked harsh criticism that policymakers were worsening moral hazard yet again.

Lehman's failure shocked financial markets. The firm had been a pillar of the U.S. financial system since 1850, and it was the largest U.S. firm in any industry ever to file for bankruptcy. Everyone on Wall Street knew that Lehman was in trouble in September 2008, but many presumed that, like Bear Stearns, the firm would be taken over by a healthier institution.

Bankruptcy meant that Lehman defaulted on its borrowings from other financial institutions. Few people knew exactly how much Lehman owed or what institutions were its creditors, so fears arose that many institutions could suffer losses that threatened their solvency. In addition to the direct effects of Lehman's defaults, the failure of such a prestigious firm suggested that *any* financial institution could fail.

The events that followed Lehman's failure were sufficiently dire that it was the last big institution to declare bankruptcy throughout the crisis. Seeking to stem the financial panic, the Fed and the Treasury acted aggressively to save other institutions from Lehman's fate.

The Rescue of AIG Policymakers' new activism began on September 16, the day after the Lehman bankruptcy. The American International Group (AIG), the giant insurance conglomerate, was the next institution in line to fail until the Fed made an emergency loan of $85 billion. In explaining this action, Ben Bernanke said that a failure of AIG "could have resulted in a 1930s-style global financial and economic meltdown, with catastrophic implications for production, income, and jobs."

A bankrupt AIG would have defaulted on the $20 billion of commercial paper that it had issued. In addition, it would not have made promised payments on the credit default swaps it had sold on mortgage-backed securities. As a result, other institutions would not have been compensated for losses on the securities. Individuals and businesses that had purchased insurance policies from AIG would have seen their insurance coverage disappear suddenly.

The Money Market Crisis A final part of the September 2008 debacle involved money market mutual funds. These funds hold Treasury bills (short-term government bonds) and commercial paper (short-term corporate bonds) and sell shares to savers. The funds generally yield low returns but are considered safe because their assets have short maturities and low default rates. Since money market funds were invented in the 1970s, almost nobody who put a dollar in a money market fund ended up with less than a dollar. Many people have come to view money market funds as similar to bank accounts, which also yield low but safe returns.

The same day as the AIG rescue, however, one large money market fund, the Reserve Primary Fund, *broke the buck*: the value of a share in the fund, which originally cost $1, fell to 97 cents. The reason was simple: the fund owned large quantities of Lehman Brothers' commercial paper, which plummeted in value when Lehman declared bankruptcy. Suddenly people were reminded that a money market fund was *not* a bank account with a guaranteed return. And unlike bank deposits, government insurance does not cover shares in money market funds.

The result of the Reserve Primary Fund's breaking of the buck was a run on money market funds. In two days, September 17 and 18, panicked holders of money market shares withdrew $210 billion from the funds, reducing the funds' total assets by approximately 22 percent. This outflow slowed on September 19, when the Treasury Department announced it would temporarily offer insurance to money market funds. But confidence remained shaky, and the funds' assets slipped further over the next few months.

A Flight to Safety The quick succession of crises at major institutions created panic. Nobody knew what shock would come next, when the crisis would end, or how devastating it would be for the economy. This atmosphere led to a *flight to safety*. Financial institutions became fearful of any assets that appeared risky, including stocks, the bonds of corporations without top credit ratings, and securities backed by any kind of bank loans. Institutions dumped these assets and bought those they considered safest: three- and six-month Treasury bills. These Treasury bills were considered safe because it was unlikely that the government would default on its debt over the next six months, even in a financial crisis.

We can see some effects of the flight to safety in Figure 19-3, which shows data from financial markets over the period 2007–2009. Starting in September 2008, the Dow Jones Index of stock prices plummeted for six months, shown in panel (a). Securitization fell dramatically as demand for securitized loans disappeared, shown in panel (b). The prices of BAA-rated corporate bonds (bonds with moderate default risk) fell, which implied a sharp rise in their interest rates as measured by yield to maturity, shown in panel (c). In contrast, the flight to Treasury bills pushed their prices up and interest rates on them fell almost to zero, shown in panel (d).

An Economy in Freefall

Much of the financial crisis played out in the Wall Street area of lower Manhattan and in Washington, D.C., where financial institutions and policymakers grappled with the crisis. In the fall of 2008, however, the problems of Wall Street spread to Main Streets across the country, plunging the economy into a deep recession.

The story followed the broad pattern outlined in our basic model of a financial crisis, Figure 19-1, and in our review of the Great Depression of the 1930s. The stock market plunge and the accelerating decline in housing prices reduced consumers' wealth. The dramatic news from the financial system hit consumer confidence hard: from September to November 2008, the University of Michigan's survey of consumer confidence revealed one of the largest drops in the survey's 60-year history. Falling wealth and falling confidence caused a contraction in consumption spending.

Financial panic also caused a credit crunch with many dimensions. Banks became fearful of lending because losses on mortgages had reduced their capital,

FIGURE 19-3

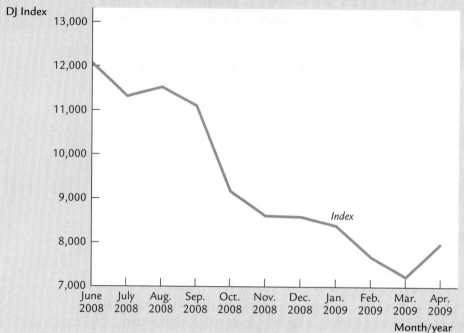

(a) Dow Jones Index of Stock Prices

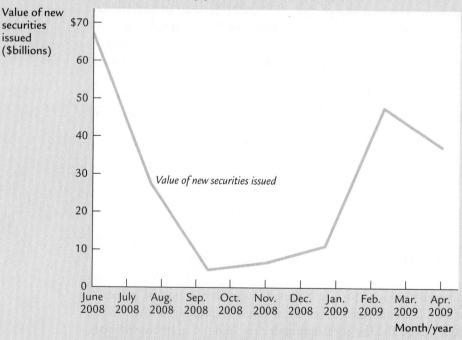

(b) Securitization of Bank Loans

The Flight to Safety, Fall 2008 In the panic following the failure of Lehman Brothers, financial institutions dumped any assets that appeared risky, causing a sharp fall in stock prices (panel a), a collapse in securitization of bank loans (panel b), and higher interest rates on corporate bonds with moderate default risk (panel c). A surge in the demand for Treasury bills, a safe asset, pushed the interest rate on Treasury bill near zero (panel d).

Sources: finance.yahoo.com, Securities Industry and Financial Market Association, and Federal Reserve Bank of St. Louis.

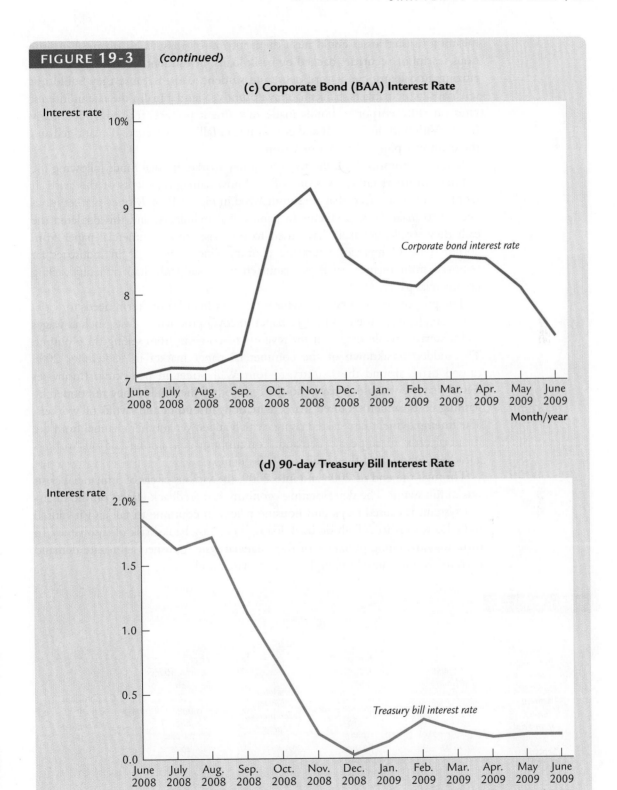

FIGURE 19-3 *(continued)*

(c) Corporate Bond (BAA) Interest Rate

Corporate bond interest rate

(d) 90-day Treasury Bill Interest Rate

Treasury bill interest rate

meaning further losses could push them into insolvency. With financial institutions fearful of securities backed by bank loans, investment banks stopped securitizing auto loans, credit-card debt, and student loans. Because they could not sell loans to securitizers, banks had fewer funds to lend. Finally, the rise in interest rates on risky corporate bonds made investment projects too costly for many firms. With both investment and consumption falling, aggregate demand fell and the economy plunged into a recession.

Some economists think the run on money market mutual funds following the Lehman Brothers failure was one of the most damaging events of the crisis. It set off a chain of effects that are summarized in Figure 19-4. Money market funds needed to make large payments to panicked shareholders, and this depleted the cash they would normally have used to purchase new commercial paper from corporations. Companies across the country—including those in industries far removed from finance, such as manufacturing—suddenly had difficulty selling commercial paper.

The purpose of commercial paper is to cover firms' short-term needs for cash. For example, firms use commercial paper to cover production costs, such as wages and materials, while they wait for revenue to come in from selling their output. The sudden breakdown of the commercial paper market in September 2008 caused firms around the country to join Wall Street in panicking. Businesses feared that they wouldn't have enough cash to pay their bills. They responded by slashing costs, which required sharp reductions in output and layoffs of workers. The unemployment rate started rising, which added yet another channel from the financial crisis to aggregate demand: consumption fell among laid-off workers and those who feared they might be laid off next.

Through the end of 2008 and into 2009, the vicious circle of a financial crisis was in full swing. The deteriorating economy had feedback effects on the financial system: it caused stock and housing prices to continue to fall and it caused more borrowers to default on bank loans, increasing banks' risk of insolvency. In turn, the worsening problems of the financial system pushed aggregate demand even lower and caused unemployment to rise rapidly.

FIGURE 19-4

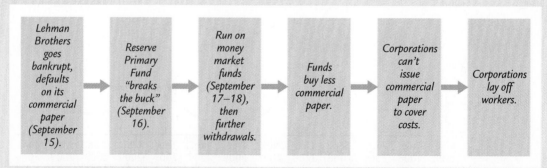

The Money Market Crisis, Fall 2008 A money market fund "broke the buck" in September 2008 and triggered a series of effects that worsened the financial crisis and increased unemployment.

The Policy Response

As the financial crisis accelerated in late 2008, so did the response of policymakers. Worries about excessive government interference in the economy were swept aside as the Federal Reserve and the Bush and Obama administrations took unprecedented actions to stave off disaster.

The TARP On October 3, 2008—18 days after the Lehman failure—President Bush signed an emergency Act of Congress establishing the *Troubled Asset Relief Program (TARP)*. The TARP committed $700 billion of government funds to rescue financial institutions.

The initial plan behind the TARP was for the government to purchase "troubled assets," primarily mortgage-backed securities. After the program was established, however, the Treasury decided to use most of the funds for equity injections: instead of purchasing the assets of financial institutions, it purchased shares in the institutions themselves. In late 2008 and early 2009, the Treasury became a major shareholder in most of the country's large financial institutions, ranging from Citigroup to Goldman Sachs to AIG.

Federal Reserve Programs Before the Lehman panic, the Fed had already sought to support the financial system with the Term Auction Facility (TAF) and the Primary Dealer Credit Facility (PDCF). In the fall of 2008, the Fed added half a dozen new programs, most with the bureaucratic title of "facility" in their names and with ugly acronyms. (This flurry of activity was reflected in the title of a speech by Fed Governor Kevin Warsh: "Longer Days and No Weekends.") The goals of the Fed's programs included repairing the commercial paper market, rejuvenating securitization, and pushing down interest rates on mortgages.

Monetary and Fiscal Policy Policymakers also sought to counter the economic downturn with the traditional tools of monetary and fiscal policy. From September to December 2008, the Federal Reserve cut its target for the federal funds rate from 2 percent to almost zero. The target was still near zero in the summer of 2010, as this book was going to press.

When President Obama took office in January 2009, one of his first priorities was fiscal stimulus. The next month, he signed a fiscal package passed by Congress that allocated about 5 percent of GDP to tax cuts and spending on infrastructure, such as roads and schools. The effects of the stimulus package are controversial, but one nonpartisan source, the Congressional Budget Office, estimated that it boosted real GDP by 1.5 to 3.5 percent.

2009 and Beyond

The Aftermath

Economists and policymakers will long debate the wisdom of Fed and Treasury actions during the financial crisis. Whatever the role of these policies, the financial system started returning to normal in 2009. Yet the broader economy remained troubled.

FYI

Specifics of Some Federal Reserve Responses to the Financial Crisis

The Federal Reserve's many actions in the fall of 2008 included the following:

➤ In October 2008, the Fed established the Money Market Investor Funding Facility (MMIFF). This program addressed the disruption of the commercial paper market after the run on money market funds. Under the MMIFF, the Fed lent money to banks that agreed to purchase commercial paper from money market funds. This arrangement helped the funds ensure that they could raise cash if their shareholders demanded it. In turn, as funds became less worried about withdrawals, they became more willing to buy commercial paper from corporations.

➤ In November, the Fed established the Term Asset-Backed Loan Facility (TALF). Under this program, the Fed lent to financial institutions such as hedge funds to finance purchases of securities backed by bank loans. The goal was to ease the credit crunch by encouraging the securitization process, which broke down during the post-Lehman panic. The Fed accepted the securities purchased under the program as collateral and its loans were without recourse, which meant the Fed took on the risk that the securities would fall in value.

➤ Also in November 2008, the Fed began purchasing mortgage-backed securities issued by Fannie Mae and Freddie Mac. The goal was to drive down interest rates on these securities and ultimately reduce rates on the mortgages behind the securities. Over a year, the Fed bought more than a trillion dollars' worth of mortgage-backed securities. Studies estimate that these purchases reduced mortgage rates by three- or four-tenths of a percentage point. The Fed hoped that lower rates would increase the demand for housing and help slow the fall in U.S. housing prices.[2]

The Financial Crisis Eases One sign that the financial system was beginning to recover was found in stock prices. The Dow Jones Index of stock prices hit a low of 6,547 in March 2009 and then rose 65 percent over the following 12 months. Fears of further failures of financial institutions waned, and institutions such as Goldman Sachs and Citigroup, which had lost billions of dollars in 2008, returned to profitability in 2009.

As the financial crisis eased, so did the need for the Federal Reserve's emergency lending programs. Borrowing under such programs as the TAF and PDCF dwindled over 2009, and the Fed quietly ended the programs in early 2010. Many financial institutions bought back the stock they had sold to the government under TARP. In the end, the government made money on many of these transactions, selling back the stock at higher prices than it paid.

Much of the money that the Fed and the Treasury poured into the most troubled institutions, including AIG, Fannie Mae, and Freddie Mac, will probably never be recouped. But overall, the direct costs of financial rescues proved modest relative to the economic damage (in terms of lost output and high unemployment) caused by the financial crisis. A government audit of TARP in 2010 estimated that it will eventually cost taxpayers $40 billion, a small fraction of the $700 billion put into the program.

---

[2] "Credit and Liquidity Policies," a page on the Fed Web site, www.frb.gov, catalogs the full range of Fed responses to the crisis.

Unemployment Persists After rising from under 5 percent before the crisis to 10 percent in late 2009, unemployment stayed high. In July 2010 (as this book was going to press), the unemployment rate was 9.5 percent, and economic forecasters predicted rates of 8 to 9 percent into 2011 and beyond.

Because the unemployment rate stayed high, more and more people found themselves jobless for long periods. In July 2010, workers who had been unemployed more than half a year accounted for 4.3 percent of the labor force, up from 0.7 percent two years earlier.

In most models of economic fluctuations—including those in Chapters 9–12 of this book—a recession causes a short-run rise in unemployment, but in the long run, unemployment returns to an unchanged natural rate. Since World War II, most U.S. recessions have followed this pattern. For example, unemployment rose from 6 percent in 1980 to over 10 percent in 1982, but then fell to 7 percent in 1984 and to 6 percent in 1987. The crisis of 2007–2009, however, may have longer-lasting effects. Chapter 12 discussed the theory of *hysteresis*, which posits that a recession can leave permanent scars on the economy, causing unemployment rates to remain high. Time will tell whether the aftermath of the financial crisis leads to a more prominent role for hysteresis in macroeconomic theory.

Constraints on Macroeconomic Policy With unemployment lingering at a high level, one might think that policymakers would seek to reduce it through expansionary fiscal or monetary policy. Unfortunately, in 2009–2010, both types of policy were severely constrained. The combination of the recession and the fiscal stimulus pushed the 2009 government budget deficit to about 10 percent of GDP, by far the highest level since World War II. This deficit exacerbated the problem of rising government debt, a long-term trend resulting from the costs of Social Security, Medicare, and Medicaid (see Chapter 14). Most economists and political leaders believed that the government couldn't afford further fiscal stimulus.

Starting in October 2008, monetary policy was constrained by the simple fact that the Fed's target for the federal funds rate was close to zero. As discussed in Chapter 11, a nominal interest rate cannot fall below zero because nobody would make a loan in return for negative interest. In 2009 and 2010, this **zero-bound problem** (also known as the *liquidity trap*) prevented the Fed from stimulating the economy. A zero interest rate was not low enough to produce a surge in aggregate demand that would push down unemployment.

As shown in Figure 13-2, a simple formula based on output and inflation—the Taylor rule—captures the broad movements in the federal funds rate from the mid-1980s until 2007. In 2009–2010, economists who used this rule to compute the appropriate federal funds rate came up with numbers around −3 or −4 percent. In effect, the zero bound was forcing the Federal Reserve to keep interest rates several points above the level needed to restore full employment.

Moral Hazard Problems Another legacy of the crisis was the precedent set by the government's rescues of financial institutions. Economists and political leaders agreed that these actions had worsened the problem of moral hazard, potentially setting the stage for increased risk taking and future crises. A consensus emerged that new government regulations were needed to protect the financial system and the economy.

UNCORRECTED PAGES

19-4 The Future of Financial Regulation

The crisis of 2007–2009 sparked intense debate about government regulation of financial institutions. How can the government prevent future crises or at least minimize the damage they inflict on the economy? Unfortunately, although many economists and political leaders advocate reform, there is little consensus about *what* new regulations are desirable. This section outlines the major ideas for financial reform in recent debates. Some of these ideas are being implemented under the Dodd-Frank Act (formally named the Wall Street Reform and Consumer Protection Act), which President Obama signed into law in July, 2010.

We can classify many proposals for financial reform within four broad categories: increased regulation of nonbank financial institutions, policies to prevent institutions from becoming too big to fail, rules that discourage excessive risk taking, and new structures for regulatory agencies. Table 19-1 lists some of the major reform proposals in each category.

Regulating Nonbank Financial Institutions

Commercial banks are heavily regulated in the United States. To reduce the risk of bank failures, regulators restrict the assets that banks can hold, impose capital

TABLE 19-1

Financial Reform Proposals

Problem	Proposed Reforms
Nonbank financial institutions are insufficiently regulated.	Impose regulations similar to those for commercial banks: restrictions on assets, capital requirements, supervision.
	Give a government agency resolution authority over failing institutions.
Some institutions are considered too big to fail.	Limit size of institutions.
	Tie capital requirements to size.
	Limit scope of institutions.
Financial institutions have incentives to take too much risk.	Require security issuers to have skin in the game.
	Reform ratings agencies.
	Restrict executive pay.
Multiple regulators lead to gaps in regulation.	Consolidate agencies that regulate financial institutions.
	Create new agency to oversee existing agencies and address systemic risk.
	Tighten regulation of financial holding companies.

requirements, and subject banks to frequent examinations to be sure they are not taking on too much risk. Nonbank financial institutions, such as investment banks, hedge funds, and insurance companies, do not face the same regulations. As a result, they have been able to engage in riskier behavior. They have held low levels of capital and high levels of risky assets, such as subprime mortgage–backed securities.

Why are banks and nonbank financial institutions treated differently? Part of the justification for bank regulation is the existence of government deposit insurance. The government is committed to compensating depositors if a commercial bank fails, so it has an interest in preventing risky behavior that might lead to failure. In addition, deposit insurance makes risky behavior more likely because it eliminates the incentive of depositors to monitor banks. In contrast, institutions such as investment banks have no deposits, so the government has not promised to pay anyone if the institutions fail. And without insurance, lenders to nonbank financial institutions have incentives to monitor their behavior.

The financial crisis has led economists and policymakers to question this traditional thinking. The crises at investment banks such as Bear Stearns and Lehman Brothers and at insurance giant AIG revealed that lenders to these institutions had not monitored them well enough to prevent excessive risk taking. And the absence of insurance did not mean the government could be indifferent to failures. The aftermath of the Lehman bankruptcy showed that the failure of an investment bank can potentially have significant adverse repercussions. To keep the financial crisis from getting worse, the government felt it had to rescue other institutions even though it was not obligated to them for any insurance payments.

To prevent this situation from recurring, many economists argue that the types of regulations previously reserved for commercial banks should be extended to other financial institutions. In the future, institutions such as investment banks and hedge funds may be required to hold more capital and fewer risky assets, and regulators may scrutinize their activities more closely.

Not surprisingly, financial institutions generally dislike the idea of greater regulation because restrictions on risky activities limit their profit-seeking opportunities. In addition, financial institutions and some economists argue that stricter regulation could stifle financial innovation. When financial engineers create new securities, their actions may appear risky but may actually improve the functioning of the financial system.

An example is the invention of junk bonds, an innovation of the 1970s that increased the number of corporations that could fund investment through the bond market. Securitization is another innovation that has, in some cases, been beneficial to borrowers and asset holders. Although the securitization of subprime mortgages proved disastrous, securitization of auto loans and student loans appears to have been a success. Securitization has provided funds for people to buy cars and go to school, and owners of securities have earned healthy returns. Overly restrictive regulations could impede such innovations, making the financial system less effective in channeling funds from savers to investors.

Ideally, regulations should be strict enough to prevent excessive risk taking yet not so restrictive that they impede productive financial innovation. Implementing this principle is difficult, however, because it is hard to predict which innovations will be successful and which will cause problems.

Another proposed reform would change how the government deals with failed financial institutions. Once again, the basic idea is to treat nonbank institutions more like commercial banks. As discussed in Chapter 18, an insolvent bank is taken over by the FDIC, which attempts to minimize the costs to taxpayers and the disruption of the economy. The FDIC can take time, for example, to find another institution that will take over the failed bank and keep the profitable parts of its business running.

In contrast, when a nonbank financial institution fails, it declares bankruptcy. This outcome may be inefficient, because it triggers a complicated legal process and increases uncertainty about the ultimate losses to creditors. Bankruptcy is also likely to bring the business of the financial institution to a halt, thus disrupting the activities of other institutions with which it does business. Bankruptcy can shake confidence in the whole financial system, as the Lehman bankruptcy revealed.

In the crisis of 2007–2009, Fed and Treasury officials felt it necessary to save financial institutions from failure with emergency loans and equity injections. Such risky rescues might become unnecessary if a regulatory agency gains *resolution authority* over nonbank institutions such as investment banks and hedge funds—the right to take them over when they become insolvent. Regulators could close or sell troubled institutions in an orderly fashion and potentially avoid a panic that threatens the financial system and the economy.

Addressing Too Big To Fail

Starting with Continental Illinois in 1984, policymakers have rescued institutions they deemed too big to fail. Institutions such as Continental, and later Bear Stearns and AIG, had large debts to other institutions and agreements such as promised payments on credit default swaps. The size of these firms and their interconnectedness with other institutions meant that their failure could trigger insolvencies throughout the financial system. Failures of smaller institutions may be less likely to pose this *systemic risk*.

One way for regulators to address TBTF is to prevent financial institutions from becoming too large or interconnected. Possible tools include restrictions on institutions' size or restrictions on their scope.

Restricting Size Some economists suggest limits on the amounts of assets or liabilities held by financial institutions. Currently, if a U.S. bank holds more than 10 percent of all deposits in the country, it cannot expand by acquiring another commercial bank. As of 2010, Bank of America was the only institution that had hit the 10 percent limit. To lessen the too-big-to-fail problem, this limit could be reduced to a level such as 5 or 2 percent. In addition, limits on assets or liabilities could be extended to nonbank institutions.

Regulators could also adopt less rigid policies. Rather than banning institutions above a certain size, they could create disincentives to growth. For example, capital requirements might be more stringent at larger institutions. The need to have more capital would reduce the risk that large institutions will fail. It would also discourage institutions from becoming overly large in the first place, because higher capital requirements reduce an institution's return on equity (see Chapter 18).

Such regulations would counter a half-century-long trend in which financial institutions have grown larger through mergers. The trend was facilitated by the repeal of past regulations, such as limits on the number of branches a bank can have and on interstate banking. Deregulation was motivated by a belief in *economies of scale*, the idea that large banks have lower costs per customer than small banks. Today, some economists argue that the danger that large banks pose to the financial system outweighs the benefits from economies of scale.

Restricting Scope Other proposed reforms would limit the scope of financial institutions by restricting the range of different financial businesses that one firm can operate. Such regulation would reduce the danger that problems in one part of an institution will hurt the other parts.

Arguably, such spillovers exacerbated the financial crisis of 2007–2009. For example, the investment banking unit within Citigroup, a giant financial conglomerate, lost billions of dollars on subprime mortgage–backed securities, reducing Citigroup's capital. The shortage of capital reduced lending in Citigroup's commercial banking units. These units include Citibank and the Student Loan Corporation, which stopped lending to students at two-year colleges. If Citigroup's investment banking and commercial banking divisions had been separate companies, the mistakes of investment bankers might not have made it harder for college students to borrow.

Like restrictions on institutions' size, restrictions on their scope would reverse a historical trend. The financial crisis of the early 1930s led to the Glass-Steagall Act of 1933, which required the separation of commercial banks from investment banks and insurance companies. This law was repealed in 1999, however, and many commercial banks merged with nonbank institutions to create conglomerates like Citigroup. Supporters of such mergers suggest that they create *economies of scope*: a conglomerate can operate as a *financial supermarket* where customers efficiently receive a range of financial services. For example, a corporation can establish a relationship with a single institution that lends to it and also underwrites its securities.

Once again, the recent financial crisis has led some economists to advocate reregulation in which conglomerates are required to break up or reduce their range of activities. Others believe that limits on institutions' scope are not necessary if regulation is improved along other dimensions.

Discouraging Excessive Risk Taking

In the view of most economists, excessive risk taking by financial institutions is a key cause of financial crises. In addition to extending regulation to more institutions and limiting their size and scope, reformers have proposed a variety of curbs on risky behavior. Here, we briefly review three of these ideas.

Requiring "Skin in the Game" Some financial reformers think that institutions that arrange risky transactions should take on some of the risk themselves: these firms should be required to have "skin in the game." For example, an investment bank that securitizes loans should have to hold a certain amount of the securities it creates. Behind this idea is the view that before the financial crisis, buyers of mortgage-backed securities were unaware of how risky the securities were. Requiring skin in the game gives financial institutions a disincentive to create overly risky products.

Reforming Ratings Agencies This idea, too, arises from the belief that buyers of mortgage-backed securities did not understand their risks. *Ratings agencies* such as Moody's Investor Services and Standard & Poor's evaluate the risk of securities and assign them letter grades. Before the financial crisis, ratings agencies gave many subprime mortgage–backed securities the highest possible rating, AAA, which greatly understated their riskiness.

Critics suggest that one reason this happened stemmed from the way ratings agencies earn money: they are hired and paid by the issuers of the securities they rate. Raters are likely to get more business if they inflate the grades they assign. This conflict of interest could be lessened through a new source of revenue for ratings agencies—a tax on financial institutions is one idea—or by having regulators review the agencies' ratings.

Reforming Executive Compensation Executives at many financial institutions receive annual bonuses of millions of dollars if profits for the year are high. This practice encourages the executives to take high-risk gambles that may yield high returns. (They aren't required to pay millions of dollars if the gambles fail.) Recall that in 2008 the Treasury imposed limits on executive compensation as a condition for equity injections under the TARP. Some economists and Congress members think that such limits should exist all the time, while others object to allowing the government to regulate pay at private firms.

Changing Regulatory Structure

A variety of federal and state agencies regulate banks in a complex system that reflects the historical evolution of regulation rather than any logical plan. At the federal level alone, some commercial banks are regulated by the Office of the Comptroller of the Currency and some by the Federal Reserve. Until 2010, the Office of Thrift Supervision regulated savings institutions.

Investment banks are regulated by the federal Securities and Exchange Commission (SEC). The Federal Reserve has sometimes resisted calls to restrict risk taking by investment banks on the grounds that they are the SEC's responsibility. Yet the SEC's main objective has been to prevent fraudulent activities by securities market participants, such as the falsification of accounting information by companies that issue stock. The SEC has not focused on ensuring the solvency of nonbank financial institutions.

Many economists argue that gaps and inconsistencies in regulation enabled the risky behavior that produced the financial crisis of 2007–2009. Some believe the government should abolish existing regulatory agencies and consolidate their responsibilities in one new agency. An alternative is to preserve existing agencies but add one that coordinates regulation. The creation of such an agency, the Financial Services Oversight Council (FSOC), was a centerpiece of the 2010 regulatory reforms. The FSOC will watch for dangers to the entire financial system, not just insolvency risk at individual institutions.

One gap in current regulation involves *financial holding companies (FHCs)*, conglomerates such as Citigroup that have units in different financial businesses. The Federal Reserve is responsible for regulating FHCs, but in the past it has largely confined itself to reviewing FHC mergers with and acquisitions of other institutions. Different units of FHCs are regulated by different agencies— commercial banking units by various bank regulators, investment banking by the SEC, and insurance businesses by state insurance commissions. As we have discussed, problems in one unit of an FHC can hurt other units. In the future, the Federal Reserve may take responsibility for monitoring risky activities in all parts of an FHC.

<h2>CASE STUDY</h2>

The Financial Reforms of 2010

In July 2010, Congress passed the Dodd-Frank Act and President Obama signed it into law. The act puts into practice some of the reform ideas discussed in this section. Its most important provisions include the following:

- As mentioned earlier, a new Financial Services Oversight Council (FSOC) will coordinate financial regulation. The Secretary of the Treasury will chair the council and it will include representatives from the Federal Reserve, the SEC, the FDIC, the Office of the Comptroller of the Currency, and other agencies. To streamline regulation, the Office of Thrift Supervision is abolished.

- A new Office of Credit Ratings will examine rating agencies annually and publish reports on their performance.

- The FDIC gains the authority to take over and close a nonbank financial institution if its troubles create systemic risk. Costs to the FDIC will be repaid through fees from financial institutions. Most failures of financial institutions—failures that do not endanger the financial system—will still trigger traditional bankruptcy proceedings.

- Financial holding companies that own banks are prohibited from sponsoring hedge funds, a step toward separating banks and securities firms.

- Issuers of certain risky securities, including mortgage-backed securities, must have skin in the game: they must retain at least 5 percent of the default risk on the securities.

The new legislation also empowers the FSOC and the Federal Reserve to create additional regulations, including stricter capital requirements and supervision of nonbank financial institutions. The FSOC and Fed can also force a large financial holding company to break up if it poses a grave threat to the financial system. The Office of Credit Ratings has the right to create new regulations governing rating agencies. In the coming years, we will see how aggressively the FSOC, Fed, and Office of Credit Ratings use their new authority.

The Senate passed the financial reforms by a vote of 60 to 39 and the House of Representatives by 237 to 192. Almost all Democrats supported the act and almost all Republicans opposed it. Democrats hailed the act as a foundation for a healthy financial system; Republicans predicted it would reduce efficiency and innovation at financial institutions.[3] ∎

19-5 Financial Crises in Emerging Economies

Previous sections in this chapter have emphasized financial crises in the United States, but crises occur all over the world. They are especially common in *emerging-market economies*—countries in the middle of the world income distribution (not as rich as the United States, but not as poor as many African countries). Crises occurred in Mexico in 1994, many East Asian countries in 1997–1998, Russia in 1998, and Argentina in 2001. In 2008–2009, the U.S. financial crisis spread around the world, and many emerging economies were hit hard.

Emerging-economy crises have much in common with U.S. crises, including bank failures and declines in asset prices. However, they also have another key element: **capital flight**, a sharp increase in net capital outflow that occurs when asset holders lose confidence in an economy. Capital flight creates additional channels in the vicious circle of a financial crisis.

Capital Flight

As discussed in Chapter 5, a country's net capital outflow is its capital outflow (purchases of foreign assets by the country's citizens and firms) minus its capital inflow (purchases of the country's assets by foreigners). In many emerging economies, net capital outflow is negative: inflow exceeds outflow. Capital inflow is high because foreigners expect the economies to grow and their assets to yield high returns.

Capital flight occurs when asset holders (typically led by foreigners) lose confidence in a country's economy. They sharply cut their purchases of the country's assets and start selling the ones they own. This decrease in capital inflow typically shifts net outflow from negative to positive, because inflow becomes less than outflow.

Asset holders' loss of confidence can have various causes, and financial crises often involve more than one. Some leading causes of capital flight are the following:

- *Government debt.* Rising debt levels create fears that the government will default, so foreign financial institutions stop buying government bonds. Foreigners also worry that default will hurt the economy, so they stop buying corporate securities.

---

[3] For more on the Dodd-Frank Act, see David Huntington, "Summary of Dodd-Frank Financial Regulation Legislation," Harvard Law School Forum on Corporate Governance and Financial Regulation, blogs.law.harvard.edu/corpgov/, posted 7/7/2010.

- *Political risk*. Political instability can bring bad governments to power or produce armed conflicts that disrupt the economy. Signs of instability make a country's assets more risky, which can spark capital flight.

- *Banking problems*. Loans to a country's banks from foreign banks are one kind of capital inflow. This source of funds is cut off if domestic banks encounter trouble, such as threats to their solvency from defaults on loans they have made.

Effects on Interest Rates and Exchange Rates When a loss of confidence causes foreigners to sell a country's assets, it drives down asset prices, including bond prices. As we learned in Chapter 16, lower bond prices imply higher interest rates on bonds.

Capital flight typically affects a country's exchange rate as well. Foreigners that sell the country's assets are paid in the country's currency, which they then trade for foreign currency to obtain foreign assets. Sales of the domestic currency cause the currency to depreciate; that is, it falls in value relative to other currencies.[4]

Contagion Just as a bank run can trigger runs at other banks, capital flight can spread from one country to others in a process called **contagion**. When asset holders see that one country's exchange rate and asset prices have fallen, they worry that the same thing could happen in countries in the same region or in countries with similar problems. Capital flight hits these countries as asset holders try to sell before prices fall.

For example, in July 1997, the East Asian financial crisis began in Thailand when capital flight caused the value of the Thai bhat to collapse. In the following months, capital flight spread to countries including South Korea, Indonesia, and the Philippines, driving down exchange rates and raising interest rates throughout the region.

Capital Flight and Financial Crises

Capital flight is often part of a broader financial crisis. It interacts with the basic causes of crises summarized in Figure 19-1. One of the typical causes—banking problems—can trigger capital flight. At the same time, capital flight causes declines in asset prices, another key feature of crises.

The increases in interest rates caused by capital flight are often dramatic; in South Korea, for example, short-term rates jumped from 12 percent in November 1997 to 31 percent in December 1997. Higher interest rates cause investment to fall sharply. In addition, lower confidence in the economy works to reduce both consumption and investment.

The currency depreciation caused by capital flight also has deleterious effects. In emerging economies, foreign loans to the government and to domestic banks

---

[4] The effects of capital flight on a country's interest rate and exchange rate can be captured in the model of a large open economy in the appendix to Chapter 5. Specifically, Figure 5-23 shows that a *fall* in net capital outflow reduces the interest rate and raises the exchange rate. Capital flight is a *rise* in net capital outflow and therefore has the opposite effects: the interest rate rises and the exchange rate falls.

and firms are usually made in U.S. dollars, so many debts are fixed in dollars. When the exchange rate falls, each dollar costs more in local currency, so debt levels rise when measured in local currency. Higher debts hurt the economy by worsening the problems of banks and pushing corporations into bankruptcy. Higher government debt increases fears of default, worsening capital flight.

In sum, capital flight adds a number of channels through which financial crises reduce aggregate demand and build on themselves. The vicious circle becomes more vicious, and economies rarely escape without a deep recession. The following case study recounts a particularly traumatic financial crisis.

CASE STUDY

Argentina's Financial Crisis, 2001–2002

Argentina has a long history of economic crises. For decades, a central problem has been large government budget deficits. The government has sometimes financed deficits with bank loans or bonds, but at other times it has not been able to borrow. In these periods, it has financed deficits with seignorage revenue—by printing money. Rapid money growth causes high inflation, which in turn hurts economic efficiency and long-run growth.

In the 1980s, Argentina's budget deficits produced annual inflation rates in the hundreds of percent. The situation deteriorated at the end of the decade, with inflation over 2,000 percent per year in both 1989 and 1990. In 1991, a new president, Carlos Menem, decided that Argentina needed major reforms. His government attacked the budget deficit with spending cuts and higher taxes. It also sought to make the economy more productive by privatizing government-owned industries and eliminating barriers to international trade.

The government's most radical action was to create a *currency board*, an arrangement that rigidly fixed the exchange rate between Argentina's peso and the U.S. dollar at 1.0. The government promised to maintain this exchange rate by holding large quantities of dollars—enough so it could trade a dollar for a peso with anyone who asked. Policymakers believed that the currency board would curb inflation: the value of the peso could not fall rapidly if it was tied to the dollar, because the value of the dollar was stable.

Initially, Menem's policies were highly successful. Inflation fell to 25 percent in 1992 and 4 percent in 1994. At the same time, output grew rapidly. Confidence in Argentina's economy soared, and capital flowed into the country. Foreign financial institutions started buying Argentine government debt, which they had shunned in the 1980s.

But then several problems developed:

- Budget deficits started to rise again. This resulted largely from spending by the governments of Argentina's provinces, which the national government could not control.

- Argentine inflation, although falling, remained above U.S. inflation for several years, affecting Argentina's *real* exchange rate. This variable equals $e \times (P/P^*)$, where e is the nominal exchange rate, P is the domestic price level, and $P*$ is the foreign price level (see Chapter 5). The real exchange rate rose because the nominal rate e was fixed at 1.0 and P (Argentina's price level) rose faster than $P*$ (the U.S. price level). The rising real exchange rate made Argentina's goods more expensive relative to foreign goods and reduced Argentina's net exports, thus slowing output growth and raising unemployment.

■ A financial crisis in Mexico in 1994 produced contagion. Capital flight occurred throughout Latin America, including Argentina, pushing up interest rates and reducing consumption and investment. Combined with the fall in net exports, lower consumption and investment produced a recession in the mid-1990s.

As usual in a financial crisis, all these different problems reinforced one another. In the late 1990s, the recession reduced tax revenue, worsening the problem of budget deficits. The currency board precluded expansionary monetary policy: policymakers could not create additional pesos because they did not hold enough U.S. dollars to back them. Without monetary stimulus, the recession worsened and the unemployment rate rose above 15 percent. Capital flight increased because of worries about rising government debt and about a possible end of the currency board. In 1999, Fernando de la Rua replaced Carlos Menem as president, but it made little difference for the deteriorating economy.

In late 2001, Argentina's problems spiraled out of control. In October, the government defaulted by failing to make promised payments on its debt. November brought a banking crisis. Argentina's banks had been weakened by the long recession and by losses on their holdings of government bonds. Fearing bank failures, and with no deposit insurance, Argentines rushed to withdraw their money.

The government's response to the bank panic was drastic: it imposed a limit on withdrawals. A depositor could withdraw only $250 in cash per week. This policy provoked a political crisis. The long recession had made many Argentines furious at the government, and the denial of access to their money was the last straw. Riots and looting erupted in December 2001: 26 people died and President de la Rua resigned. In January 2002, an interim president, Eduardo Duhalde, ended the currency board.

The immediate economic consequences were disastrous. The value of a peso fell from its fixed level of $1 to 27 cents in 2002. This exchange-rate collapse caused a large rise in import prices, reducing living standards for Argentine consumers. It also caused a huge rise in the peso values of dollar-denominated debts, leading to a wave of corporate bankruptcies. Output fell by 15 percent from 2000 to 2002, and unemployment rose above 20 percent.

At the time, some economists predicted a long depression for Argentina. However, the fall in the exchange rate set the stage for more-rapid-than-expected recovery. It made Argentine goods cheap relative to foreign goods, and exports boomed. From 2003 to 2007, output grew rapidly and unemployment fell below 10 percent. During this period, the government also managed to reduce budget deficits, the problem underlying Argentina's history of instability. Time will tell whether strong growth and low budget deficits prove to be durable. ■

Recent Crises

The U.S. financial crisis of 2007–2009 triggered crises in many other countries, largely by causing capital flight. As we discussed, the panic following the failure of Lehman Brothers produced a flight to safety, with financial institutions selling any assets that appeared risky. These assets included many in emerging economies, where assets are generally considered risky because the economies are less stable than advanced economies. Countries in eastern Europe and Asia, for example, experienced capital flight and sharp recessions.

In 2009–2010, a financial crisis struck Greece (which is sometimes categorized as an emerging economy, because its income is low by western European standards). The trigger for this crisis was rising government budget deficits, which produced fears that Greece might default on its debt. Asset holders around the world dumped Greek debt, pushing up the interest rates that Greece had to pay on new debt. In May 2010, Greek long-term government bonds paid 8.0 percent, compared to 2.7 percent for German government bonds (see Figure 19-5).

In the summer of 2010, it appeared that Greece was heading for a severe recession. Making matters worse, Greek policymakers could not support their economy with traditional policy tools. They could not pursue expansionary fiscal policy because that would worsen the problem of rising debt; indeed, Greece's government was trying to cut its spending. Policymakers could not

FIGURE 19-5

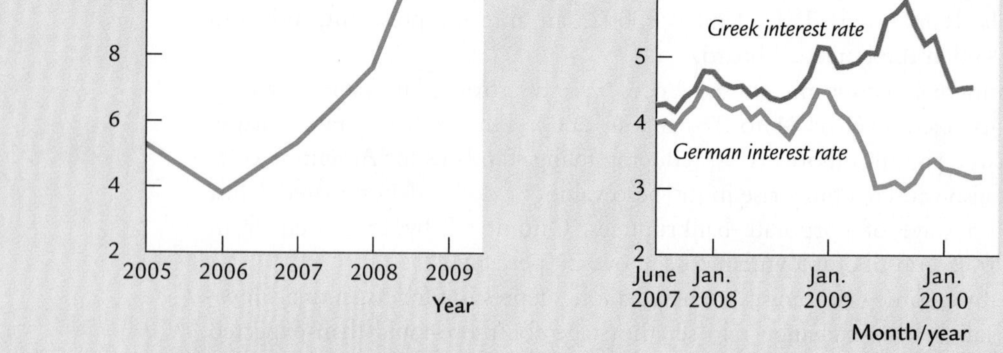

(a) Greece's Government Budget Deficit as a Percentage of GDP

(b) Interest Rates on 10-Year Government Bonds

Greece's Crisis, 2009–2010 Greece's financial crisis was triggered by rising government debt, which created fears of default and pushed interest rates on Greek government bonds above other European bond rates.

Source: OECD.

pursue expansionary monetary policy because Greece does not have its own currency. Its currency is the euro, which it shares with 15 other European countries. Monetary policy for all euro countries is set by the European Central Bank, so Greece has no independent policy tool to wield against recession.

As Greece's government struggled to make debt payments, Europeans worried that the crisis would worsen dramatically if the government actually defaulted. In addition to wrecking Greece's economy, a default could produce contagion. Some other European countries, such as Spain and Portugal, also have high debt levels. Default by Greece would shake confidence in these countries' debt, and they could be hit by capital flight. Uncertainty hangs over Europe's economies as this book goes to press.

The Role of the International Monetary Fund

When financial crises threaten the United States, the Federal Reserve and Treasury Department try to contain them. When emerging economies experience crises, governments and central banks often don't have the resources to respond. In particular, they lack foreign currency, which is needed to pay debts set in dollars. Therefore, countries in crisis often seek help from the **International Monetary Fund (IMF)**, an international institution that lends to countries experiencing financial crises.

The IMF was established in 1944 to oversee a system of fixed exchange rates among 44 nations, including the United States and other leading economies. That system ended in the 1970s, and since then aiding countries in financial crises has been the IMF's primary function. Most of the world's countries are members of the IMF and contribute funds to it, but rich countries provide most of the money. A country's votes on the IMF board of directors are proportional to its financial contribution, so rich countries hold most of the power.

In recent decades, the IMF has intervened in most crises involving capital flight, including those in Argentina and Greece. As we've seen, private financial institutions are wary of lending to countries in crisis. These countries turn to the IMF for emergency loans, which are made in dollars. The IMF is sometimes called the "international lender of last resort."

Countries use IMF loans in various ways depending on their circumstances:

- The government can use the loans to make payments on its debt, preventing default.

- If a country's banks have debts denominated in dollars, the central bank can lend them dollars to repay those debts.

- The central bank can use dollars to buy its own currency in foreign-exchange markets (if, unlike Greece, the country has its own currency). Increased demand for the currency dampens the fall in the exchange value of the currency.

Each of these actions attacks a part of the financial crisis. In addition, IMF loans are intended to boost confidence in the economy, reducing capital flight. The overall goal is to slow down the vicious circle and hasten financial and economic recovery.

Most IMF loans have strings attached. To obtain a loan, a country must sign an economic agreement with the IMF. The country agrees to reforms that address the problems underlying its crisis. For example, a government with a high debt level may be required to cut spending. This condition was a key part of the IMF's agreement with Greece in May 2010. Loan provisions may also include stricter bank regulation, monetary tightening to control inflation, or privatization of government-owned industries.

IMF loans are controversial. Some economists believe they significantly reduce the damage caused by financial crises, for example, by curbing the length of recessions. Others criticize the IMF on the grounds that it creates moral hazard. They criticize IMF loans to countries for essentially the same reason that many criticize rescues of U.S. financial institutions by the Federal Reserve and the Treasury. Aid to countries that get in trouble encourages other countries to behave the same way. Still others criticize the IMF for the conditions it imposes on loans, which can be painful. Reducing budget deficits, for example, may force governments to cut spending on antipoverty programs. The IMF argues that painful reforms are needed for long-run economic growth, but again, not everyone agrees.

19-6 Conclusion

Financial crises have caused many of history's worst recessions and highest unemployment rates, both in the United States and around the world. Often monetary and fiscal policies are inadequate tools for ending these recessions. To stem crises, governments and central banks take drastic actions, ranging from a bank holiday to emergency loans and equity injections for financial institutions. When emerging economies face a financial crisis, the International Monetary Fund lends to the countries' governments.

The events of 2007–2009 drove home the lesson that, despite its strong financial institutions and extensive regulatory system, the United States is susceptible to severe financial crises. Seeking to reduce this risk, economists and political leaders have proposed many reforms of financial regulation. Some of these proposals, such as a new government agency to monitor financial risk, were enacted in 2010. It remains to be seen how greatly these reforms will change the behavior of financial institutions, how effective they will be in preventing crises, and whether further changes in regulation will occur. You will surely hear much about these issues in the years to come.

Summary

1. A financial crisis typically begins with declines in asset prices, failures of financial institutions, or both. Failures can result from insolvency or liquidity crises. A financial crisis can produce a credit crunch and reduce aggregate demand, causing a recession. The recession reinforces the causes of the crisis.

2. Policymakers may seek to stem a crisis by rescuing troubled financial institutions. Rescues range from riskless loans to institutions facing liquidity

crises to giveaways of government funds. Risky rescues, including risky loans and equity injections, are an intermediate type of policy that may or may not cost the government money.

3. Financial rescues are controversial because of their potential costs to taxpayers and because they increase moral hazard: firms may take on more risk, thinking the government will bail them out if they get in trouble.

4. Over 2007–2009, the subprime mortgage crisis evolved into a broad financial and economic crisis in the United States. The stock market fell drastically, some of the country's most prestigious financial institutions failed or came close to failing, lending was disrupted throughout the economy, and the unemployment rate rose to 10 percent.

5. The 2007–2009 crisis produced an intense debate about government regulation of financial institutions. Many proposals for financial reform fall into four broad categories: increased regulation of nonbank financial institutions, policies to prevent institutions from becoming too big to fail, rules that discourage excessive risk taking, and new structures for regulatory agencies.

6. Financial crises in emerging-market economies typically include capital flight and sharp decreases in exchange rates. Causes of capital flight include high government debt, political instability, and banking problems. Capital flight adds new channels to the vicious circle of a financial crisis. The International Monetary Fund makes emergency loans to countries struck by capital flight.

KEY CONCEPTS

Financial crisis	Too big to fail (TBTF)	Contagion
Credit crunch	Equity injection	International Monetary Fund (IMF)
Lender of last resort	Zero-bound problem	
Discount loan	Capital flight	

QUESTIONS FOR REVIEW

1. What two types of events are the typical triggers for financial crises?

2. Explain how a financial crisis leads to a fall in aggregate demand and a recession.

3. Explain how the central bank can ease liquidity crises at solvent financial institutions.

4. How can the central bank or government prevent failures of insolvent financial institutions or reduce the costs of failures to the economy?

5. Why are some financial institutions "too big to fail" and what are the implications for central bank and government policy?

6. Is the following statement true or false? Explain your answer. "The only costs of financial rescues are the direct payments from the government."

7. List the four broad categories of financial reform. Describe a proposed reform in each category and explain how it would help prevent a financial crisis.

8. What effects does capital flight have on interest rates and exchange rates? Explain these effects.

9. What are the leading causes of capital flight?

10. Describe the IMF's role in the financial crises of emerging economies.

PROBLEMS AND APPLICATIONS

1. Many economists argue that a rescue of a financial institution should protect the institution's creditors from losses but *not* protect its owners: they should lose their equity. Supporters of this idea say it reduces the moral hazard created by rescues.

   a. Explain how this approach reduces moral hazard compared to a rescue that protects both creditors and equity holders.

   b. Does this approach eliminate the moral hazard problem completely? Explain.

2. What could U.S. policymakers have done to prevent the Great Depression or at least reduce its severity? Specifically:

   a. What government or Fed policies might have prevented the stock market crash and bank panics that started the financial crisis? (*Hint:* Think of policies that exist today.)

   b. Once the crisis began, what could policymakers have done to dampen the effects on the financial system and economy? Explain.

3. Some Congress members think the government should not risk taxpayer money to rescue financial firms whose highly paid executives have behaved irresponsibly. Instead, the government should aid middle- and low-income people hurt by the financial crisis, such as homeowners facing foreclosure. Discuss the arguments for this position and against it.

4. In 2010, Senator Blanche Lincoln (D-AR) proposed that commercial banks be forbidden to trade derivative securities. Discuss the arguments for and against this proposal.

5. Of the proposed financial reforms discussed in Section 19-4, which would have significantly dampened the financial crisis of 2007–2009 if they had been in place before the crisis? Could any of the reforms have prevented the crisis entirely? Explain.

6. Draw an expanded version of Figure 19-1 (the outline of a typical financial crisis) for emerging economies. The figure should include capital flight and show how this phenomenon interacts with the other elements of a crisis.

7. In the late 1990s, some economists advised Argentina to dollarize, that is, to eliminate the peso and use the U.S. dollar as its currency. Discuss how dollarization might have changed the course of events in 2001–2002.

8. Find out what has happened to Greece's financial system and economy since this book was published. Has Greece's crisis worsened or eased? Has the crisis affected other European or non-European economies? Have events followed the typical pattern of financial crises described in this chapter? Explain.